SHORT STORIES FOR SENIORS

101 Heartwarming and Funny Large Print Tales to Create Joy, Stimulate Memory, Cognition, and Relieve Stress for Elderly

TABLE OF CONTENTS

CHAPTER 10

BONUS

Manuscript 1
Short Stories for Seniors

51 Heartwarming Stories for Stimulating Memory, Cognition, and Relieving Stress

INTRODUCTION

Everyone has a story, one worth remembering and recounting to others. Sometimes we only become aware of how poignant and influential particular moments in our lives have been long after they have passed.

This book contains 51 heartwarming and endearing short stories to take you on the most important journey of all. You can enjoy these stories from the coziest, comfiest sofa in your home and with the company of someone willing to hold your hand and listen, or perhaps read these stories to you. With so many amazing tales inside these pages, your still-vibrant heartstrings are sure to be pulled as you read or hear about moments in the lives of others that will rekindle the spark of moments that have passed but are still very much alive in your consciousness.

CHAPTER 1

FIVE STORIES ABOUT FAMILY

DURNWIN

David had never seen the toy store so busy. Several young children, all about the same age as him, were running around admiring their favorite toys. Some children quickly grabbed the plastic boxes they wanted, whether they contained an action figure or perhaps a dinosaur figurine, and handed the box over to their parents as they pleaded for what they enthusiastically explained was a very necessary purchase.

The crowded, congested feeling was only pronounced by the small size of the store.

However, David knew exactly where he needed to go.

Still holding his father's hand, David pulled him through the narrow aisles, dodging other families until they got to where they needed to be: right in front of Durnwin.

"Here it is, Dad!" David exclaimed as he pointed his small index finger at the plastic, medieval-looking sword resting inside a box almost the same size as David himself.

John, David's father, put one hand on his tie as he leaned over to survey the sword before ultimately looking at the price.

"That's quite expensive for a toy…" he said.

This statement was of no consequence to young David, who was practically vibrating with excitement. He explained to his father that it was a magic sword like the one in the movies he watched at home, but that didn't excite his father quite as much as David had hoped.

"I'll make you a deal," John began as he stood up straight and looked at David stoically. "When you manage to ride your bike across the grass field outside our house, I will give you the money to buy the sword."

David's expression turned grave with disappointment.

"But it's the last one they have! Someone else might take it!" he whined.

"You said you're tired of being the only one of your friends who can't ride a bike, so this should be as important to you as it is to me," said his father.

David regretted having expressed his frustrations about not knowing how to ride a bike and not practicing like he had promised his father.

After a brief but fervent protest, David acquiesced to his father's terms and ambled back to the car with a look of utter defeat.

Once they got home, it seemed later than it was due to the rain clouds forming in the sky. However, David's worry that another lucky child (with perhaps a more reasonable father) would buy the sword was so intense that he got his bike and headed to the grass field opposite his house.

"David, it's going to rain; let's practice tomorrow!" John exclaimed, but David insisted.

Once both father and son made it to the field, they noticed it was muddier than usual.

"I don't have the right shoes for this, David. Let me go home and change. They're going to get muddy, and this is what I wear to the office."

"NO!" David exclaimed as he pulled his bike onto the far end of the field.

Visibly frustrated, John accompanied his son—dirtying his leather shoes in the process—to where David would begin biking.

The air was cold, and the clouds were beginning to make threatening sounds, but David was unfazed by the approaching tempest.

At first, the mud made it nearly impossible for David to find his balance—let alone move the bike forward.

John kept bending down to help David back up, but David pulled away from his father angrily. He was still indignant over not owning Durnwin, the magic sword.

After several minutes, rain began to fall, but John said nothing; he knew his son was determined to ride his bike to the end of the grass field.

"You can do it; I believe in you!" yelled John.

David looked at the gray sky and felt the cold droplets hit his nose and cheeks.

This time, he leaped onto the bike and rode it flawlessly across the entire field. When he got off and turned to see if his father had been watching,

John was already running towards him with arms wide open.

David and John hugged jubilantly. They were oblivious to the pouring rain soaking both of them.

***

The next afternoon, John was in a particularly dreadful mood when he returned from work. However, he was looking forward to seeing David brandishing Durnwin, which he had surely purchased with his mother while John was at the office.

John went into his son's room and asked him about the sword.

David smiled and ran to his closet, where he pulled out a cardboard shoebox and handed it to his dad.

John was confused, since the box would have had to be about three times that size to contain the sword. After noticing the look of utter joy in his son's eyes, John opened the box and saw a pair of new leather shoes resting inside.

"I chose to buy these for you instead. Thank you for helping me learn to ride a bike," David exclaimed gleefully.

THE KITTEN

"You're wrong!" Tom protested as he sat in the backseat of his parents' car, cradling the small kitten in his arms.

"Buddy is a very energetic dog, and you know it's not safe for the kitten to be around him," Tom's mother reasoned as she drove toward the nearby forest, where she had instructed her son to drop off the young stray that kept venturing into their home.

"We've had Buddy for two years, and he's never hurt another dog. How can you think he would hurt a kitten?!" argued Tom.

"We literally saw him with his mouth over her little head!"

"He was just playing!" Tom exclaimed.

The argument continued for the entire drive. Tom's mother was not an animal person. Finally convincing her to allow Tom to have Buddy, their playful golden retriever, had been a long and arduous effort, but Tom finally had the dog he had always dreamed of.

For the past week, a tiny gray kitten who couldn't have been more than a year old kept venturing into their front yard, which Buddy frequented. Tom reveled with joy every time he saw the kitten. His mother, on the other hand, did not.

Tom ignored the sound of twigs and leaves under the tires as they reached the forest; his gaze was on the kitten, which he did not want to relinquish to the woods. He sat silently stroking the kitten, which he hadn't even named yet, until his mother exited the car and opened the passenger seat.

A part of Tom wondered if his mother was right: if Buddy would one day hurt the kitten—by accident, of course. After all, Buddy was still very young, and he shared Tom's zest for adventure, which sometimes led to the occasional mishap.

Once Tom and his mother were deep inside the forest, Tom knelt and gently put the kitten down. Before he could say goodbye to the kitten, it had already darted behind the trees, quickly moving out of sight.

The ride back home was the opposite of the ride to the woods. Tom was utterly silent, looking out the window and hoping to see the kitten again.

"STOP!" Tom suddenly exclaimed, which made his mother jolt and swerve the car.

"What is it?!" she gasped.

"There are dogs! Big angry dogs!"

"What?!" Tom's mother asked as she stopped the car and looked at her son, her face turning red.

Tom explained that he had seen two very intimidating-looking dogs running toward the spot where they had dropped off the kitten and that they needed to go back to rescue her.

Before his mother could finish explaining why that wasn't going to happen, Tom opened the door and ran back to where he'd released the kitten, ignoring his mother's screams for him to come back.

Once he made it to where they'd left the kitten, he called out to the young feline desperately. He had only been looking around for a few minutes before his mother ran over to him and forcibly pulled him back to the car.

"Do you want those dogs to hurt you?!" she exclaimed as she slammed the door shut, walked over to the driver's side, and slid in.

She was right. Tom hadn't considered the danger of calling out in the middle of the woods and potentially attracting the attention of the large dogs he'd seen earlier.

Once Tom and his mother got home, Tom refused to exit the car.

"I was worried about you. I didn't want you to get hurt, Tom. I'm sorry," she apologized.

"I don't want the kitten to get hurt, but maybe it's too late."

Without saying anything, Tom's mother made her way to the backseat and sat by her son's side, putting her arm around him and stroking his hair. They stayed this way for a long time before they decided to go inside for a snack.

Tom entered the house and saw something in the front yard through the sliding glass door. He darted toward it and slid it open.

"Mom, look!"

Tom's mother came running and put her hand over her mouth when she saw what Tom was pointing at.

The kitten was fast asleep on Buddy's fluffy stomach, its little head gently moving up and down as Buddy breathed in and out.

Buddy opened his eyes and looked at Tom, his mother, and finally at the kitten sleeping on his belly before closing them again and going back to sleep.

Tom knelt and began stroking them both. He looked up at his mother, who was smiling at the sight in front of her. Without saying anything, Tom knew from his mother's satisfied expression that he and Buddy now had a new, lifelong friend.

THE BOX HOUSE

Albert parked in front of his house and stayed inside the car for a long, contemplative moment as he looked at the small, white house he would maybe never see again. He had built this house, just like he'd built many others—some even currently inhabited by his nephews or friends.

It always brought Albert great joy remembering that he had built the houses that were giving shelter and keeping many of his loved ones warm. However, now that he was due to move to the big city to join a multinational architecture firm, he felt his heart twinge with sadness over the loss of the first home he had ever built: his own.

Once inside, Albert was greeted enthusiastically by his daughter Ella, whose blonde pigtails bounced as she ran to greet him in her little pink Minnie Mouse dress.

"Do we get to stay?" Ella demanded with a smile so bright and intoxicating that it seemed as if she was confident the answer would be the one she was hoping for.

After yet another moment of hesitation, Albert sheepishly shook his head in denial.

Ella's green eyes filled with tears upon hearing this devastating news. However, she did not protest like she had the previous days. Instead, Ella bowed her head in sullen acquiescence and disappeared, probably into her room.

Albert called to her, but she ignored him, which bothered Albert much more than her vehement demands that they stay. Ella had always relished the fact that she lived in the very first house her father had built—so much so that she constantly announced to everyone that one day she would grow up to be an architect like her father and that she would build a house just for the two of them.

Albert became tormented by the worry that perhaps this move would make Ella lose sight of those childish, yet poignant and heartfelt aspirations.

***

A couple of days later, on a particularly wet and downcast Saturday morning, Albert ensconced himself in his bedroom. He was surrounded by so many cardboard boxes that it was impossible to see what the actual floor of the bedroom looked like anymore.

He had initially requested Ella's help with packing, but given the way she had been willfully ignoring him for the past couple of days, he had rescinded his invitation to make packing a family affair.

The door to his bedroom opened and Ella walked in. Her hair was down, and she had a determined look on her face. She made her way through the spacious bedroom and gathered up as many cardboard boxes as she could carry with her little hands before disappearing through the open door.

Albert surmised that she must be worried that her things would be left behind unless she helped pack, which made him smile. He wondered whether he should try and help her, but ultimately decided to let her have her space.

After a couple of hours of packing, the white carpet was once again visible. There were cardboard boxes everywhere, making Albert feel more melancholy than he had expected. He felt the urge to grab a box cutter and free his belongings, but he knew that he had to be strong, especially in front of Ella.

As Albert slowly made his way to Ella's bedroom, he pondered how to make her understand that all of this was happening because he wanted to keep building houses for other people and that he was sorry for breaking the promise he'd made many years ago that they would never leave their home. As much as he tried to think of the right thing to say, he realized that words could not explain his sorrow.

Before Albert could open the door, it swung open by itself, which frightened him.

"Are you ready?" Ella asked, her eyes once more glimmering with joy.

"For what?"

"Come inside!" Ella replied as she pulled her father into the bedroom.

Once inside, Albert noticed about six cardboard boxes taped together to form what seemed like a makeshift castle. There were flowers, vines, and windows drawn on the first four boxes, which were stacked on top of each other, and the two boxes on each side had a fence drawn on them.

"What is this?" he asked.

"This is the house I built for us. We can take it with us and live in it wherever we are in the world!" Ella rejoiced.

Albert smiled and followed his daughter. He sat down in the space she'd built inside the first four boxes and looked at all the drawings of kitchen utensils and bookshelves she'd made.

"It's perfect. We'll take it with us wherever we go," Albert said as a tear ran down his cheek.

MAGIC MOUNTAIN

Maggie repeatedly nodded as she listened to Matthew, her six-year-old son, continuously explain how amazing Magic Mountain was. Initially, she thought Matthew was referring to the amusement park ride, which made it very confusing when she heard that the teacher had read a book about it to the entire class at school.

"No!" Matthew protested, "Magic Mountain is a place with a secret castle that only appears for children who are ready to become king and rule Magic Mountain forever!"

Maggie smiled as she listened to Matthew's excitement about the stories he heard in school. Matthew had always had a vibrant imagination that took him places she could not always follow. As she drove to their favorite restaurant, she wondered if the baby currently growing inside her would have an imagination that was just as active; after all, it was going to be another boy.

"And what does the king have to do in his kingdom?" Maggie asked as she parked the car on the gravel road leading up to the steakhouse.

"He protects the castle from dragons and teaches his knights how to fight and be brave!" Matthew proclaimed.

"That's an enormous responsibility!" Maggie responded.

"That's why the castle only appears on the mountain when the rightful king appears. It doesn't show up for just anyone!" enthused Matthew.

Mother and son got out of the car and walked up the gravel path toward the large steakhouse, holding hands as they made their way through the verdant pastures. At this point, with her belly the size it was, Maggie felt that it was her son helping her walk rather than the other way around.

Once seated, Maggie sighed. She was relieved to be off her feet. Both of them perused the menu, even though neither of them would ever consider deviating from their usual order: nachos to start and a Hawaiian steak for both.

"Can I go play outside?" Matthew requested.

"Do you know what you're going to order?"

Matthew responded with a cheeky smile.

"Same as always, huh? Ok, but don't go far, and don't take too long," admonished Maggie.

Matthew's mother hadn't even finished her sentence before he slipped away from the red leather booth and dodged a couple of waiters dressed in black and white as he bolted out the door toward the nearby green hills.

Matthew always came back exhausted after running circles around the restaurant, which is what she was hoping would happen this time too. She enjoyed hearing his fantastical stories, but they often went over her head and she became frustrated at herself for not knowing how to respond.

The large platter of nachos arrived, and Matthew was still not back. He was too young to have a phone, but he never spent longer than 10 or 15 minutes running around the pastures outside the restaurant. Luckily, Maggie's pregnancy meant she was always hungry enough to polish off whatever was in front of her.

More than 30 minutes had passed since Matthew left, which began to worry Maggie. Matthew had a proclivity to imagine impossible yet imaginative scenarios, while Maggie tended to envision the worst-case scenario for each situation.

Is he lost? Is he hurt? she wondered.

As her imagination began to get the better of her, she almost involuntarily and rather awkwardly slid out of the booth and crossed the gleaming hardwood floors as she headed out of the restaurant.

Once outside, she could not see Matthew anywhere. She called his name but heard no response.

Suddenly, her mind recalled all the articles she'd read about child abductions.

Maggie called out for her son furiously as she struggled to walk over to the nearby hills, where she hoped she would finally find him.

Although the hills were not too steep, her pregnant belly made her move slowly and awkwardly, and she had no one to hold her hand as she climbed. Maggie tried to control her thoughts, but she couldn't help herself from beginning to plan what she'd do in case she couldn't find Matthew or, worse, if she found him unconscious or injured.

Her fear spurred her to try to move faster until she finally reached the top.

Matthew was sitting at the summit of the hill, resting his back against a tall elm tree under the shade the branches provided.

"Matthew!" Maggie yelled, "do you have any idea how worried I was?!"

Before Maggie could elaborate, she noticed Matthew look up with tears in his eyes.

"The castle didn't show up for me. I'm not fit to be a king…" he sobbed.

It took a lot for Matthew to cry, so she knew he was genuinely upset. As angry and tired as she was, she couldn't bring herself to scold him further.

Maggie took a couple of deep breaths and walked over to her son.

"I was worried about you…" she began.

"I knew the castle wouldn't show up for me. I found the mountain, but not the castle…" cried Matthew.

Maggie held onto the thick branches of the tree and lowered herself to sit by her son. She struggled to find the right words to say. She could not fault him for the emotions caused by his imagination; after all, in a way, she had fallen victim to the same thing when catastrophizing possible reasons for her son's absence.

Maggie smiled as she realized that her imagination was not that far off from her son's, and they were both upset over things that were not real.

"Do you know why the castle didn't reveal itself to you?" she inquired gently.

"Why?" Matthew asked as he wiped his tears on his muddy, grass-stained jeans.

"Because you have an even bigger responsibility than being a king waiting for you," explained Maggie.

"What responsibility?"

"Being a big brother. Your little brother will need you to teach him to be brave and fight against dragons. The castle knows your brother would be lost without you; that is why it is letting you stay with us," elaborated Maggie.

Matthew smiled at his mother and then looked at her pregnant belly.

"Don't worry, little brother, I will keep you safe," Matthew declared as he wrapped his arms around his mother's belly. "I'll be your protector."

THE VISIT

Dan paced his small bedroom frantically until he realized he needed more space to pace. He walked over to the living room, which was not significantly larger but had fewer clothes on the floor. His girlfriend was away, so the apartment was messier than usual.

Great, now I'm going to have to clean up the apartment as well, Dan lamented.

His father, Sebastian Hawkes, an erudite and very financially successful businessman, was visiting him for his birthday. Initially, Dan was excited about seeing his dad after such a long time, but he was also nervous about what Sebastian would say about his lifestyle.

Sebastian was an old-fashioned man who had become very powerful through hard work and perseverance. He also believed his son could do great things if he just put his mind to it, which is exactly what Dan was trying to do.

Dan had been trying to turn his life around for the past few years. After years of frivolous living as a carefree teenager and happy-go-lucky young adult, Dan had found the love of his life and was dedicated to working as hard as possible to one day becoming as successful as his father, or at least getting close to being that successful.

***

Dan had taken the day off work from his job as a finance executive to be with his dad. During the sporadic calls he got from his father, he would inform him of how happy he was at work and how much responsibility he had. However, this wasn't strictly true. Dan was not enjoying the work as much as he thought he would and was looking for a change, but he was not ready to divulge this to his judgmental father.

During their breakfast at the coffee shop down the street, Dan's father kept questioning him about work, regardless of how hard Dan tried to change the conversation and talk about anything else.

"It's great; I'm thrilled," Dan declared as he fiddled with the paper coffee sleeve in his hands and tried to relax, readjusting his position on the green polyester sofa.

Sebastian was in his usual business attire, even though he had retired from working years ago. He loved blue, which was made apparent by his blue tie and dress shirt. He glanced around the coffee place Dan frequented with his girlfriend on the weekends, and Dan began to worry that he disapproved of the setting.

"Do you like this place?" Sebastian asked.

"I do, very much," replied Dan.

"What do you like about it?"

Dan successfully stifled a sigh of frustration.

***

The night was dark, but the city was brightly lit by the streetlights and the glowing windows of the tall buildings. There were no stars in the sky. The bustle of Friday night traffic provided the backdrop to Dan's stroll through the city with his father.

Dan zipped up his brown coat while his dad continued to walk in just a blazer, seemingly unaffected by the cold.

"What is special about your job? Why do you like working there?" Sebastian asked again.

Dan shook his head in disbelief that his father would be so brazen in his questioning; it was as if no matter what Dan did in life, his father would never approve.

"I work with people who don't judge me," Dan responded rather harshly.

"But do these people drive you to become a better version of yourself?" pestered his father.

"That's it!" Dan snapped as he turned around to face his father just before they approached the pedestrian crosswalk in front of them.

Sebastian looked at his son, bewildered. Dan could feel the anger rising in his throat.

For a brief moment, both father and son stood in silence, just looking at each other, as people loudly came in and out of the burger joint only a few feet from where they were awkwardly standing.

Dan put his hands in his pocket and looked around, unsure of what to say next.

"What's the matter?" Sebastian asked his visibly flustered son.

"Why are you so critical? You kept looking around at the coffee place I took you to this morning, and now you keep asking me why I'm happy at my job. All I ever do is try to make you proud of me, but I never will!" shouted Dan.

The light turned green, and Dan stormed across the crosswalk. When he got to the other side, he noticed his father hadn't moved from where they had previously been standing.

He knew his father would be surprised to see him react this way, but he didn't expect his face to express such bewilderment.

The light remained green and people continued to cross, oblivious to the emotional staredown happening between father and son on opposite sides of the street.

After a few more seconds of inaction, both men hastily started to cross the street at the same time until they met in the center of the crossing.

"I'm sorry," Sebastian apologized after almost bumping into his son, "I had no idea it was affecting you this way."

"I just want you to be proud of me," mumbled Dan.

"I am. I am very proud of you. That's why I've been asking you all these questions," explained Sebastian.

"What do you mean?" Dan replied incredulously.

Sebastian ushered his son back to the other side of the street to continue the conversation.

"I am finally setting up my café. It's been a dream of mine for years, and I've been putting everything in place to start getting it up and running next year."

"That's why you were so interested in the café this morning..." murmured Dan to himself.

"Yes. I want you to run the business..." Sebastian said tentatively.

"What?" Dan gasped.

"That's why I've been asking you about work. I don't want to take you away from a job that makes you happy. As much as I would like you to run this business, I only want what's best for you," his father offered.

Everything about the day with his father was now making perfect sense; however, Dan had never expected this kind of revelation.

"I've never run a business before…" muttered Dan.

"I trust you," Sebastian replied wholeheartedly.

Dan looked at his father, then at the busy street, and smiled. Regardless of his decision, his father's approval was the most important revelation of the day.

"Thank you," Dan said fervently.

In reply, Sebastian pulled his son into a heartfelt hug.

Chapter 2

Five Stories About Friendship

The Decision

Natalie had been John's friend for many years. They were inseparable, like brother and sister— only without the fighting. Natalie was a few years younger than John, but it was clear to all their mutual friends and anybody else who knew them that she was the more mature one of the two.

As close as they were, John hadn't actually seen Natalie in years. The last time he'd seen her was at the airport when he left their hometown to pursue a postgraduate degree in Spain and stayed after being offered a job there.

John was happy in Spain, but had yet to find a friend like Natalie. What he had found, however, was Laura, a girl he loved very much: so much so that he was planning to marry her one day in the not-so-distant future.

Laura was everything he dreamed of in a woman, and he would constantly talk about her to Natalie during their weekly phone calls.

However, as time passed and their relationship developed, John began noticing strange behaviors in Laura that bothered him. Laura would constantly ask John where he was, even though it was obvious he was at work. She would also get suspicious whenever he chatted with anyone on his phone.

When Natalie asked how things were going, John still very much professed his love, but found it hard to focus on anything other than Laura's blinding good looks.

"But how is the relationship going?" Natalie would insist.

"It's strange. I feel like she doesn't trust me. I am 100% faithful to her, and I don't understand why she doesn't see it," lamented John.

It was true that John was faithful, and he spent most of his days confused over the lack of trust between him and the most beautiful girl he had ever been with.

One afternoon, after John arrived home from work and was having dinner with Laura at the round wooden table in their cramped studio apartment, he got a text message from Natalie.

Much to Laura's chagrin, John opened the text and read it.

"WHAAAT?!" John exclaimed as he shot up from his seat in disbelief, almost knocking over the steak and potatoes he'd cooked for himself and Laura.

Laura's beautiful brown eyes beamed at John, unsure how to react to his unexplainable outburst.

"Natalie is coming to live here! She's also going to do a postgraduate like me!" celebrated John.

Laura's reaction was not the one John had been hoping for. In fact, it seemed like she refused to react at all.

"Why?" she asked, looking down at her food as if she had found a hair in it.

***

As trepidated as John was over Laura's jealous behavior, he never would have expected her to have such a big problem with Natalie's arrival in Spain.

As the day John was due to pick up Natalie from the airport drew nearer, the tension between John and Laura reached its boiling point. They were fighting so much that Laura decided to go on a yoga trip with her ex-boyfriend.

"So, I can't hang out with my best friend, but you can go on a yoga retreat with your ex-boyfriend?" steamed John.

"He's the instructor!" Laura would yell. The same fight happened repeatedly until Laura eventually left for her yoga retreat the night before Natalie was due to arrive, leaving John alone in the apartment.

When morning came, John got up and excitedly raced to the airport. As happy as he felt, he was also saddened by the tension in his relationship with Laura.

The reunion between John and Natalie turned heads at the airport, making many people believe that the grinning girl John was embracing was his girlfriend.

After the airport, John took Natalie to the café where he and Laura often went on Sundays.

"So, how are things going?" Natalie asked.

John explained everything to his best friend, who was immediately concerned by how clear it was that Laura and John's relationship was causing John a lot of sadness and worry.

They talked for almost two hours before Natalie invited John to stay over at the small apartment she was renting so that he wouldn't have to be alone.

John agreed to stay with Natalie, although he had no idea how he would break the news to Laura.

***

On the last day that John was staying with Natalie, a couple of days before Laura arrived back from her yoga trip, John got a call from his mother. They spoke about many things, and John told her that he was staying with Natalie at her apartment.

"But she was supposed to be on an induction trip with her future classmates this weekend. She was so excited about going!" John's mother said.

"She was?" John asked, dumbfounded.

Once the conversation ended, John confronted Natalie about the trip.

"Is it true?" he asked.

Natalie nodded.

"You missed out on that for me? And you weren't going to tell me about it?"

Natalie nodded again.

"I knew you were in pain, so I wanted to be there for you," she said simply.

John didn't know what to say. He contemplated the difference between Natalie's decision to stay home to help him feel better and Laura's decision to leave on a yoga trip with her ex-boyfriend.

It didn't take long before things became very clear to John, which made him smile.

"Can I stay here a little longer?" he asked softly.

"Of course! How much longer?" Natalie said, grinning.

"A couple of weeks. Depends on how long it takes for either Laura or I to move out."

"Move out?" Natalie asked in astonishment, putting down her white coffee mug a little too hard and sloshing coffee onto the table.

"If I look at the difference between what you chose to do for me this week and what Laura did by leaving me to go on a yoga retreat with her ex-boyfriend, regardless of if he is the instructor or not, the distinction is clear. I should be with someone who's there for me and doesn't abandon me out of jealousy," John explained.

Natalie smiled. Her green eyes contentedly rested on John's determined smile.

John ended up staying much longer than a couple of weeks. He finally moved out a year later—but with Natalie, as they found another apartment together and began to build the life that they continue to share to this day.

THE REUNION

Diego hated the idea of going to his high school reunion.

"It's going to be fine!" his fiancée Deborah insisted from their en suite bathroom as she did her hair in front of the oval-shaped mirror.

"It's not going to be fine. I don't know why I let you convince me to do these things!" Diego protested as he sat on the double bed and tied the shoelaces of his favorite brown leather shoes, which he only wore on special occasions.

"Because deep down, you know that you'll regret not going. It's been ten years; surely it will be nice to see your friends again!" countered Deborah.

"I was only there for two years. I hardly even remember anyone!" insisted Diego.

That statement wasn't strictly true.

One of the main reasons Diego felt flustered about attending his high school reunion was that he had been bullied for those final two years of school.

As a high schooler, Diego was a hypersensitive and introverted kid who found it very hard to relate to others. People sometimes wondered if perhaps he was autistic, but it was just a case of Diego constantly moving to different countries due to his father's job. He'd never been able to develop any close friendships, and therefore had missed the necessary social skills to survive high school.

Diego turned around to look at his fiancée as she got ready. Diego and Deborah had been engaged for a year and a half, and all his thoughts of starting to plan their wedding were put on hold over the anxiety he was feeling about the reunion.

"I don't know if I should go. Maybe you go without me, honey…" Diego suggested.

"It's YOUR high school reunion!" Deborah retorted as she exited the bathroom and switched off the lights. She sat next to her fiancé and held his hand. She was wearing the gold and silver watch he'd gotten her for her last birthday, which she only wore on special occasions.

Deborah put her arm around her fiancé and lowered her head to meet his worried expression.

"It's going to be ok. Let yourself be surprised," she said softly.

***

The first person Diego noticed at the reunion was his old acquaintance Greg. Greg had always been popular. He was tall, good-looking, and girls had always been interested in him back in high school.

With Diego's recent promotion and engagement to Deborah, he felt he had a lot to be proud of, but he was worried his achievements would be undermined by Greg—just like everyone had undermined Diego's accomplishments back in school.

Greg noticed Diego and immediately honed in on him like a missile.

"It's so good to see you, D!" Greg exclaimed as he surveyed Diego quickly. "You look great!"

Diego and Greg continued to make small talk until Diego decided to get another drink.

***

After a couple hours, Diego had had a little too much to drink and was finally starting to feel comfortable talking to classmates he'd known back in the day.

From the corner of his eye, he saw Greg signaling Deborah to come speak to him, which seemed very odd.

Diego watched his fiancée walk over to Greg as he began to whisper things in her ear.

"What's going on there?" Diego asked as he looked at his fiancée speaking to Greg in such close proximity.

"Maybe Greg is up to his old ways with that absolute beauty…" one of Diego's classmates asserted as he took a sip of his champagne, unaware that the "absolute beauty" he was referring to was Diego's fiancée.

Rather than inform his old classmate that he was speaking about Diego's fiancée, Diego continued to assess the situation.

After a couple minutes, Diego turned to check on Deborah and Greg once more, but he could not find either his fiancée or Greg, which prompted him to go looking for them.

He found Greg and Deborah talking, their heads very close together, behind one of the room's large columns.

"What's going on here?!" Diego demanded as he pushed his way between them. "Are you chatting up my fiancée?"

Diego got really close to Greg's face (or chin, rather).

"Honey!" Deborah called out.

"Why are you hiding from me and talking to this guy?!" challenged Diego.

"D, calm down...." Greg began.

"No! You stole all my girlfriends in school and I won't let you do it again!" growled Diego.

"Diego, he was asking me how to approach you about asking for business advice and if you could help him professionally!" Deborah explained, looking frustrated and slightly embarrassed.

"What?" Diego inquired, dumbfounded.

"I'm so sorry, D. I just heard how successful you were these days, and I was wondering if there was a chance you could help me. I haven't been doing so good lately ever since I was fired from the garage..." mumbled Greg.

Diego took a couple deep breaths and looked at his fiancée before backing away from Greg in shame.

"I'm really sorry, Greg. I had no idea…" he started.

"It's ok. I'm sorry for being an idiot back in the day. You have every right to be mad," Greg admitted.

Diego looked up at Greg and felt a wave of sympathy flow through him. Luckily, not too many people noticed the altercation.

"You wanna go have a drink and talk business?" Diego asked.

Greg's face lit up immediately, and the two men headed off to refresh their drinks.

BUCKLEY AND BAILEY

Buckley was the second dog I'd ever had. The first had been a golden retriever when I was very young, too young to feel any ownership over a dog that belonged to the entire family more than it did to me. It had been my older brother who had petitioned to get a dog back then. But this time I was living alone, and I could say without a shadow of a doubt that Buckley was my dog.

It took almost half a year to find the right dog for me. I found the breed I liked fairly quickly, but finding a Stabyhoun breeder near me was a challenge. I was living in Europe at the time, and Stabyhouns are a Dutch breed, but I was living in Spain and the only way to get a Stabyhoun was to live either in the Netherlands or England.

However, after about a month spent trying to find a way to get one of these beautiful dogs, I spoke to my brother, who lived in Germany and said there was a Stabyhoun breeder near him.

I hadn't spoken to my brother in many years due to a falling-out, which upset my parents, but I knew that if I tried to force the relationship we would only be making matters worse. The only reason we spoke this time was that my parents had informed him of what I was searching for, and—after what I imagined took a lot of coercion and convincing from my parents—he reached out to me and told me about the breeder.

Long story short, I took my remote job abroad to Germany for a while to get Buckley.

I spoke no German and had visited the country a couple of times as a child, but never stayed longer than a week. In fact, I once visited Germany with my parents and the golden retriever we had back then.

I moved about an hour away from my brother, and although I told my parents that I would gladly visit him or that I would be happy to have him stay with me for a while, I was correct in assuming that that would not happen.

The connection between Buckley and me was not instant. However, once I spent enough time with him, I found myself missing—and often needing—his presence. It became clear that I was genuinely falling in love with the little guy.

I was due to stay in Germany for six months before returning to Spain with Buckley. I enrolled myself in an immersive German-language course, and during those classes, I met a girl named Anne. Anne was American and had a dog, a three-year-old German Shepherd named Bailey, who was almost bigger than she was.

We took our dogs on our first date. They were particularly tired that day and did not interact with each other very much. We continued to see each other almost every day, and eventually, I moved into Anne's apartment, which was bigger and better located than mine.

I did not know what my plans were now that Anne was in my life, but that was something I would contemplate during the months I had left in Germany. However, a couple of weeks after moving in with Anne, I began to feel highly frustrated with how Bailey would behave around Buckley.

I was unsure if something had changed, or if I had just previously been unaware of this behavior between the two dogs. Still, Bailey was much more territorial and temperamental than Buckley.

My blood would boil whenever Bailey barked at Buckley for taking his toy or going outside to the terrace where Bailey was sunbathing. Things never got past the point of barking. Still, the issue was that Buckley didn't bark at any other dogs, so I was afraid Bailey's aggressive behavior would negatively affect Buckley's serene and passive nature or that, eventually, the situation would escalate.

The dogs' interaction quickly became a point of contention between Anne and I. Anne proclaimed that this was normal behavior and the two dogs loved each other. Still, my overprotective nature made it difficult for me to accept that.

My parents kept trying to persuade me to reach out to my older brother for advice since, for the past seven years, he'd had two dogs and was more knowledgeable on these matters than I was, but I was still reluctant to speak to him.

One day, Anne and I took the dogs to the park for some exercise. Anne and I were sitting on a bench arguing yet again about me thinking that Bailey needed an attitude adjustment while she maintained that the problem only existed in my mind.

At one point, a huge dog—even bigger than Bailey—began chasing Buckley around the park. Suddenly, I saw Buckley stop running and recoil in fear as the large dog continued to bark and snap at him.

Before I could react, Bailey ran to Buckley's defense and began barking at the larger dog. The two got so loud and close to each other that everyone noticed and a commotion erupted. Luckily, the owner of the larger dog arrived in time and pulled his dog away from the scene.

When Anne and I got home, we found a little blood coming out of Buckley's thigh, which must have been from the incident at the dog park.

Thankfully, the cut was not deep, and we knew it would heal without a trip to the vet.

I spent the rest of the afternoon sitting alone in the kitchen, pondering my worries about Buckley and Bailey. Suddenly, I received a text message from Anne asking me to come to the living room, which I did. Once I got there, Anne had her index finger pressed against her lips. She signaled me to be quiet and to follow her.

Anne led me to the bedroom where Bailey's large bed was located. On the bed was Buckley, taking up about 10% of the bed, with Bailey lying just off the bed next to Buckley's head. Bailey had wedged himself in the little space in the corner of the room and was licking Buckley's head; Buckley was either fast asleep, or about to be.

I watched the two of them and immediately knew that Bailey was comforting his brother and that it was working. I also appreciated how Bailey had stood up for Buckley at the dog park against the aggressive dog.

As Anne and I stood together, we witnessed Buckley waking up and putting his head on top of Bailey's, which was both funny and endearing.

The next day I apologized to Anne and explained to her that I had been wrong to doubt the loyalty and love between the two dogs. Anne smiled.

"I think there's one more person you need to consider in this realization of yours…" she said.

About an hour later, I called my brother to ask about visiting him. He insisted I bring Anne and the dogs. I smiled, filled with joy at the thought.

THE TREE

Fabienne and Anna were best friends and completely inseparable. They had been in the same class for the past four years of elementary school and were excited about spending the summer vacation together.

Every summer, they would venture into the woods and climb their favorite oak tree, which technically was in a backyard belonging to an older lady who never left her house and never bothered anyone.

Last summer, they'd built a swing around one of the branches and carved their initials into the bark. This year, they were determined to build a tree house, something they'd been dreaming of doing for a long time, but they were advised against it since the tree was the older lady's property, after all.

"But no one even knows her name!" Anna protested to her mother.

"Her name is Tamara, and she is a very kind woman," replied her mother.

"I've heard she's an evil witch. Witches should not be allowed to have nice trees!" Fabienne joined in.

Anna's mother shook her head in disapproval and sent them on their way to the forest; she knew once they joined forces, there was no stopping them.

Once they arrived at the tree, they began circling it to imagine how they wanted the tree house to look.

"I think it should be pink, and boys shouldn't ever be allowed!" Anna declared as she looked up at the prodigious branches.

Fabienne tore her gaze away from the tree and shot a look of disapproval toward her best friend.

"No boys?" she asked skeptically.

"Yeah, only girls…" insisted Anna.

"What about the boys we like?" countered Fabienne.

"Not even them!"

Fabienne was visibly displeased by this suggestion.

"What if I want to bring my little brother?" she asked.

"Not even him," Anna retorted.

"What if I want the treehouse to be blue?" contended Fabienne.

The discussion ensued to the point where both girls became frustrated with each other and began fighting for the first time since they'd known each other.

The fighting got so loud that it even attracted the attention of the mysterious old lady who lived in the decrepit house nearby.

Her appearance shocked Fabienne and Anna into silence.

"What are your names, young ladies?" Tamara asked as she beckoned them over.

"I'm Fabienne, and she is Anna..." supplied Fabienne hesitantly.

"Then you are the two girls who have been damaging my tree with your carvings. That tree is beautiful and should be preserved and treated respectfully," commented Tamara.

The two girls apologized.

"You're going to have to make it up to me. I want you to rake the leaves off my front yard and weed my garden beds every morning for ten days. If you do that, I won't tell your parents about what you've done," said Tamara.

***

To both Fabienne's and Anna's surprise, Anna's mother ultimately agreed with Tamara.

"I warned you, girls. Now you have to face the consequences!" she admonished.

As the days passed, Anna and Fabienne silently raked the leaves and worked in Tamara's garden. They refused to speak to each other the entire time they were there, which was about an hour each day.

This uncomfortable situation continued for most of the time they were forced to clean up Tamara's yard and garden.

Finally, on the last day, Anna broke the uncomfortable silence they were getting so accustomed to.

"You can bring your brother to the tree house if you want. And we can paint it blue if you want," she offered shyly.

Fabienne looked surprised but felt compelled to reply.

"Thank you. I think pink would be a nice color for the treehouse…" she said hesitantly.

"Maybe we can find a color we both like… what do you think about yellow?" asked Anna.

"I would LOVE yellow!" Fabienne exclaimed.

'We're going to have to find another tree to build it in, though…" mused Anna.

After a couple of minutes, the girls continued to talk like nothing had happened. They were right back to where they had left off before the argument. They began enjoying each others' company so much again that they were disheartened when the chores ended and they could no longer clean Tamara's garden.

As they finished up, Tamara came outside and announced, "You did well. I am very proud of you girls."

"We're sorry for damaging your tree; we won't do it again," chorused the girls.

"What do you mean? I thought you were going to build a treehouse," said Tamara.

Fabienne and Anna looked at each other, befuddled.

"I thought you didn't want us near the tree anymore…" Anna inquired.

"All I wanted was for you two to stop fighting and remember how much you love being friends. And look, my plan worked. You have my blessing to build a treehouse," declared Tamara.

Anna and Fabienne ran up to Tamara and hugged her simultaneously.

Later, they ran home, excited to tell Anna's mother what had just happened. Once they did, Anna's mother laughed and confessed that she knew about the plan all along because Tamara had called her and explained everything.

"Just never forget what you mean to each other. It's one thing to carve it on a tree; it's another to work at the friendship every day, even when times are tough," Anna's mother reminded both girls before walking back to the kitchen to get them some well-deserved snacks.

SHOW-AND-TELL

It was show-and-tell day at school, and Zachary was excited about showing his dinosaur toy his father had gotten him during one of his business trips.

However, Zachary was not excited about having to escort the new kid, Tony, through the school campus yet again. Tony had just been enrolled a couple of days ago, and Zachary had been assigned to be his chaperone for the week.

The problem wasn't so much the chaperoning, but the fact that Tony seemed to be a very strange boy who didn't like to talk or interact with others.

Zachary was the complete opposite. Zachary had always been the loudest, most extroverted boy in class—the one everybody wanted to play with, which might have been the reason why they thought he would be the best choice to guide the new boy around the school.

The problem was that for the last couple of days, ever since Zachary had been spending time with Tony like he'd been instructed to do, the other kids who usually loved playing with Zachary had been keeping their distance. In Zachary's mind, the problem was obviously Tony.

"I brought a drawing I did for show-and-tell," Tony declared worriedly as he walked through the halls alongside Zachary, "but I don't know if the other kids will like it."

"You'll be ok, so don't worry about it. Everyone is going to be paying attention to my toy anyway…" boasted Zachary.

"What did you bring?" asked Tony.

"I brought a T-Rex; my father got it for me, and it's red!" bragged Zachary.

"Can I see it?" Tony said.

"You'll see it in class when I show it. Everyone is going to love it," Zachary declared.

Zachary walked down the halls with his chest held high, but he was still worried that Tony being next to him was keeping everyone else away from him.

"Are you sure people are going to like my drawing?" Tony asked.

"They're going to love it. Don't worry about it," answered Zachary.

"Thank you," said Tony.

The time finally came for show-and-tell, and all the kids sat on the multicolored carpet excitedly as they anxiously waited for show-and-tell to begin.

Because of Tony's last name, he was due to be one of the first ones presenting, but he declared that he wanted to go after Zachary. That made Zachary cringe with embarrassment.

As the children took their turns for show-and-tell, they enthusiastically presented their various objects and artifacts in great detail. One child had even brought a live tarantula, which he kept as a pet at home.

"My dinosaur is way cooler than that spider!" whispered Zachary.

"I'm sure it is!" Tony responded.

"Are you sure you want to go after me? Maybe going a few before me would be better..." suggested Zachary.

"I'm scared. I'd rather go after you if that's ok," said Tony.

"That's fine," Zachary reluctantly accepted.

It was finally Zachary's turn to present. He noticed several children around him begin whispering and smiling as he got up and walked over to his backpack to retrieve the dinosaur. Once the sizable red T-rex was in his hands, he ran over to stand next to the teacher on her wooden stool in front of the semicircle of children.

Children were already smiling and giggling among each other, which Zachary took as a good sign at first. At this point, he was glad to finally be separated from Tony.

"This is Rexy," Zachary began, "I've had him for about a year now, and he is my favorite dinosaur. They did not have a lot of red dinosaurs in the store where my father was, so he got this one because he knew it was special."

As Zachary continued talking, the murmurs and the giggles got louder, so much so that the teacher had to tell everyone to quiet down. Tony was the only person paying attention to Zachary instead of laughing.

The commotion continued despite the teacher's protestations, which made Zachary feel progressively more uncomfortable. The only thing that calmed his nerves was looking at how attentive Tony was throughout his show-and-tell.

"Can we call you dinosaur boy?" a boy cried out, which gave way to rapturous laughter from the other children.

Zachary became overwhelmed with shame and humiliation as the teacher tried to calm the children. Zachary promptly finished his show-and-tell and sat beside Tony, feeling deflated and defeated.

"Tony, you're next," the teacher called out.

Zachary was too busy looking down at the ground to notice Tony take his dinosaur from him and take it with him as he took his place in front of the classroom.

"Today, I want to talk about my friend Zachary," Tony declared, which caught Zachary's attention and prompted him to finally look up.

"When I first arrived here, I was very nervous. Zachary was with me the entire time, and he answered all my questions and helped me feel better. I think he is a great friend, and I'm very happy he has helped me feel better," explained Tony.

Tony continued to describe how thankful he was to Zachary as he held the dinosaur in his hand. This time, nobody laughed or even made any sound; it was clear that Tony was speaking from the heart. His words were especially poignant considering this was the first time anyone other than Zachary had heard him speak.

Once the presentation finished, the students clapped as Tony sat beside his friend.

Zachary smiled and no longer felt ashamed to be sitting next to Tony; in fact, he felt quite the opposite.

Once class finished, Zachary and Tony walked to recess together and have been doing so as best friends ever since.

CHAPTER 3

FIVE STORIES ABOUT LOVE

BALTO

Joey knew that Flo loved dogs. The truth is, Joey loved dogs too, but he had never considered getting one himself. Sure, whenever there was a dog around—either at a friend's house or perhaps in a restaurant near his table—he loved being around the dog and playing with it, but the thought of getting a dog of his own had never crossed his mind until about a month ago, when he was talking to his ex-girlfriend Flo.

Joey and Flo had broken up a couple of months ago due to all the fighting they'd been doing, but after about a week of silence, they decided to talk again and see if they could work things out.

It had been Flo who had suggested taking things slowly instead of getting back together right away. She thought they should see if it was a good idea to reunite without any idea of how to avoid continuing to fight in such an impassioned way.

While Joey could see she was right, he felt miserable without her. Every day that passed made him feel more certain that breaking up was a mistake.

After some time deliberating what would be the best way to get Flo back, Joey came up with the notion of getting a dog. Flo had always wanted a dog, and he had never seen her get more excited than when a dog was in her general vicinity.

The original plan was to surprise Flo with a puppy that would initially live with Joey but could also spend time at Flo's place, since they lived so close to each other. Joey even contemplated insisting that the dog live with him the whole time, thinking that might be an effective way of getting Flo to move in with him—which he'd wanted her to do for some time.

As it turned out, getting a puppy was nowhere near as easy as Joey thought it would be. Joey tried many different kennels, but they always seemed to have an endless waiting list. Finally, he found one with a newborn chocolate labrador puppy.

Joey went to see the puppy and knew that Flo would love it.

"He's a little meatball!" Joey exclaimed to the woman as she handed him a chubby and excitable three-month-old puppy. His eyes were yellow and full of character. Although he was very young, he was heavier than Joey had expected.

"You are a chubby little guy, aren't you?" Joey asked what could potentially be his new dog.

The puppy wagged his tail enthusiastically, and as he did, Joey decided that this was the one.

"I'm gonna call you Balto," he informed the puppy in his hands, smiling broadly.

When he got home, he could not contain his excitement. He immediately told Flo all about the puppy, and she reacted just as joyfully as he'd hoped.

***

A couple of days before Joey was due to pick up Balto from the kennel, he and Flo had yet another fight. This one was more heated than any fight they'd ever had before, leading Flo to declare that there was no way they could get back together.

Joey did not get much sleep after that incident, so he showed up to pick up Balto with bags under his eyes and dragging his limbs a bit. However, once he was handed Balto, he quickly realized he needed to wake up, as the newborn pup behaved as if he had had all the sleep in the world and was ready to take on the world.

Joey struggled to keep the brown puppy in his arms as he headed to the car and drove home.

To make matters worse, raising Balto did not allow Joey to catch up on any of the sleep he'd missed worrying about what had happened with Flo. He hadn't even managed to tell her about Balto. However, as the days passed, Joey found it impossible to think about anything other than Balto.

Joey was waking up every three hours to let him out and spent the rest of his time running around cleaning up whatever mess Balto had made in the two minutes Joey went to the bathroom.

The first week was very taxing for Joey. One day, after Joey had been standing outside in the pouring rain for 20 minutes with Balto so that he could go to the bathroom on the grass, Joey gave up and headed back inside. Almost immediately, Balto squatted on the welcome mat by the front door and went to the bathroom in the house.

Joey screamed as loud as he could, which made Balto squeal in fear and run away from him.

Once he collected himself, Joey searched for Balto for a long time before he finally found him hiding under the dining table.

"I'm so sorry, Balto. I will never scream at you that way again," Joey promised.

After that incident, Joey went for a walk through the woods with Balto and realized that in the entire time that Balto had been at the house, he had never once thought about Flo. As sleep-deprived and frustrated as he was, at least he was no longer obsessing over Flo the way he thought he would be; his mind was too focused on Balto.

Almost a year later, Flo reached out to Joey. He got her call when he was at the dog beach with Balto. Flo asked Joey if they could talk about maybe getting back together after all.

Joey couldn't believe it. He had dreamed about getting this call from Flo one day, but for some reason, he did not feel as euphoric or excited as he had imagined he would.

Balto was chasing his canine friends all around the beach. Joey had kept his promise to Balto and never screamed at him again; in fact, he had never felt the same need to scream ever since that promise was made.

"I'm sorry, Flo, but I don't know if we will be able to stop being so aggressive to each other, and I promised Balto that I would never let him see me scream ever again," he finally said.

This response shocked Flo. She insisted that Joey reconsider his decision, but he couldn't.

Once the phone call ended, Joey opened his arms and contracted his core to prepare for Balto as the dog ran toward him as fast as he could and leaped into his arms. Joey hugged Balto and kissed the top of his head.

"It's you and I forever, buddy," Joey said as he looked into Balto's yellow eyes. "Thank you for everything."

MARIE

It had been a couple of weeks since Joey had rejected Flo's petition to get back together. Although he was initially confident that he had made the right choice, he eventually began to doubt whether he had inadvertently made a mistake and might have lost his chance to be with the woman he was truly supposed to be with.

The more people Joey spoke to about the uncertainty he felt, the more he heard about how it was normal to feel doubt. Although Joey believed those voices to be right in their assessment of the situation, he was still riddled with doubt.

One particularly dark and gloomy day, which fitted Joey's tormented state of mind, he headed to the dog beach with Balto to think about his situation.

Once there, he spotted a red-haired girl with a cocker spaniel who refused to get into the water no matter how hard she tried to get him to join her for a swim.

It didn't take long for Joey to approach her and start giving her advice on how to get her dog to stop being scared of the water.

"I'm a dog trainer," she informed Joey as she tried her best not to giggle.

After a couple of minutes of playful banter, the two exchanged numbers and arranged to meet the following day for lunch. The girl's name was Marie.

Both Joey and Marie brought their dogs to lunch, and to Joey's exultation, the dogs became immediate friends.

The date went very well, except for an unfortunate incident involving Joey spilling water on his white shirt, but he played it off as a joke and made Marie laugh in a way that he appreciated.

After the date, Joey dropped Marie off at her apartment and kissed her on the cheek before she stepped out of the car and grabbed her dog from the back seat.

Joey went to bed that night happy, replaying the date in his head over and over until he fell asleep thinking about it.

The following day, Joey woke up late, but he saw he had a disturbingly lengthy message from Marie on his phone. Still in bed and only half awake, he read Marie's confession that she was due to leave the country in 24 hours to return to Germany, where she was from, and that she hadn't mentioned it before because she was having such a lovely date.

Joey called Marie immediately and arranged to meet her for coffee that afternoon.

During their second encounter, Marie apologized profusely and explained why she was too scared to tell Joey the truth.

"Is there any way that you could stay a little longer?" Joey asked.

"I would need a place to stay, and I would need to tell my parents. They would have so many questions," she said hesitantly.

Joey and Marie continued to discuss the matter until Joey realized what he had to do.

"I won't let you go. If you want, you can stay with Balto and me, but I can't let you go like this," he declared.

Marie smiled at Joey as if that was exactly what she had wanted to hear all along.

"Ok. I will stay," she agreed.

Marie and her small dog stayed an extra week. She temporarily moved in with Joey and Balto, and the four of them went sightseeing and on long walks almost every day.

When it came time for Marie to return home, she hugged and kissed Joey as if it was the last time she would see him.

"Call me when you land," Joey told Marie.

Once Marie landed safely and was back at home with her parents, she called Joey, and they spoke all day on the phone. They continued to speak virtually every day that week until Joey built up the courage to ask Marie to be his girlfriend. She accepted gleefully.

Joey ended up moving to Germany with Balto to be with Marie, and he lived there for three years until the relationship ended.

Joey moved back home with Balto after those three years but never stopped loving Marie. He still talks to her from time to time, but misses her every day.

When it has been a particularly tough day or something happens that makes him think of Marie, he calls her and reminds her what he told her that day after their first date when they discussed what she revealed to him about having to fly back to Germany.

"That day, I told you I wouldn't let you go. I want you to know that all these years later, it's still true, and my heart will never let you go," Joey told Marie, who cried and told him she felt the same.

Sometimes the most beautiful and invigorating relationships do not last forever, or at least they don't last outside of our hearts, but that does not mean that they are any less important than the ones that do.

Joey still visits the dog beach to this day, and every time he does, he thinks of Marie and no one else.

BIRTHDAY WEEK

Anne could tell that I was upset.

"What's wrong?" she asked once I hung up after talking to my parents.

Anne and I lived together in a small apartment about a four-hour drive away from my parents and most of my extended family.

"They originally said they would be here tomorrow, but now they're saying they can't make the drive until next week," I told her.

"How come?" she inquired.

"They said it's because my dad has a medical appointment they had forgotten about. I don't understand how they can do this just one day before they are due to get here," I complained.

Anne and I had spent the entire weekend buying groceries for all the meals we were planning to cook for my parents, and Anne had spent the majority of the past two days cleaning the apartment. She'd worked so hard that I was barely allowed to even get a drink of water just to preserve how immaculate she wanted to keep it.

"This is typical!" I protested as I sat at the round, wooden kitchen table, which had never gleamed the way it did then.

I somewhat aggressively slammed down my favorite white porcelain coffee mug on the table. Anne shot me a look of disapproval, which quickly communicated to me that there was something I was doing wrong. At first, I thought she disapproved of my mild outburst, but then I quickly realized the problem. I grunted and promptly grabbed a cork coaster to place under the mug so the integrity of the table she had worked so tirelessly to clean remained intact.

Anne looked content. She walked over to the table and sat next to me. She put her hand on my leg and looked at me. Her green eyes always looked their best when the sun shone upon them and highlighted the freckles surrounding them, which was the case on that particular morning.

"You have to be more patient. You know your parents love you, and that's what matters. You only know half of the story…" Anne suggested in her faint German accent, which always rose to the surface when she was speaking from the heart or she was worried about me.

"That's the problem; they didn't even want to tell me what the appointment was about or why they forgot. They just seemed so uninterested in providing context. Now we'll have to buy all these groceries and clean the apartment all over again for when they actually do come… if they ever do!" I complained.

"Well, that gives you a chance to help out with the cleaning next time," Anne proposed as she brushed her ginger hair back with a smile. I smiled, too.

For the rest of the day, my parents continued trying to get in touch with me, but I kept brushing them off, telling them I was too busy to talk. In reality, though, I was just upset that they had done exactly what I had predicted they would do: cancel at the last minute.

Finally, while I was lying on the green sofa in the living room with Anne later that day, I got a message from my parents saying that they would be there early the next morning.

"Ok, you clean the bathroom. I'll do the kitchen!" Anne exclaimed as she shot up so quickly that her blue flannel pajama pants almost fell off.

I glanced at the kitchen to my right, which was still so clean you could perform invasive surgery on the table, and chuckled. It was amazing how much importance Anne gave to ensuring a clean apartment for her in-laws and how nothing they ever did could detract from that.

***

It was the fourth day of my parents visiting Anne and me, and only two days until my actual birthday. Everything had been going well, until things blew up that evening.

While I was out running errands that evening, I got a call from my mother informing me that she had forgotten an important document back home and had to drive back with my dad.

"So you're leaving now and you won't be here for my actual birthday?" I asked.

"We will do our best!" she replied.

The conversation turned hostile, and I hung up the phone in anger. When I got home, Anne did her best to comfort me. We sat together on the sofa as she stroked my head, which normally always calmed me down but didn't work this time.

"I can't believe they are canceling yet again!" I steamed.

"They did come here, though!" Anne reminded me.

"Yes, but they aren't going to be here for my actual birthday. What frustrates me the most is that I am always right when I predict these things will happen!"

My phone continued to ring as my parents called me repeatedly, but I refused to answer.

Anna looked at me in a way that made it obvious many conflicting thoughts were running through her brain. I waited silently to see if she would share whatever was troubling her.

"There's something I'm not supposed to tell you, but I feel like I have to at this point..." she finally said.

"What is it?" I grumbled.

Anne hesitated to reveal what was on her mind, but then acquiesced to her own desire to divulge some truth I was unaware of.

"Your parents were on their way to pick up your uncles, aunts, and cousins to bring them here to surprise you..." she admitted.

"What?!" I exclaimed.

"They managed to get the confirmation from everyone right after they got to our place, and since they have the biggest car and know how to navigate city traffic the best, they'd planned on picking everyone up to drive them here," she shared.

"And now they're not coming back? Because of what I did?!"

"They are. Your parents are driving back home tonight, and tomorrow morning they will drive back here with everyone else. They wanted to surprise you," she reassured me.

I looked at Anne in disbelief. I felt like a terrible son. My immediate reaction was to call my parents and apologize for everything, but Anne stopped me.

"I have an idea," she said.

***

Anne and I quickly changed from our pajamas into regular clothes and packed our bags. We hopped in the car and headed towards the highway. I called my parents while Anne drove.

After about half an hour spent apologizing, I informed them that we were driving to their house that evening and that we would be celebrating my birthday back home.

"I'm so sorry; I didn't know the whole picture. Anne told me, but I still haven't learned to accept that she's always right," I said remorsefully.

Anne smiled.

We drove all the way to their home that night, and Anne and I slept in my childhood bedroom. The following day, Anne and I woke up to the sound of all my aunts, uncles, and cousins arguing downstairs in my parents' kitchen about what to make for breakfast.

"See where I get it from?" I jokingly asked Anne, who smiled in bed next to me.

THE PETER PAN STATUE

I was reeling from the graduation ceremony I had just left. I had finished my master's degree and was enjoying how proud my parents were of me, which did not happen as often as I would have liked.

I was also thrilled to finally be back in London. I had completed my master's almost two years ago but was only now attending my graduation ceremony. I had been away working, but I had constantly daydreamed about returning to my favorite city in the world—and now it was finally happening, and for the best reason possible.

After leaving the university my parents and I went to dinner, where they repeatedly asked me about Carole. Carole was the girlfriend I had been living with during my studies in London. Our relationship had lasted for a little under two years, and she was the person who was responsible for pushing me to complete my master's.

As much as I loved Carole when we were together, my parents might have loved her even more. Carole was a kind, intelligent, and beautiful girl who always supported me and showed me the right way to go about my problems.

Carole and I tried to make a long-distance relationship work when I left London, but it was too hard. Furthermore, when I left she could no longer afford to live in central London and she had to move back in with her parents, which always made me feel guilty for leaving.

I didn't tell my parents that when I had left London two years beforehand, Carole and I had made a deal that if we were truly meant to be, we would meet by the Peter Pan statue in Hyde Park on the seventh day of the seventh month at seven in the evening.

A couple of weeks after the ceremony, I made my way over to Hyde Park, expecting to see Carole there. I had avoided talking to her during my visit because I wanted to see if she would show up at the statue without knowing I was already in the country.

I was very excited, but equally nervous. If she showed up, it would be a very romantic story that we could tell for the rest of our lives. If she were not there, that would be very disheartening, considering that I managed to make it even though it required that I get on a plane to get there. Granted, I was already in the city for my graduation—but I like to think that even without that excuse, I would have shown up.

What was unclear was what the implications of our meeting up would be. Even if we both showed up and got back together, how would we make the relationship work when I would still eventually need to fly back to where I was living?

I also wondered if she perhaps was angry at me for leaving. Carole had a very conflicted relationship with her parents, and moving back in with them once I left was something she was unwillingly forced into due to the high cost of living in London. I worried that maybe living with her parents all this time had changed her and somehow made her less interested in seeing me or following through with romantic gestures.

As I entered Hyde Park, I looked around at all the families and friends spending time under the warm summer sun and contemplated the crazy situation I was in. I looked at my watch and noticed it was already seven, so I began walking a little faster, dodging pigeons, squirrels, and sprinting children in the process.

It did not take long for me to realize that I was wrong in thinking I'd be able to find the statue. I was already terrible at directions, and I had only visited Hyde Park once before with Carole. It was quite a voyage to get there, which meant that my foolish belief that I would be able to remember the way to where we had agreed to meet was a mistake.

I ran around the park so much that I felt I was doing more exercise than the litany of joggers out for their evening run. I stopped to get some air and to look at my watch. It was fifteen minutes past seven, and I had no idea where to find the statue.

I asked someone for directions, and they told me I wasn't even close to the statue. Once the person finally stopped explaining what paths to take and where to turn, I sprinted as fast as possible to where he indicated I had to go.

I finally arrived at the statue with sweat pouring down my face. I was half an hour late, but even more disheartening was that I could not see Carole anywhere.

I sat down on a nearby bench and waited. Perhaps she had come and gone? Had I ruined the romantic gesture?

It did not take long for me to start kicking myself in frustration.

"Excuse me?" a short, red-haired girl with glasses asked me.

"Yes?" I responded.

"Are you Joel?" she inquired.

"Yes, I am," I replied worriedly.

The girl smiled and informed me she had been sent to the statue on Carole's behalf.

"Why?" I asked.

"She was too scared about what she would feel if you didn't show up and broke her heart. And she told me to wait a long while because she knew you would get lost," the girl said.

"So she isn't here?" I asked.

"She's home, but can be here in two minutes," answered the girl.

"Two minutes?" I repeated.

"Yes. We live two minutes away. I'm her roommate," she explained.

Roommate. Upon hearing that Carole was living in central London once more and had remembered our rendezvous at the statue, I experienced a joy even greater than the one I had felt when receiving my master's diploma.

I smiled and waited as the girl excitedly informed Carole I was there. I looked up at the Peter Pan statue and felt an immense sense of gratitude that Carole still had a heart that was open enough for her to be scared of it getting hurt.

The next time I left the country was ten years later, with Carole by my side as my wife.

CAMILLA

Camilla had blonde hair and blue eyes. She was French, but spoke English with an enchanting British accent because she had studied in England for both her bachelor's and postgraduate degrees.

I couldn't remember what she had studied, but it must have been something important since right after graduation, she was employed by one of the most famous and reputable fashion houses in the world.

I, on the other hand, was still struggling to find work after graduation. I was staying at the house of a very wealthy friend who was out of town for a couple of months and was letting me sleep at his home while I looked for an apartment.

It had been years since I'd left Europe, and now I was finally back in Spain, the country where Camilla also lived and worked.

I met Camilla in a club several years ago when I was still a student. I was with a friend, and she was with one of her friends too. I approached Camilla that night and started talking to her. One of the things that impressed me about her immediately, aside from her evident and intoxicating beauty, was the fact that she informed me that she did not want to leave her friend alone and would only continue talking to me if I could find someone for her friend to talk to as well.

Although I immediately became stressed about locating my friend and convincing him to join us, I found her loyalty to her friend very moving. Luckily, I quickly found my friend and asked him to speak to Camilla's friend as a favor to me, which he did begrudgingly.

It was now several years after that meeting, which unfortunately never culminated in anything more than one date. (And that one date was cut short only an hour after we met up because Camilla had forgotten about a previous commitment and had to leave.)

Camilla had written to me that she was excited that I was back in Spain, and we were due to meet up in a club that night to go on our long-awaited second date. Camilla told me she'd be with a friend and asked if I could bring a friend too, which I did.

***

Seeing Camilla again was overwhelming, but in a pleasant way. As beautiful as she looked, nothing was more attractive than the way she spoke so softly and in such an attractive accent. I once again introduced my friend to Camilla's friend Caroline.

It was summer, and there were a lot of people at the club the four of us were in. Every time Camilla and I spoke, I wondered if this would finally be the moment when we officially became a couple. I was also very excited to surprise her with the fact that it was my birthday and that I had chosen to spend it with her.

"So, how come we never went on a second date?" Camilla asked me as both of us stood by the bar waiting for our drinks to be served.

"Because I would always see pictures of you with other guys, and I became jealous. I should have spoken to you about it, and I'm sorry. It was my mistake," I humbly responded.

Camilla smiled, but didn't respond. We continued to chat until I felt it would be a good time for me to divulge my secret.

I looked around me and saw that Caroline was by herself. I knew that if Camilla saw her friend alone, she would go over to her and stop talking to me.

"Excuse me, I'll be right back," I said to Camilla before making my way over to Caroline.

"Hey, how are you?" I asked Caroline, who did not look as happy as I was at that moment.

"I'm ok. No thanks to your friend. I think he saw some girl who was more interesting to him and left me by myself," she grumbled.

As frustrated as I was, I was not surprised.

"I'm sorry, he's like that sometimes. I say we just leave him and go somewhere else. Do you want to stay, find some other bar, or go home?" I asked.

"What about you and Camilla?" she responded.

"I'm sure Camilla would just want you to be comfortable. Besides, I am about to tell her something that hopefully will make her realize how much I like her," I admitted.

"What's that?" Caroline asked.

"It's my birthday today. She has no idea. I want her to know how much I like her," I said.

Caroline looked very surprised.

"It's your birthday, and you would go home right now if we wanted?" she questioned.

"Well, if you're uncomfortable, yes, of course! Besides, the only thing that matters to me is being around Camilla, and I don't need to be out in the city to do that!" I responded enthusiastically.

Upon hearing my response, Caroline looked at me with a strange expression, as if feeling sympathetic for me.

"I love Camilla because she's one of my best friends in the world," Caroline began, slurring her words slightly as a consequence of all the drinks she'd had that night, "but I think there's something you should know."

"What is it?"

Caroline seemed reluctant, yet equally determined to say something more.

"Is it about Camilla?" I asked, worried that there was something I'd missed in my plan to surprise her and make her realize how attracted to her I was.

Caroline nodded.

"What is it?" I inquired anxiously.

"She has a boyfriend. She's been seeing someone for a couple of years now. I'm very sorry. I thought she had told you," whispered Caroline.

First I felt as though Caroline was wrong and was saying things that weren't true due to all the drinks she'd had, but then I realized that didn't make sense. It didn't take long for me to understand that Caroline's confession finally provided me with the answers I was searching for when I wondered why Camilla never responded to any of my messages and always ran away from me whenever she got a phone call from home.

Many thoughts ran through my head, mainly regarding how I could make Camilla immediately end the relationship with whoever she was with and choose to be with me instead.

"You're a great guy. I just think you deserve to be happy," Caroline said.

I sheepishly walked back to Camilla and confronted her about what I'd just learned. Camilla said it was true, seemingly without any remorse. It made me angry that she didn't seem to understand how I could be upset over this obviously devastating revelation. However, it was at that moment that I decided to see things from a different and healthier perspective, one which I still carry to this day.

"What do you feel?" Camilla asked.

Even though this unexpected realization hurt me, I smiled. For a brief moment after Caroline informed me of Camilla's boyfriend, I had contemplated spending my time with Camilla trying to convince her to leave who she was with and be with me. However, I suddenly decided to do something different.

"I've been trying to be with you for many years. I canceled spending my birthday with my family and friends to see you. I need to start loving myself more," I announced.

Camilla's blue eyes widened, and she looked at me as if impressed.

"I'm so sorry. You're right. The truth is I'm not happy; I don't think he deserves me!" Camilla quickly added, edging slightly closer to me.

"Well, I'm not sure you deserve me," I replied before turning around and leaving. I stopped for a second to say goodbye to Caroline, who was smiling as if impressed, and then exited the club.

After that night, Camilla continued to write me and insist that we speak, but I refused. I had finally learned to love the one person I had been disregarding for many years—myself.

Chapter 4

Five Stories About Loss

Alexander

I remember the day I arrived at school and could immediately tell that something was different. I was very young—I'm not sure exactly how young, but everyone in the classroom was still at the age where we'd sit in a semicircle around the teacher to listen to her read a story before being released to play at recess.

Furthermore, I was at the age where you are friends with whoever is nearby and wants to participate in the game or activity you are engaged in that day. There was no one I would call my best friend, and if I had been pressed to answer who I considered my closest friend, it definitely would not have been Alexander.

There was nothing bad about Alexander that would deem him unfit to be a good friend; we just never happened to be playing the same game or share any of the same interests at the same time.

I knew who he was, of course. He was the nerdy-looking boy with the bowl haircut and glasses. He always seemed to wear the same green and blue sweater and a radiant smile that never waned, except for that day in the principal's office.

As a young child, when you are asked to go to the principal's office, you immediately assume you'll be reprimanded even if you cannot recall doing anything wrong. Then again, with most of the things you do wrong as a kid, you only learn they are wrong after the fact.

I walked in somewhat sheepishly and fearfully, but was immediately relieved when I saw

Alexander sitting inside with his mother and a couple more adults. I didn't know who they were, but they worked at the school. Although I was not friendly with Alexander, there was no denying that his positive energy was infectious. However, when I walked up to say hi to Alexander, I noticed his smile was not as bright as usual.

Alexander was not the only one who seemed to be troubled by something. The adults had very grave expressions on their faces, which once again made me worry that I was unknowingly guilty of some terrible crime.

The principal began speaking but struggled to get the words out as she became visibly upset. She explained that the plane bringing Alexander's father back home from a business trip had crashed and that there were no survivors.

Everyone except Alexander and I began crying. If it hadn't been for Alexander remaining stoic and seemingly unaffected by the news, I would have felt guilty for not sharing in their grief—but when you are that young, you cannot comprehend the implications and emotional considerations of such a tragedy.

After the adults managed to compose themselves, the principal explained that I was the designated support person for Alexander during what remained of the academic year. I looked at Alexander, surprised, considering I couldn't remember ever having played or conversed with him.

Alexander smiled at me, and I smiled back. I was unsure how to react, so I put my hand on his, making the adults even more teary-eyed.

The principal explained that I was deemed the best person in the class to be around Alexander and keep him company during this challenging time.

Before the meeting concluded, Alexander was given a chance to speak. At first, he spoke very pragmatically and stoically about what had happened, but when he mentioned how he knew his father would always be with him in spirit, he burst out crying harder than any of the adults.

When I got home, I told my parents about what had happened. My father surmised that they must have chosen me because I was doing so well academically.

I remember spending time with Alexander after that. He wanted to talk more than anything about his father and what he remembered about him.

Unfortunately, not too long after the accident, my mother was due to give birth to my little brother. Since we were living in a foreign country where she did not speak the local language, she opted to fly back to our home country for a few months to give birth surrounded by her extended family inside a hospital where she could communicate with the doctors.

The day I left school to fly back to our home country, I remember Alexander looking at me, confused. I was also confused; I had no idea when I would return to that school, if ever.

I was enrolled in a public school during the 12 months that we lived in my home country and I hated every second of it. I rejoiced when we finally moved back to the country where we'd been living and I could return to my old school.

I remember walking back to my old school full of doubt, wondering if people would remember me or like the fact that I was back.

The first person to greet me was Alexander, who ran over to me with open arms and a radiant smile. From that moment on, we were best friends. We were even best men at each other's weddings.

Unfortunately, after that I became immersed in work, which was very demanding. Alexander and I lived in different countries, but I always did my best to stay in touch.

When I was told by a mutual friend that Alexander had been diagnosed with a terminal illness, I could not believe that he'd been sick for months and I hadn't found out until that point. I quickly hopped on a plane to be with Alexander and stayed until he passed away almost a year later.

One of our last conversations involved a lot of apologizing from my side, first for leaving the country for my brother's birth during our childhood, and second for not having been a better friend the last couple of years.

Alexander smiled. "Do you know why you were selected to be my support person when my father died?"

"No," I responded.

"Because of your kindness. Whenever I asked you about the toys you were playing with, you would just give them to me and let me play with them. You also always answered my questions whenever I couldn't do a difficult math problem."

Alexander put his hand on mine. "Because of your kind heart, I knew you would come back now—just like I knew you would come back then."

After losing Alexander, I slowed down everything at work and learned to focus on what matters. Although he passed on, Alexander always remains with me in spirit, just like his father always remained with him.

THE GREEN HANDKERCHIEF

Orlando had not planned on his son Daniel being sick and unable to attend school on the day of his important interview. Before finding out about his seven-year-old son's unfortunate illness he had had a very productive morning, which instilled an advantageous sense of confidence in him that he hoped would stay until he'd completed the interview that he'd spent weeks preparing for.

Since quitting his previous job, Orlando had been going through a rough time. He had not been able to secure as many interviews as he originally believed he would, and the few he'd had did not culminate in a job offer.

However, he was sure his luck was turning around now that he had had a personal friend vouch for him with the head of HR for a huge multinational company. They had a vacant position that Orlando knew he'd be perfect for.

"Are we almost at Grandma's?" Daniel asked from the backseat.

Orlando hadn't accounted for having to drive his son to his mother-in-law's place, so he was already feeling stressed and increasingly worried every time he looked at his watch. Luckily, the traffic was light, and he thought he could get to the interview just in time if everything went according to the plan he'd hastily devised after getting a call from the school.

Things would have been significantly easier if Daniel had stayed at school instead of being sent to the school nurse's office, where the nurse had taken his temperature and called Orlando to pick him up, or if Orlando's wife had been at home instead of at a doctor's appointment.

"About seven minutes away, Danny!" Orlando bellowed. He wasn't particularly fond of seeing his mother-in-law, yet he drove as fast as possible to get there.

Orlando glanced back at his son and wasn't surprised when he saw him playing with the green handkerchief. Ever since Daniel discovered the green handkerchief that Orlando sometimes wore with his black suit, he had been carrying it around with him and twiddling it between his thumb and index finger as if it were the most exciting toy he had ever gotten.

In fact, Daniel was so enamored with the handkerchief that Orlando was worried that this was symbolic of some sort of emotional problem his son might be having. Still, he was informed by a professional that there was nothing to worry about. When Orlando and his wife asked Daniel about the handkerchief, he responded with, "It makes me feel calm. I need it by my side."

Although quite stressed, Orlando smiled as he saw how much peace that green handkerchief brought his son.

Once Orlando arrived, he raced out of the car so fast he nearly fell and hit the pavement, which would have been bad considering he was wearing his lucky white shirt and didn't have time to run home and change if it got dirty.

Orlando helped his son out of the car, rang the doorbell once, and restrained himself from jabbing the bell repeatedly until his mother-in-law opened the door.

Of course! Orlando thought to himself as he surveyed the house and tried to peer through the windows to see what was taking his mother-in-law so long to come to the door.

"Is she not home?" Danny asked.

"She said she would be!" Orlando replied as he rang the doorbell a second time.

After about five excruciatingly long minutes, the door finally opened. Orlando's mother-in-law smiled when she saw little Danny and not so much when she saw Orlando.

With someone to watch over his sick child, Orlando raced back to the car and drove as fast as he could to the interview.

Luckily, he made it there with just five minutes to spare.

Orlando sat down in the waiting room and tried to slow his breathing.

"Can I get you something to drink?" the receptionist asked him, probably noticing his discomposure.

"Yes, please," Orlando replied, taking a deep and calming breath.

The receptionist came back with a paper cup filled with ice-cold water.

Orlando smiled and took a generous swig.

His throat was so dry that he coughed up the cold water and spilled an embarrassing amount all over his white shirt.

Orlando looked around, but the receptionist didn't notice until she hung up the phone and notified him that they were ready to see him.

"Oh no. Do you want to go to the bathroom first?" she asked.

"No, I'm ok, thanks!" Orlando replied foolishly as he buttoned his blazer, hoping it would cover the wet spot. Unfortunately, it didn't hide the spot at all.

***

"How did it go?" Danny asked as he looked down at his handkerchief.

If anyone else had asked, Orlando would have ignored the question to avoid his bad temper getting the better of him.

"Not as good as I was hoping," Orlando replied, omitting the part about everyone immediately noticing the giant wet patch on his chest when he entered the interview room.

"Why not? Didn't you have your lucky shirt?" Danny queried.

"I did. It turns out it's not as lucky as I thought…" muttered Orlando.

"Maybe you need a lucky handkerchief like me!" Danny suggested as he held up the green handkerchief a little too close to the open window.

"NOOO!" Danny wailed as the wind pulled the handkerchief out of his hand.

"What happened?" barked Orlando.

"My handkerchief just flew out the window. We have to stop!" sobbed Danny.

"We can't stop, Danny. I need to get home and change."

"Please… you have to turn around,"begged Danny.

"NO! Sit down!" Orlando exclaimed, his temper finally getting the best of him.

Once the sun went down and the house was quiet, Orlando was inundated with guilt. He began to see how unfair he had been to his son and wished he would have reacted better.

Orlando walked up to his son's bedroom and stood by the door for a few minutes, unsure how to apologize or explain why he had been in such a bad mood when driving home.

Instead, he decided to search for the handkerchief.

It was late and traffic was heavy, but Orlando stood on the sidewalk, looking as hard as he could for something green. He walked through the edge of the forest by the side of the road until leaves and twigs stuck to his socks and pants.

After thirty minutes of wandering through the road where his son had lost his handkerchief,

Orlando decided to go home empty-handed and simply apologize.

When he got back, his wife Emma immediately greeted him.

"You need to see this," she said the second Orlando walked through the door. She guided him to Danny's bedroom and opened the door.

Danny was sitting on the floor holding Orlando's lucky white shirt and playing with it precisely as he had played with the handkerchief.

"What are you doing with my shirt, buddy?" said Orlando.

"It's just like my handkerchief," Danny replied excitedly.

"It is?" Orlando asked, confused.

"Yes, it is!" Danny replied as he held the shirt up to his face and smelled it. "It smells just like you. The handkerchief did too!"

"You liked the handkerchief because of the smell?" repeated Orlando.

"Yes, your smell makes me feel like you are next to me," Danny replied.

Orlando walked into the room and knelt by his son's side before embracing him and apologizing for what had happened earlier.

"It's ok. The water didn't ruin the smell..." Danny told his father happily. "Can I keep it?"

"Of course. Now it's *our* lucky shirt." Orlando smiled.

EMILIA

David thought about other ways of getting the money he needed without selling his favorite guitar, but couldn't think of anything.

As much as he wanted to ask for his girlfriend's advice about what to do, he was reluctant to do so because he believed she would probably be the first to encourage him to sell the instrument. In the early stages of their courtship, Anna loved hearing David serenade her and exclaimed over his talent.

However, as the years passed, she would grumble about the noise late at night and complain about the time he spent practicing instead of with her.

David had been fired from his job and struggled to make ends meet. His guitar, which he called "Emilia," had been a gift from his parents before they passed away. It had cost about half a year's salary at his old job.

Reluctantly, he posted his guitar for sale online at a price so high he hoped no one would be able to afford it. Unfortunately, only 24 hours after posting the ad, someone offered to buy it for the listed price.

David initially ignored the offer and proceeded to play Emilia all day instead of looking for a job, as he had intended.

When Anna asked why he was playing even more than usual, David replied defensively.

"Don't worry about it; soon, you won't have to hear me play anymore because I'm selling Emilia to someone next week," he snapped.

"Yeah, right," Anna scoffed. "There's no need to get aggressive with me. I'm just saying that you haven't been able to focus on looking for a job because all you do is play guitar. You aren't going to find anything if you don't devote the same energy to getting an interview."

"I'm serious. I need the money, and this is the best way to get it," David muttered.

Anna looked at her boyfriend incredulously.

After a few more attempts to find out if he was serious, Anna went from annoyed to shocked.

"I told you that my parents are willing to help you if you ask them to. You don't need to be so proud; you know that they love you," Anna said.

"It's not pride; I just don't want the relationship to become uncomfortable because I owe them money. Besides, they hate me," rebuffed David.

"You know that's not true!" insisted Anna.

"They do. If I asked them for help, they would just say no because it's me who's asking."

This was not the first time Anna and David had argued about money. The discussion ended the same way it always did, except this time Anna expressed sympathy for how David must be feeling about giving up his guitar—something he sometimes appeared to appreciate even more than his own girlfriend.

"Now all my attention can go back to you," David said.

"The attention shouldn't be on me, and you know that," argued Anna.

The following day, just as David was about to contact the buyer, he noticed that someone else had also made an offer for the guitar. This person lived in the same city, which meant that David would not need to spend any money on shipping.

David contacted the second buyer, who was very keen on buying the guitar. This comforted David because it made him feel that at least this person understood the value of the guitar and would treat Emilia with reverence.

It was tough to make the deal, but David agreed to meet the buyer by the train station near his home the next day to complete the transaction.

"It's a done deal," David informed Anna, who seemed to be significantly less shocked about David's decision today.

"I know how much the guitar means to you, but perhaps this really is the right thing to do," she told him.

David didn't answer. Whenever he thought about how much his girlfriend must revel in this sudden turn of events, he became too frustrated to even speak to her.

The next morning, David got up early and headed to the train station with Emilia safely in her hard case. If he wouldn't have felt so silly doing so, he would have cried the entire walk from the apartment to the station.

The buyer, a tall, bald businessman, was already waiting by the station with a big smile on his face. That infuriated David, who was considering making a run for it at the last minute before handing over the guitar.

The interaction was short but definitely could have been sweeter. David sat on a wooden bench by the station next to the businessman and the guitar, which he held very tightly. The transaction was immediate, and when David handed over the guitar, he felt an immense sorrow that he carried with him all the way home. He fell into bed and napped the rest of the day.

As the days passed, David became obsessed with the idea of one day making enough money to seek out the guitar he had sold and purchase it again. He knew that the more time that passed, the more the guitar would be worth, which made him work even harder to find a well-paying job.

After a couple of months of focused determination, David finally got a job that allowed him to declare himself on the road to getting his guitar back.

Anna had never seen David so happy. He got home from work every day excited to be doing something with his life.

One evening, as David entered the apartment after work, he noticed a long, rectangular cardboard box in the middle of the hallway. As soon as he closed the door behind him, Anna ran to greet him with an excited smile that was clearly about the box.

"This is for you; open it!" Anna exclaimed.

David did not hesitate to do as he was told. It did not take long for him to recognize the guitar case inside the box. David shot Anna a look of disbelief.

After ripping the box open and unzipping the guitar case, he reunited with the guitar he had been forced to sell.

"How did you find Emilia?" David asked.

"I didn't have to look for it. It's always been at my parents' place," said Anna.

"Your parents' place?" David repeated incredulously.

"My dad offered to buy it and hold onto it to protect you from yourself and your desire to sell it. He knew once you got a job, you would regret selling it, so he's been holding on to it this entire time," explained Anna.

David was speechless.

"The man who bought it from you is just a friend of his. You can't say that they hate you anymore, because they did this just to protect something you enjoy, s"he continued.

David ran to Anna, and they embraced tightly.

"So, your old man does like me, huh?" he murmured.

"Yeah, but you still need to pay him back for the guitar…" Anna replied.

CHOCOLATE-COVERED RAISINS

The first thing I noticed about my new school was that everything was made of brick and smelled like paint. To my great dismay, I'd had to leave my old school in Poland, where my family was living, to return to my home country of Colombia. Although I was technically Colombian because that's where I was born and my parents were from, I hadn't been back since we moved to Poland when I was four.

Every day I went to my new public school, I kept reminding myself that this change was only temporary and that I would be back in Poland in no time. We had returned to Colombia because my mother was pregnant with my little brother and was reluctant to give birth in Poland due to her inability to speak the language.

At first, I was excited about wearing a uniform to school, even if it was a dreary shade of mossy green. However, like almost everything else in that school, I grew tired of it fairly quickly.

Every day after school, I would come home and feel like the only one struggling with the new living situation. My mother was very happy to be reunited with her sisters and brothers, but I missed my old school where I could speak English and not be forced to speak Spanish—even though Spanish, in theory, was my native tongue. Still, I had no previous experience speaking the language for longer than five minutes at home.

One of the few aspects of this new school I preferred to my school back in Poland was that there was a mini market within the school grounds that you could access after exiting any classroom, since it was in the center of the building.

For the first couple of weeks, I didn't buy anything because even the snacks seemed so foreign to me that I was nervous about using the little money I had on foods I might not like. After a month of being the only one not snacking on something during recess, carefully observing what everyone was eating, and being given a taste of a few different snacks, I decided the chocolate-covered raisins were worth the investment.

I couldn't remember who was the one who had let me try quite a few raisins from his bag, but whoever it was had been right when they assured me that I would immediately fall in love with them.

After purchasing my first bag of chocolate-covered raisins, I was hooked. In a strange way, having a clearly defined snack for your recess purchase was a way for people to identify you among the vast amount of uniformed children.

One Friday, I was sitting on the brick floor with my classmates during recess. As I munched down on some raisins, a particularly boisterous boy named Carlos, who I had been consciously avoiding because of how different he seemed, approached me.

"Are those the chocolate-covered raisins?" he inquired as if he had found an oasis in the middle of the desert.

For a brief moment, I feared that perhaps I was not allowed to have the same snacks he ate on a regular basis, but then I realized how absurd that sounded.

"Yes," I admitted.

"They're so good, aren't they?" he enthused.

"Yeah!" I agreed.

"Can I have some?" he asked.

"Sure," I replied, handing him the packet and watching him take a generous handful.

"Thanks!" Carlos thanked me without even looking at me.

Carlos kept asking me to give him some chocolate-covered raisins for the rest of the day. The first couple of times, I said yes, but then I decided to stand my ground and tell him no.

"What do you mean, no?" Carlos asked, interrupting the teacher—who was in the middle of reading from her textbook to the class.

"I have barely any left now. Buy your own!" I told him.

Carlos then tried to snatch the bag from my hand, but I pulled it away from him, which caused the teacher to scream at both of us.

***

After that day, Carlos and I never spoke again. We would avoid walking past each other or sitting next to each other in class or during lunch break. Things continued like this until it was finally time for my family and me to return to Poland with my little brother.

The incident with Carlos that day had caused me to miss Poland a lot, and I could not wait to leave this school, regardless of how good their chocolate-covered raisins were—which I'd stopped having altogether ever since Carlos tried to snatch my bag from me in class.

On the last day, I was waving goodbye to everyone in my class as my dad waited for me outside the school, ready to take me home, when

Carlos walked up to me and handed me a folded note.

"I'm sorry," he said before walking back into the classroom.

Unsure of what was happening, I opened the letter and read the following:

> I'm sorry for what happened. My sister loves chocolate-covered raisins, and I used to bring her a bag every afternoon after school. My dad recently got fired from his job and hasn't been able to give me money for snacks. I didn't want to disappoint my sister, and I was too embarrassed to explain why I couldn't buy them for myself anymore. I hope you understand, and I am sorry.

My dad looked at me with concern. He got out of his car, walked up to me, and put his hand on my shoulder.

"Is everything ok?" he asked.

"Yes, I just need to do something first," I replied as I stuffed the note in my pocket and ran to the snack area to buy as many chocolate-covered raisins as my lunch money would allow.

THE WRITING COMPETITION

Sarah had never been to an event like this one before. Or if she had, it had been as someone else's guest as opposed to a prize nominee.

After about a year of laborious work, she had finally finished the third draft of her novel and felt it was worthy of sending out to various writing competitions around the country. However, she was filled with doubt. This was her first time trying to make it as a writer, and she was competing with other writers who had already published books and won previous competitions.

Sarah was proud of the book she had written, but had been assured by her family and friends that she shouldn't get her hopes up too high considering this was her first outing as a novelist. She had written a romance novel based around a tempestuous and troubled relationship she had had with her latest boyfriend, who she had broken up with a couple of years ago.

Unsure about how to cope with the end of a toxic relationship that still meant a lot to her, Sarah wrote a fictional story based on her experience with her ex-boyfriend Luke.

She struggled most with the ending of the story. In real life, she was still suffering a lot over Luke and constantly debated whether she should reach out to him and see if they could make it work this time, or finally allow herself to have a healthy relationship with someone who treated her better.

As much as she wanted to write a happy ending for her novel, she found it hard to do considering the emotional space she was in when writing the story. Therefore, she chose to end her romance with the lead female character living the rest of her days alone and saddened by the loss of the person she loved most.

The few people that Sarah showed her manuscript to said they enjoyed the book but felt the ending needed work. For the most part, Sarah agreed and didn't argue that her ending was inconclusive and somewhat tragic.

"How can I write an ending to a story I am still living? If I do that, I'll have to wait until I marry the right person, and finding them could take years," Sarah would always argue.

Regardless of her concerns about the ending, Sarah valiantly sent her manuscript to as many competitions as possible. After a month of waiting, she was finally nominated as a finalist and invited to an awards ceremony.

As Sarah walked around the event hall's reception area, she looked around the room and wondered which people around her were competitors and which were the staff.

Her friend Scarlett was next to her the whole time, looking at everyone disapprovingly.

"Everybody here looks so pretentious!" Scarlett exclaimed, speaking a little too loudly for Sarah's liking.

"Don't say that so loudly; someone will hear you!" shushed Sarah.

"Why would you want to work with people like this?" asked Scarlett.

"I wouldn't be working with them. Do you not know what a novelist is?" hissed Sarah.

Before Scarlett could respond, she became transfixed by someone walking past her.

"I wouldn't mind working with him!" Scarlett exclaimed—once again speaking a little too loudly.

Sarah turned and saw the man Scarlett was referring to. A tall, dark-haired man wearing a white T-shirt and jeans passed by and disappeared into the crowd.

The man was very handsome, which made Sarah worry that Scarlett would continue to attract attention to them by flirting outrageously.

Scarlett kept making jokes that made Sarah uncomfortable, prompting her to pull Scarlett forcibly along to find the open bar the event invitation had promised.

***

Once both women were seated in the auditorium, Sarah realized she was more nervous than she had anticipated. The stage was much larger than she had imagined it would be. As the minutes passed, more and more people filled the auditorium until there were no empty seats left.

"I can't believe so many people are here," Scarlett said as she looked around in amazement.

"I know. I can't imagine getting up on that podium if I win," Sarah admitted.

"Do you have a speech prepared?" whispered Scarlett.

Sarah turned white as she realized she hadn't even considered preparing a speech. At this point, regardless of how much hard work she had put into the manuscript, she was still determining if she even wanted to win and face such an enormous audience without a speech prepared.

As the night progressed, Sarah became increasingly nervous and almost suggested they should leave when her category was announced.

Sarah and Scarlett held each other's hands so tightly that their arms began to feel numb.

"I should have prepared a speech. What if I win?!" moaned Sarah worriedly.

Scarlett was too nervous to reply; it was apparent that despite her jokes regarding the people present at the event, she genuinely wanted her best friend to win—with or without a speech prepared.

***

"Come on, what better way to celebrate your loss than to have a drink with me and everyone else from the event? Maybe we'll meet a cute guy!" Scarlett implored.

"No one celebrates a loss!" Sarah responded as she put on her coat and tried to remember where to find the subway station that would get the two of them back to the hotel.

"Of course you do. You didn't even have a speech prepared. If you would've won, that would've been pretty embarrassing for me to watch!" countered Scarlett.

Sarah smiled and eventually consented to her friend's request.

Once they arrived at the bar, they sat down at a table by themselves and ordered drinks.

Sarah and Scarlett talked about the event and how the competition had made a big mistake by not giving Sarah the prize she deserved.

As Sarah got up from the table to head to the bathroom, she saw the handsome man from earlier. Sarah pretended not to feel overwhelmed by his presence, but failed as he approached her and stood inches away from her nose.

"I remember you. I wanted to talk to you after the event, but you left so quickly," the man said.

"Excuse me?" she stammered.

"I'm Luke."

Sarah didn't know how to react. She couldn't believe what was happening or that the handsome stranger shared the same name as her ex-boyfriend, who was also the basis for her manuscript.

Scarlett watched in awe as her friend talked to the attractive man.

Sarah returned to sit with her friend, utterly oblivious that she had never actually made it to the bathroom.

"What was that?!" Scarlett inquired.

"I have a date later tonight…" Sarah replied, still visibly shocked.

***

The date with Luke went better than Sarah ever expected. She called Scarlett as soon as she left the restaurant to give her all the juicy details.

Once Sarah arrived at the hotel, Scarlett had Sarah rehash her date over and over until it got so late that Scarlett fell asleep on the hotel room sofa.

Sarah sat down with her laptop and opened the third draft of her manuscript. She scrolled down to the end, where the main protagonist resigned herself to a life of sadness and depression after having lost the man she loved.

With a confident smile, Sarah deleted the last five pages of the document—finally ready to create a new, and hopefully better, ending to her story.

CHAPTER 5

FIVE STORIES ABOUT CHILDHOOD

TWO LARGE DOGS

Cole had always been obsessed with his childhood. He thought about it so much that he began to wonder if other people did the same. However, every time he brought it up with his friends, everyone would assert that they did not have the same relationship with their childhood that Cole did.

Perhaps the reason for this strange dynamic was that Cole still very much felt like the immature boy he had been before landing his very high-paying job and getting married. In fact, Cole felt like he was finally living the life he had envisioned for himself back when he was young. Cole had achieved everything he had ever wanted to achieve, except for getting rid of his stutter.

Cole had had a stutter for as long as he could remember. Whenever he went to stuttering support groups, he would listen to other people with a stutter talk about the age they began to stutter or even the exact moment they stuttered for the first time. Cole had never been able to speak so specifically about the origin of his stuttering, which bothered him.

It had occurred to Cole that perhaps the reason why he hadn't been able to get rid of his stutter, despite his immense success as a businessman and as a husband, was that he had no idea how his stutter had originated. Maybe finding out the source of his speech impediment would not rid him of it completely, but it might help him talk more fluently.

Cole had recently even started going to a speech therapist. During their fourth session, two things happened that made it a day he would never forget. The first thing that happened was a breakthrough when he and his therapist were talking about Cole's obsession with his childhood.

"Maybe you want to be a child again because there is something in your past that you have forgotten but need to remember," Anna, Cole's therapist, suggested. She adjusted her gold-rimmed, round glasses that were nestled between a freckled nose and two striking, blue eyes.

"Like what?" Cole asked.

"What is the earliest memory you have of when you were a child?" Anna probed.

Cole and Anna began tracing key moments in Cole's childhood until they finally arrived at a memory that Cole had completely forgotten about up until that moment.

"When I was a child," Cole began, "I couldn't have been any older than four. I was left alone in the bedroom of my parents' friend's summer villa. It was a particularly rainy night, and I woke up and went looking for my mom and dad. I jumped out of bed and ran outside into the rain, hoping to see them there. I was standing outside in the garden by a large swimming pool with fluorescent lights. Before I could make my way inside the house again, two very large, angry dogs appeared out of nowhere and began circling me and barking at me."

"Then what happened?" prompted Anna.

"I was too scared to move, so I just collapsed on the ground and started crying. That continued for a very long time until finally someone heard me and took me inside away from the dogs and dried me," remembered Cole.

Anna and Cole continued talking about the incident, and it became clear that that might have been one of the earliest causes of Cole's stutter.

The second thing that he'd never forget occurred after he got home that day. Upon arriving home, he found his wife crying by herself on the kitchen table with a half-empty bottle of red wine by her side. It did not take long for Cole's wife to confess that she wanted to move out and get a divorce.

The divorce hit Cole so hard that he stopped going to work, eventually leading to him being fired from his job.

Cole went from being at the height of success to being at his lowest point in under a year, and the worst part was that he could not understand how something like that could have happened. The more he thought about it, the more anxious he became, so at a certain point, Cole decided to stop trying to fix what was broken and simply accept things.

Cole began to obsess over returning to his childhood more than ever before. As the weeks passed and Cole began to recognize the reflection in the mirror less and less, he began to wish more than anything that he could go back to the carefree life of a child.

After finishing an entire bottle of wine by himself one night, Cole fell asleep on his black leather sofa. He had a nightmare about the night the two large, angry dogs had ambushed him. The memory felt so real that Cole woke up with a jolt and nearly fell off the sofa onto a half-finished bag of potato chips.

After regaining his composure, Cole stood up and turned on all the lights in his apartment. He then walked over to the window and gazed at the city below him. It was raining furiously, just like it had been that night in his childhood.

Even through the violent rain, Cole could hear dogs barking below him, and the noise made his skin crawl. Cole looked out the window for a long time until a thought occurred to him. Perhaps this was a way to go back to his childhood and fix things. Cole thought about how the last time he had felt this scared and alone was when the two large dogs were circling him. Maybe there was no need to go back in time because life always finds a way to present you with similar situations from the past, with the hope that you will learn how to face them as you grow older.

Cole tried to give a name to the fears that were crippling him daily. He was scared that he would never find love again, and he was scared that he had just lost the best job he would ever have. Once Cole could give his fears a name, he immediately recognized them as manifestations of the two dogs that had terrorized him as a child.

I don't need to stay paralyzed with fear this time, Cole reasoned.

Cole ran to the bathroom to shave and shower, then combed his hair and neatly tucked in his shirt.

Once he was dressed, Cole picked up all the trash from his apartment and put it into a large trash bag to take downstairs. The apartment needed a lot of work to become presentable again, so Cole decided to brave the rain and make his way out into the street in search of cleaning products.

Although the rain was falling hard, Cole did not fall to his knees and cry like he did the last time two large and scary dogs surrounded him. This time, Cole kept moving forward and has been doing so ever since.

Cole never did get rid of his stutter completely, but another thing he never did again was give up in the face of adversity. The more he worked on facing the proverbial dogs that come barking during the hard times in everyone's lives, the more fluent his speech became—to the point that he would often forget he even had a stutter.

COURAGE

Rodrigo had had a crush on the British girl next door ever since he'd first laid eyes on her. Rodrigo was too young to have a girlfriend. Still, the moment the new family moved into the empty house next door and Rodrigo's family made their way over to welcome them into the neighborhood,

Rodrigo was smitten by the blonde girl with blue eyes and brown freckles.

"What do girls like?" Rodrigo would ask his older brother Sebastian, who was already in high school and therefore had a lot more experience with girls than he did.

"They like boys to be brave. If you can be brave in front of a girl, they will like you," Sebastian told him.

"What else?" Rodrigo asked.

"They like athletic boys. Boys who can run fast," shared Sebastian.

Rodrigo pondered what his brother had told him all day and the next day too.

During school, Rodrigo thought about the things that scared him most in the world.

Dogs, Rodrigo thought. Luckily, no one in the neighborhood owned any dogs, and even if they did, Rodrigo knew he would not have the courage to face a dog just to prove himself in front of the British girl.

At one point during school, Rodrigo realized he did not even know the girl's name. As soon as he arrived home, he asked his mother, who smiled and asked him why he wanted to know.

"Just curious," Rodrigo replied, which made his mother smile even more.

"Emma," she shared.

"Ok, thank you!" Rodrigo exclaimed less than a second before disappearing from the kitchen. Rodrigo ran up to his older brother's room and continued to ask him for advice about what girls liked.

After getting all the information he needed, Rodrigo returned to the kitchen, where his mother had just gotten off the phone.

"Guess what?" she asked. "We've been invited to have dinner at Emma's house tomorrow. Would you like to come?"

"Yes!" Rodrigo replied as he punched the air triumphantly.

***

Rodrigo's nerves were getting the better of him. He was sitting on the floor of Emma's room directly in front of her, and he could not think of anything to say.

"Are you scared of dogs?" Rodrigo asked.

Emma nodded enthusiastically.

"What scares you about them?" he wondered.

"I'm scared because they are fast, and they can chase me…" Emma replied.

Despite wholeheartedly agreeing with Emma and beginning to feel a little bit nervous just even thinking about the prospect of a dog chasing him, Rodrigo tried to seem calm and collected.

"I guess that might be scary…" he replied.

The door to Emma's room opened, which made Rodrigo jolt a little in fear as he had not managed to shake the thought of a dog chasing him completely out of his mind yet.

"Would you two like to go outside and play? I think some of the neighborhood kids are out there too…" Emma's mother, Monica, asked.

"Yes!" Rodrigo replied, hoping that Emma had not seen him jump in fear and trying to sound as confident as he could.

As he and Emma trooped out the door, Rodrigo decided that he did not like Emma's mother. Rodrigo never hung out with the neighborhood kids because they were older than him and, therefore, more athletic and intimidating.

As he and Emma stood outside, Rodrigo devised a plan to impress Emma and avoid embarrassing himself by trying to keep up with the older neighbor kids.

"Do you want to go to the grassy area?" Rodrigo asked, to which Emma nodded in acceptance.

Rodrigo smiled and led her a couple of blocks further to a vast grassy field that seemingly never ended. Together, they walked farther than Rodrigo had intended, but he wanted to prove to Emma that he was not scared or worried about being so far from home.

As the children walked together, they talked about the things they liked. Rodrigo listened to Emma talk about her new school and what she felt about moving to a new city. Rodrigo did his best to impress Emma by talking about how he ran a lot during recess and was one of the fastest boys in his class.

"My best friend from home has a brother who is a professional basketball player," Emma said as she opened her hands wide to feel the long blades of grass on her fingertips.

"Oh," Rodrigo replied, somewhat dejected.

Emma continued to talk about the basketball player, which began to frustrate Rodrigo.

"Do you have a boyfriend?" he interrupted.

"No. Do you have a girlfriend?" she answered.

"No, not yet," Rodrigo replied.

"Do you want one?" she prodded.

"I think so..." he said hesitantly.

Thinking that this was the best opportunity to make Emma like him, Rodrigo set out to put his plan into action. Rodrigo looked around and saw nothing but the tall grass surrounding him and Emma. He stretched up on his tippy-toes to see their houses just a few yards away.

Rodrigo then turned around again and pretended to be seeing something that was not there.

"Oh no, a giant dog! It's chasing us. We have to run!" Rodrigo screamed, trying as hard as he could to sound brave and not make it obvious that there was no dog in sight and that he was only pretending.

"What?!" Emma exclaimed.

"Come on, I'll protect you!" Rodrigo said as he grabbed Emma's small hand and pulled her forward. "I will get you home. Don't worry!"

Rodrigo ran as fast as he could and as fast as Emma would allow him to. As they ran back home, Rodrigo continued to say things that he believed would impress Emma.

"When we get home, I'll stand in front of you and make sure the dog is gone!" Rodrigo screamed as loudly as he could.

Although he was doing his best to make it seem like both he and Emma were in grave peril, Rodrigo could not help but smile as he felt that his plan was working perfectly. Emma was behind him, so he couldn't see her face, but he could feel how anxiously she was grabbing his hand. Rodrigo imagined how appreciative Emma would be once they finally got home and he could victoriously tell everyone in the house that he had protected Emma from a huge and dangerous dog that was no match for his speed and athletic abilities.

"I've never seen such a big dog. It really looks angry, but I'm not scared!" Rodrigo yelled, not worried about the fact that there was no way he'd actually see the size of the dog since his gaze was focused exclusively on the path before him.

Once both kids made it from the field to the street, Rodrigo stopped running and turned around to smile at Emma and put on a brave face. Before Rodrigo could even say anything about the fact that he was ready to stand in front of the grassy field and wait for the dog to come at him, he immediately became genuinely frightened when he saw how distraught Emma was.

Emma was crying hysterically. Her face was red and tears were running down her freckled cheeks, which made her blond locks stick to her face.

"What happened?" Rodrigo asked, as if completely oblivious to the fact that he had just informed Emma that a very dangerous and large dog was chasing them.

Emma was too scared and despondent to answer; she continued running home and left Rodrigo outside by himself, looking on in bewilderment. Rodrigo saw the door open, and Emma's mother worriedly scooped up her daughter and took her inside the house.

"Oops," Rodrigo mumbled to himself.

***

"That little girl told you she was terrified of dogs. Is that why you made up the story about the giant dog chasing you both, just to scare her?" Rodrigo's mother asked.

Rodrigo was back home, sitting at the round, wooden kitchen table with his head slouched down and both his parents giving him looks of disapproval.

Out of shame, Rodrigo had been reticent about divulging the truth behind his motives. He knew his parents would never make fun of him for failing so miserably at making a girl like him, but he still felt too embarrassed to even talk about it.

"That little girl is very upset. You had her thinking she was about to be attacked by a scary animal. Do you think that was a nice thing to do?" Roger, Rodrigo's dad, asked. He was still in his office clothes and had his hands on his hips as he lectured Rodrigo.

"I didn't mean to scare her or to make her cry," Rodrigo mumbled.

"I think it would mean a lot to that little girl if you went over to their house and apologized," his father said sternly.

"No!" Rodrigo replied.

"Why not?" Roger demanded.

Rodrigo struggled to tell the truth, but realized that if he didn't, then his parents might think he simply wanted to make Emma sad, which was not the case at all.

"I'm scared…" he said softly.

Rodrigo's reply seemed to assuage his parents' concerns.

"What scares you?" Roger asked, bending down to be at eye level with his son.

"I'm scared she hates me and that her parents hate me," whispered Rodrigo.

"I'm sure no one hates you. You just need to do what's right and apologize," Roger said firmly.

Rodrigo struggled to find a way around needing to go over and apologize, but couldn't think of one. Eventually, he acquiesced and got up from the kitchen to put on his coat.

***

With every step Rodrigo took toward Emma's house, which were not many since they were neighbors, he contemplated running back home.

Once at the house, Rodrigo struggled to look anyone in the eye due to the overwhelming shame he was carrying. The only time he mustered the courage to look up was when Emma came down the stairs to stand before him.

With all the emotions about coming over to Emma's house to apologize, Rodrigo had forgotten how pretty Emma was.

"Hi, Emma," he said quietly.

"Hi," Emma replied sheepishly.

"I wanted to apologize for what happened. I didn't mean to scare you…" Rodrigo began.

Before continuing to speak, Rodrigo looked around and saw both his and Emma's parents looking at him. Rodrigo let out a deep sigh.

"I was trying to impress you because I like you. I wanted you to think I was brave," he said in a rush.

"Ok…" Emma replied, seemingly unphased.

"That is very sweet…" Emma's mother said as she put her hand on Rodrigo's shoulder.

On the way back home, Rodrigo complained that Emma didn't seem to care about the fact that he had confessed his crush on her. Once he was back inside, Rodrigo ran upstairs to his brother's room to tell him what had just happened.

"But don't you see, little man?" Sebastian asked. "You did exactly what you wanted to do!"

"I didn't want to make Emma cry!" protested Rodrigo.

"Not that! You were brave. You were scared to go and apologize and you did! Not just that, but you told a girl you like her; that takes a lot of courage. *I* wouldn't even be brave enough to do that!" said Sebastian.

Upon hearing his older brother's words of encouragement, Rodrigo smiled.

Sebastian continued, "And I know you were also trying to prove that you are athletic, but I think the few steps you took from our house to Emma's were more impressive than your entire sprint through the grass field because those were steps of courage."

"But Emma wasn't impressed that I was brave and told her I liked her," said Rodrigo.

"That's OK, because you shouldn't do it for her. You should be brave for yourself," reassured Sebastian.

Rodrigo jumped up onto his older brother's bed and sat down next to him.

"Thank you." Rodrigo thanked Sebastian with a beaming smile. "How did you get so good at explaining things?"

Sebastian smiled back and said, "Girls also like a poet… but don't start devising any new plans."

THE HAUNTED HOUSE

Rodrigo was invited to accompany his father and mother to a work-related dinner. Roger, Rodrigo's father, was being honored by his coworkers and given an award for his many years of service to the company.

Rodrigo was indifferent about attending the event. But while sitting in the car with his parents, he heard his father say something that bothered him so much that he could not think about anything else after hearing it.

"You know something, buddy?" Roger asked as he drove everyone to the event, which was taking place in the country club of a gated community not too far from their house.

"What?" Rodrigo asked, struggling to feel comfortable in the first suit he had ever worn in his life.

"In my speech, I'm going to talk about you, so get ready to have all the spotlight," enthused Roger.

At first, Rodrigo became excited about the prospect of having a room full of people looking at him and hearing about him. However, once they arrived at the event, there were so many serious-looking grown-ups walking around that Rodrigo felt intimidated and overwhelmed.

There were also a lot of lights and loud sounds, which made Rodrigo start to feel terrified about having all the attention turned on him. Rodrigo decided to ask his father not to mention him, but his dad was busy greeting everyone in the near vicinity. Every time Rodrigo tried to speak to his dad, another person approached Robert and began congratulating him.

Before he knew it, Rodrigo was seated inside a very large auditorium with his parents. The room was so loud that it was virtually impossible for Rodrigo to speak to his father, who was not seated directly beside him.

Rodrigo saw one of his friends at the event, whose dad also worked with Robert.

"Mom, can I go play with Mitchell?" he asked.

"OK, but don't go too far!" his mom cautioned.

The idea was not to go far but to stay away from the conference room for long enough that no one would look at him, even if his father did mention Rodrigo in his speech.

***

The night was cold, and things were much more peaceful and quiet outside the auditorium.

"You know, I heard that this place has a haunted mansion. Apparently, it's not far, and if you go inside and stay long enough, you come out braver," Mitchell said as he wandered around the grounds with Rodrigo.

"Awesome. Can we see it?" Rodrigo asked.

"Sure!" Mitchell led Rodrigo a few yards away and stopped in front of what looked like an abandoned house. The walls looked like they may have originally been white but were now streaked with sooty gray, as if the building had survived a great fire.

No lights were visible inside, and the boys could tell it would not be any warmer inside than outside.

There was no denying that the building was creepy. The darkness inside seemed to be even more pronounced than the darkness outside.

"Yeah, if you ask me, that place is definitely haunted," Rodrigo asserted.

"I don't even like looking at it!" Mitchell added, quivering as he spoke—partly due to the cold, but mainly because of the haunted house.

"I bet it looks better from the inside," said an older and more confident voice behind Mitchell and Rodrigo.

Unable to contain his fear, Mitchell yelped before turning around to face a group of five older boys surrounding them, all with mischievous smiles on their faces.

"Who are you?" Rodrigo asked.

"The Harleys," Mitchell responded somewhat regrettably. "They live here."

"We don't call ourselves that, but it's not the worst name for a group. I think it has something to do with the awesome bikes we have. My name is Axl," explained the gang's tallest and most confident-looking member.

"Motorcycles?" Rodrigo asked excitedly.

"Sure. Motorcycles, why not?" Axl responded as the rest of his gang laughed. "In fact, I'll let you look at mine and have a ride on it if you go inside that house and stay there for at least five minutes."

"No way!" Mitchell responded, as if the dare was directed at him.

Rodrigo looked at the scary building.

"And like your little friend said. You don't have to worry about ever being scared again in life because once you go inside, you come out fearless," Axl said.

After a few contemplative moments, Rodrigo smiled and turned to face the Harleys.

"I'll do it!"

***

The inside was not as scary as it looked on the outside. However, Rodrigo couldn't help but think of all the scary films his older brother had made him watch a couple of years ago and how this decrepit, squalid old building would be exponentially more terrifying with some eerie background music accompanying Rodrigo's every trepid step.

There was light coming in from somewhere and loud voices in the distance, but he couldn't make out exactly where they were coming from. The more he tried to listen to the voices, the more frightened he became, so he decided to ignore them and simply make his way up to the second floor, which was the deal he had made with the Harleys.

Rodrigo made his way up a long, spiral staircase that wound past a hole-infested wall filled with oil paintings of stern-looking people. Rodrigo tried to ignore their intimidating looks as he approached the balcony.

Once he made it to the balcony, he looked down and saw Mitchell standing by himself, appearing highly distressed.

"Where are the Harleys?!" Rodrigo cried from the top of the balcony, which was nowhere near as high up as he thought it was.

"They left! And they did something to lock the door shut!" Mitchell replied anxiously.

"What?!" Rodrigo exclaimed, immediately regretting speaking so loudly—just in case his voice might wake up whatever ghosts were still slumbering inside the haunted house he was trapped in.

"I don't know what they did, but they just got on their bikes and left. Can you find a way out from inside?" called Mitchell.

Even if there was another way to exit the building from the inside, Rodrigo was not overly keen on exploring the house out of fear of discovering things that could end up haunting him more than the films his brother had inflicted upon him.

But, not wanting to sound too frightened in front of Mitchell, Rodrigo told him he'd find a way out and darted back downstairs to see if there was another door.

After a few minutes of slowly inching across the floor, Rodrigo decided to move faster.

The deeper Rodrigo went into the house, the louder the sound of people talking became, and the more light emerged from the cracks in the wall.

Suddenly, Rodrigo heard footsteps approaching him. Rodrigo's heart began to race as the footsteps got louder and continued moving toward him. A tall, human-like silhouette began to emerge from the shadows, making Rodrigo scream and run toward the thread of light emanating not too far from where he was standing.

The farther Rodrigo ran, the brighter the light became until he realized it was coming from the other side of a large door that was slightly ajar.

Rodrigo stopped in front of the door and heard the footsteps running toward him.

Almost involuntarily, Rodrigo pushed the door open and darted through. He immediately became blinded by the light, and the loud noises and voices emanating from the other side suddenly went silent.

After a couple of seconds, Rodrigo's eyes adjusted to the light enough for him to notice where he was standing. Although he was now immersed in light and surrounded by people who were definitely not ghosts, Rodrigo felt no less frightened. Then, he realized that his father was standing at a podium in front of him.

"Rodrigo?" Roger asked as he looked away from his notes and stopped speaking to his friends, family, and colleagues.

Noticing that his son could not speak, Roger turned back to his microphone and once more addressed the room full of people.

"Everyone, I want to introduce you to my son Rodrigo. The bravest boy in the world," he announced.

Roger ushered his son to come toward him and join him at the podium. Rodrigo ran to his dad as the entire room clapped.

Roger continued making his speech with his son by his side and, when he was done, they returned to the table to join Rodrigo's mother.

"So, your solution to not wanting your dad to direct people's attention to you was to run on stage in the middle of his speech?" Rodrigo's mother asked.

"It wasn't on purpose!" cried Rodrigo.

"Were you scared?" she continued.

"No," he stated.

"How come?" Roger asked.

"I guess staying inside the haunted house for five minutes does make you brave," said Rodrigo.

Although Rodrigo's parents did not understand what their son meant by that statement, they could tell by the smile on his face that he was no longer nervous. Instead, he was ready to have a lovely, relaxing evening.

AXL

Axl had just moved into our gated community and was already more popular than me. He was more athletic, better-looking, and more outgoing. However, since our mothers had been friends back when they were in grade school, Axl and I were introduced one day so that we could become friends and so I could show him around the neighborhood.

To my chagrin, Axl ended up introducing me to kids in the neighborhood I had known for several years but had never become friends with due to my introverted nature. I admired Axl for his social, charismatic personality.

One day, I invited Axl to my house. He was the first person I had ever invited over, and the fact that the most popular boy in the neighborhood would be at my place was overwhelming.

At first, we played around and had fun scaring each other and making crazy drinks from what we could find in my parent's fridge and the storage area.

During a particularly long game of hide-and-seek, where I was hiding and Axl was supposed to be trying to find me, I heard my baby brother crying frantically in his crib. This was not a particularly strange occurrence, but the way he was crying and the way he did not stop started to worry me.

I quickly ran up to his bedroom and found Axl throwing toys into the crib at him from a distance. Almost out of instinct, I screamed at Axl to leave the house, which he did immediately.

I picked up my brother and sat on the sofa next to his crib, holding him in my arms until he calmed down. I learned that day not to try and be friends with people just because they are considered popular or exciting by others.

THE BLACK SLOPES

Dana had never spent so much time with adults in his life. When his parents had invited him to join them on a ski trip with his father's work colleagues, Dana had said yes because he had always wanted to learn to ski.

It was the last day, and he was now standing at the top of the black diamond run with his father's work colleagues because Dana's parents had gotten food poisoning the night before and could not join them.

"So, Dana, last night you said you would be fine with the black diamonds. That's why we're here. Are you still sure you can hang?" Rob asked with a condescending tone.

It immediately dawned on Dana that saying yes to skiing the black diamonds had been a mistake, but he would never show fear in front of five grown men.

After nodding their heads in approval, all the men began skiing down the run with Dana right behind them.

Dana screamed every second of the way down but miraculously managed not to fall even once, even though he sometimes downright closed his eyes to avoid seeing what he believed was about to be his ultimate demise.

The four adults kept skiing around him to ensure he was fine. It was easy for them to spot Dana, since he was the only person screaming the entire way down the mountain.

Once the group made it to the bottom of the mountain, Dana collapsed in a heap on the snow.

"Dana, you were doing so good! You only fell at the last moment," called one of the men.

Dana was breathing heavily but finally managed to get himself up with the help of Rob and the others.

"I was just too exhausted from all the screaming to stay standing up!" Dana exclaimed.

CHAPTER 6

FIVE STORIES ABOUT WORK

THE NEW JOB

Lorena was nervous about starting a new job in Mexico. Although she was technically Mexican, she hadn't been back since she was four years old and her family moved to Europe.

Lorena had just graduated from a very prestigious university but had failed to find a job. Instead, she had spent the six months after graduation partying and socializing with her friends, despite her parents' protests.

Whenever Lorena's parents would insist that she focus on finding a job, Lorena just responded that she would do it later and that she deserved to have fun with her friends after finishing her studies.

Fearing that their daughter would not understand the responsibility she had to be independent and self-sufficient, Lorena's parents decided to cut her off financially. When Lorena failed to find a job and could no longer rely on her parents to maintain her lifestyle, she decided to accept a job her uncle was offering her back in Mexico.

Although she was nervous about flying back to Mexico by herself, she was confident that this would only be a temporary solution and that she would indubitably find a job back in Europe in a year or so.

Once she arrived at her uncle's company, she was introduced to everyone. The office was tiny, and the people working there were very unlike the people she was used to hanging out with back home. First of all, no one spoke English, and Lorena's Spanish was not that great. No one in the office, except for Lorena's uncle, had ever left Mexico. Most had not even been to college.

Lorena immediately felt out of place, which made her nervous. Even if she could speak Spanish fluently, or if her coworkers could speak English, she worried that they would prefer not to speak to her.

Whenever she walked into the office, everyone either got quiet or started whispering to each other in Spanish. Lorena had never felt ashamed of her lifestyle until moving to Mexico and working for her uncle. Everyone there seemed reluctant to engage with her because of all the countries she had lived in and all the opportunities her parents had given her to live a comfortable, privileged life.

The most popular person in the office was a younger guy called Fernando. Fernando usually talked loudly and made a lot of jokes but would become visibly more apprehensive whenever Lorena would arrive at work.

Lorena usually went out for lunch, while everyone else brought Tupperware containers filled with food. Her parents advised her to do the same, but she was worried that it would be devastatingly humiliating if she brought leftovers from home too. Still, she always ended up sitting by herself in the dining hall, away from everyone else in her office, while they all ate together.

Every day when Lorena arrived home from work, the first thing she would do was apply for jobs back in Europe—she was desperate to leave the situation she was in.

One day, Lorena was driving to work in a car that belonged to her parents. It was a Thursday and there was heavy traffic, as usual. Lorena was about twenty minutes from the office when a taxi driver cut her off a little too aggressively. Lorena did not see the taxi in time, which meant the driver had to brake very loudly and suddenly.

Lorena gasped. The braking noise had been so loud, and the cars were so near each other, that she was unsure if they had collided.

Before she could do anything, the driver got out of the taxi and began violently banging his large, greasy hands against the window of Lorena's car.

Unsure of what the angry driver was saying, Lorena just recoiled back in her seat and waited for the abuse to end, which it finally did after a very long two minutes of being screamed at.

The driver kicked Lorena's car before storming back over to his taxi and driving off.

Seeing the light in front of her turn green, Lorena had no option but to continue driving to work. Once she arrived at work and parked her car in the outdoor parking lot, she burst into tears, hands still on the steering wheel. Suddenly, every frustration she had been harboring regarding her new life rose to the surface until she was overcome by a wave of emotion.

After a couple of minutes of despondent crying, there was a knock on her window. Lorena could not see who it was before wiping the tears from her eyes. It was Fernando.

Lorena ashamedly rolled down the window.

"Are you OK?" Fernando asked. Lorena was shocked to hear him speak English, albeit with a strong accent.

"Yes, I'm fine," Lorena responded, failing miserably to compose herself.

"What happened?" queried Fernando.

Lorena explained the incident with the taxi driver, but left out the part about feeling alienated at work.

Fernando scoffed in frustration.

"The taxi drivers think they are the kings of the street. I am so sorry!" he sympathized.

After a couple of minutes, Fernando invited Lorena to grab some coffee before heading into the office. She hesitantly accepted.

Lorena finally confessed to Fernando about how she had been struggling with the move to Mexico, which made her cry again regardless of how hard she was trying to control her emotions.

"Why don't you sit with us during lunch?" Fernando asked.

"I'm scared that you don't want to talk to me…" Lorena replied, once again wiping tears from her face.

Fernando explained that the office thought she did not hang out with them because everyone else came from more humble beginnings. After half an hour, Fernando and Lorena agreed that they had both been making false assumptions about each other and decided to stop doing so.

Fernando invited Lorena to lunch with the entire team. At lunchtime, when he explained what happened with the taxi driver, everyone began defending Lorena.

"They think they can do whatever they want!" someone shouted in anger.

The next day, Lorena walked into the office and was greeted kindly by everyone. The team invited her to drinks after work, and she happily accepted.

From that moment on, Lorena learned to enjoy her work. Lorena began to work on her Spanish and helped Fernando and the others with their English.

About a month later, during a long weekend, Lorena got an email from a company back in Europe saying that they wanted to interview her for a job. After a couple of minutes spent deliberating her options, Lorena replied that she was no longer available for an interview.

After replying to that email, Lorena felt relieved and satisfied. She picked up the phone to call Fernando and invite him over for some lunch or a coffee.

Fernando told her that he would love to come but asked her to stay inside when he arrived. When Lorena asked why, he cheekily replied that he would have to take a taxi to her place and didn't want Lorena to start crying uncontrollably when she saw the taxi driver.

Lorena laughed to herself. To her surprise, she was thankful that she had almost collided with the taxi that day. If it hadn't been for that incident, she might have never found a way to connect with her coworkers, who in time became better friends to her than any other friends she had ever had.

FRIEND BOSS

Alan had been working at the same marketing agency as Tatiana for three years. Tatiana had been hired about a year after Alan and was initially supposed to report to him. However, only a couple of months after Tatiana joined the company, the CEO made some changes in the company and promoted Tatiana to become an account manager for a different client, meaning she had similar responsibilities as Alan.

Although they did not work on the same account, it did not take long for Alan and Tatiana to become best friends. They would routinely go to lunch together and hang out after work. Alan and Tatiana became such close friends that people would often gossip and speculate that they were secretly dating, which was completely untrue. Alan and Tatiana kept lecturing everyone on the importance of not making false assumptions because it could lead to conflict in the workplace, but at the end of the day, they did not care what people thought about their friendship. The truth was that they never had any intention of evolving their relationship from friendship to romance, regardless of what people said behind their backs.

Even on the most challenging days in the office, Alan and Tatiana always supported each other emotionally. They sometimes even helped with some of the work that the other person had to do.

One day, Alan was called into his boss's office along with Tatiana. This was new, since they didn't work on the same account. For a brief moment, Alan was worried that the gossip regarding their false love affair had been brought to his manager's attention and that there would be repercussions because of it.

As Alan and Tatiana sat in front of Leo, Alan's boss, Alan began to prepare how he would convince Leo that nothing was going on between him and Tatiana.

"Alan, we've lost your account. The client has decided to go look for another agency," Leo explained with a frustrated look.

As anxious as Alan was before hearing this news, now he felt even worse.

"Don't worry; you are not getting fired. Instead, you are going to join Tatiana's account. Since she is the account manager, you will be reporting directly to her. She is now your boss," continued Leo.

Alan and Tatiana looked at each other, trying to contain their laughter. As bad as this revelation was, at least Alan still had his job, and he would be able to work closely with his best friend.

However, as the weeks and months passed, the dynamic between Alan and Tatiana began to change—and not for the better. Alan started to feel reluctant to hang out with Tatiana, considering they were constantly together at work and she continuously gave him work to do. Even when it was time to have lunch, Alan was scared that Tatiana would get mad if he stopped for lunch before she was ready to take a lunch break.

Alan stopped having lunch with Tatiana altogether and would often come back down to the office to see her still working, which made him feel guilty.

After some time, the two stopped speaking to each other as friends. One night in the office, when everyone had already left and it was only Alan and Tatiana working, Alan realized just how awkward the relationship between him and Tatiana had become.

It was very late, and he needed to finish up within the hour if he wanted to catch the last bus home. There was still some work to be done, but he figured he could do it at home or early the next morning. However, considering he always left for lunch before Tatiana, he felt guilty leaving the office first, too.

Alan worked as fast as he could but kept getting distracted by the clock. If he missed the last bus, he would need to take a taxi, which would be very expensive.

"Is there somewhere you have to be?" Tatiana asked as she noticed Alan continuously looking at his watch.

"No, just hoping I manage to catch the last bus," Alan replied, trying to sound as amicable as possible.

Tatiana grunted as if someone had just handed her a lot more work to do that night.

"Just go home and get some rest. I'll finish up," she said gruffly.

"No, it's ok. I can stay…" offered Alan.

"Don't worry. If it's the last bus, you should take it," ordered Tatiana.

Alan wanted her to know that he was willing to stay, but decided it would be best for him to leave the office.

Feeling somewhat ashamed, Alan left the office and waved goodbye to Tatiana. As he closed the translucent door behind him, he heard Tatiana sigh with exasperation. He stood by the door for a minute and heard Tatiana pull out her phone and make a call.

He could not make out exactly what she was saying, but he heard enough to realize she was complaining that she was disappointed. As much as Alan wanted to hear more, he eventually had to run to catch the last bus—thankfully making it just in time.

***

The next morning, Alan walked into work and saw Tatiana in Leo's office, looking frustrated.

"Why is she in there?" Alan asked the person in the cubicle next to him.

"No idea, but she doesn't look happy…"

Alan suddenly felt angry. He had a suspicion that Tatiana was complaining to Leo about how Alan had left the office before finishing his work the night before.

Unbelievable, he thought and decided he was no longer going to worry about ever being friends with Tatiana again.

Not long after that, Alan was called into Leo's office. As Alan walked in, Tatiana left.

Alan sat down, angry that the situation between him and Tatiana had gotten to such a bad place.

"There is going to be some restructuring going on. In light of some new information given to me today, you are no longer going to be working for Tatiana…" began Leo.

Before Leo could finish his sentence, Alan abruptly—almost involuntarily—stood up from his chair in a rage. He opened the door behind him and yelled at Tatiana.

"Was it so hard to just speak to me?" Alan protested. "Now you are getting me fired?"

"What?" Tatiana asked incredulously.

"We used to be friends, and now you are making me lose my job because I leave the office minutes before I miss the last bus? That is so unfair!" snapped Alan.

"No one is losing their job," Leo exclaimed as he appeared behind Alan. "This is just a demotion."

"Why should I get demoted?" Alan protested.

"You are not getting demoted!" Leo responded.

"I am," Tatiana added.

"What?" Alan asked, confused.

"I think you two need to have a talk…" Leo suggested.

***

"I don't understand," Alan said as he took a sip of his coffee.

"I have just been feeling so frustrated and ashamed about how you see me as your boss and not your friend anymore. Last night I became angry at myself when I watched you almost miss your bus because of me," Tatiana responded.

"That's why you were upset last night?" asked Alan.

"Of course. I stopped joining you for lunch because I want you to relax, and I know that you can't do that around me anymore, which is why I asked Leo for a demotion," shared Tatiana.

"You asked for a demotion?!" sputtered Alan.

"Yes. I just want to be friends with you again, even if it means that I'm not the account manager anymore. Leo is going to find someone new to replace me; that is what he meant when he said this was just a demotion," explained Tatiana.

Alan was in shock. He had no idea Tatiana had been suffering so much over the loss of their friendship, or that it meant so much to her.

"I am so sorry. I completely misread the situation. I have missed you as a friend, too," Alan confessed.

Tatiana and Alan hugged and ended up staying at the café longer than they probably should have. Tatiana explained that she believed Alan hated having her as a boss and was trying to distance himself from her as much as he could.

After settling their issues, Alan convinced Tatiana that she should stay on as the account manager instead of asking to be demoted. Instead, they agreed to communicate better instead of making assumptions without asking each other for the truth.

As they walked back to the office, Tatiana laughed to herself.

"What's so funny?" Alan asked.

"You know what we can't do anymore?" she told him.

"No, what?" he replied.

"Lecture everyone about the importance of not making assumptions about people…" Tatiana replied. Alan smiled in agreement.

THE CALL CENTER

After working at the same marketing agency for over five years, Alan was finally promoted to an account manager position. His new account was a pharmaceutical client that ran a call center. Alan had never even been inside a call center, but he was excited about his new, expanded responsibility.

Alan had been waiting years to get promoted. There were several other accounts in the agency he worked in that interested him and that he felt he would be more comfortable managing than the pharmaceutical call center account he was given. However, Alan was eager to prove himself worthy of the opportunity and to learn as much as he could from the experience that awaited him.

After a quick conversation with his boss Leo, Alan assured Leo that he would improve the call center and make the account one of the most profitable for the company.

One day, Alan was tasked with visiting the call center to meet the agents he would be working with. Alan was more nervous than he had expected. The client would be there waiting for him to make the formal introductions.

When Alan arrived, he felt overwhelmed with nerves, but was determined to conceal his nervousness from the client. The client showed him around and introduced Alan to three call center agents who would be his daily points of contact.

Alan spent the entire day at the call center learning about what the job entailed. There was a lot of information to process, but Alan acted as if everything he was hearing was being retained in his memory. Unfortunately, it wasn't.

Before the day was over, Alan noticed a beautiful, young, blonde call center agent sitting on her desk taking calls and writing things down. As much as he tried to focus on the work, Alan couldn't stop looking at the gorgeous blonde.

When the day ended and Alan was preparing to follow the client out of the building, he went up to the girl he had been admiring for hours and asked for her name.

"Jess," the girl replied.

"Can I have your number?" he asked.

Jess seemed reluctant at first but eventually wrote her number on a piece of paper and handed it to Alan, who was overjoyed.

Once Alan arrived home, he sent a message to Jess and asked her out on a date. It took a couple of hours for her to reply, but Jess finally answered that she'd meet up with him.

***

"The client wants to move the call center to this building. I need you to set up these empty offices as a call center so that the new agents can come in next week and start making their calls from here," Leo informed Alan the next day.

Although Alan had no idea how to do that, he once again purposefully exuded false confidence to appear comfortable in his new position and assured Leo he would come in on Saturday and have the space ready for the call center agents before Monday.

***

It was now Friday evening, and no matter how much research Alan did, he did not feel remotely confident about setting up a call center. He hadn't informed Jess about his predicament because he was still hopeful that he would manage to finish his work on time and be able to meet her for a dinner date on Saturday evening.

After arriving home that evening and realizing that he would need the entire weekend to set up the call center, Alan begrudgingly picked up his phone to cancel his date with Jess.

However, before doing so, a thought occurred to him. Alan pondered whether asking Jess to come to the office with him on Saturday to help him would be a good or terrible idea. In terms of what he needed to accomplish at work, it made sense.

Jess had experience working in a call center and could potentially advise him on what needed to be done to set one up successfully. This way, he would not fail his first big assignment and also would be able to spend time with Jess on Saturday, even if it wasn't what would typically be considered a date.

Alan pondered the right thing to do until he realized there was no other option.

Alan called Jess and informed her of his predicament. Jess laughed and said she would be willing to help him tomorrow afternoon at the office.

"It's a date! Thank you so much!" Alan exclaimed on the phone.

"Is it?" Jess asked on the other line.

"Sort of…" Alan said tentatively.

***

Much to Alan's dismay, Jess arrived a little late to the office. Although Alan had already been there for two hours, he hadn't managed to get anything done other than pace frantically as he tried to calm his nerves.

"It's ok… don't worry. I will help you," Jess reassured him.

Alan tried to act like he knew what he was doing, but soon realized it was better to simply let Jess take control of the situation.

After about an hour, Jess had completely set up the communication lines and said that the call center was fully operational.

Alan tried it out the way Leo instructed him to do once it was finished, and everything worked the way it was supposed to.

"I owe you big time!" Alan exclaimed as he wiped the sweat from his forehead.

Jess looked at him and smiled.

"What is it?" Alan asked.

"You know, I was about to cancel our date before you called me and asked for my help…" Jess confessed.

"How come?" wondered Alan.

"When you walked into the call center, you were acting so arrogant. I was unsure if we would get along. But today, you seemed completely different, so I'm glad we met up," Jess told him.

Alan explained that he had been trying to portray the image of someone who knew what they were doing as a way to protect their job. Jess laughed.

"I get that. Maybe next time, just be more humble; there are always people willing to help people who need it," Jess suggested.

Alan nodded in agreement.

"Especially if you ask someone who is an absolute master of their craft—like me," Jess quipped as she smiled and exited the office.

THE BLOG POST

Miranda had been working as an accountant for over ten years. Although the work was somewhat monotonous and easy for her, Miranda relished the security it provided.

It was a sunny Friday afternoon. There was positive energy in the office as people prepared for the start of the weekend. All the windows were open, and a soft summer breeze and bright sunlight drifted into the office and made the few people still working even more eager to leave.

Miranda was typing away on her laptop as she answered the last few unread emails in her inbox. Once she was finished, Miranda took a sip from her translucent plastic water bottle and shut her laptop with a triumphant smile.

The sound of her laptop closing on a Friday afternoon was one of her favorite sounds in the world. Miranda looked around the office and saw that everyone was too focused on getting their work done as quickly as possible to notice that she was about to leave.

Before Miranda could take the few steps over to the coat rack to put on her green coat, she heard one of the sounds she detested most in her life: the sound of her boss's office door opening.

"Miranda, can you come into my office?" her boss Leo asked as he poked his head through the door and then disappeared back inside.

"Coming!" Miranda replied as she quietly winced and shut her eyes in dismay. This time, everyone in the office saw her and smiled sympathetically.

Miranda took another sip of water and then slammed the water bottle down on her mahogany desk a little too aggressively. As she made her way to Leo's office, she hoped that she was about to be given some great news that would make her ride home all the more pleasant.

Once the pleasantries were out of the way, Leo asked Miranda to sit—something he rarely did unless he wanted to talk about something serious.

Miranda sat down and noticed everyone outside was looking at her through the transparent glass walls of Leo's office. Even though she felt quite nervous, Miranda smiled at everyone stoically.

"We're going to have to let you go. I am so sorry," Leo said gently.

At first, Miranda was convinced she had misheard her boss, but then she saw an expression of guilt on Leo's face that she had never seen before.

"I really am sorry, but it is out of my hands. Losing the pharmaceutical account put us in a bad place, financially, that we are still scrambling to get out of. I tried my best, but I have to follow orders," Leo explained.

Miranda couldn't help but turn around to look at her coworkers through the glass wall. Once they noticed her confused and shocked expression, they stopped smiling and turned away as though they felt embarrassed for watching.

Unsure of what to do or say, Miranda began rubbing her hands along her blue jeans and making noises that she hoped would, at some point, turn into words. When nothing comprehensible came out, Leo continued explaining the situation and trying to make it seem like it was not his fault. Even though Miranda knew he was right, nothing Leo said assuaged the anxiety rising in her chest at the prospect of no longer having a job.

"I'm sorry," Leo said, his dark brown eyes locked on Miranda as if worried that she would at any moment start screaming, "but maybe you can make something positive out of this."

That night, Miranda canceled her plans as soon as she got home. She camped out in her TV room with a big plate of her favorite snacks and watched reruns of her favorite comedy show until she fell asleep on the sofa without even changing out of her work clothes.

***

It had been over a month since Miranda had been fired. She had taken a week off to relax and enjoy the freedom she had never asked for. Miranda's friends and family had reassured her that she would find a new job in no time. However, after her one-week break, Miranda had been applying to at least ten jobs every day and still was not getting any interviews.

Trying not hard not to crumble under the pressure she was feeling, Miranda went out for a walk by herself to clear her mind. During her walk, she thought about what her ex-boss had said to her, about how maybe she could "make something positive out of this."

What does that even mean? Miranda pondered, feeling frustrated.

She thought about what her younger, more rebellious self would have thought about leaving her accounting job and smiled. When Miranda was still a student, she loved to write stories. The only reason she had become an accountant instead of a writer was that she was pressured into it by her parents, who did not believe in her literary abilities.

The more Miranda thought about her situation, the more frustrated and worried she became. To ensure she didn't succumb to a panic attack, Miranda decided to go back home and figure out something that might calm her nerves.

Once she was back home, she thought about what her old writing teacher used to tell her about the best way to go about writing. She had always told Miranda, "Whenever you feel there is so much inside you that it cannot be contained, let it out onto the page."

Miranda sat by her desk and began writing her frustrations down on the white computer paper that she pulled out of the printer next to her feet. To her surprise, she did not struggle at all to write and very soon needed to pull out another five sheets of paper from the printer to keep writing down her thoughts.

Miranda continued to write every day for the next week. When she wasn't writing, she was reading what she wrote and laughing at how silly some of her ideas were. Miranda spent hours flopped on her white sofa, editing some of the things she had written to make them flow better— even though she had no plans of allowing anyone other than herself to read them.

***

Another two weeks had gone by, and Miranda had nothing to show for her job-hunting efforts other than the frustrations she kept building up and then releasing onto the page. Her bedroom was starting to look like a stationery store, what with all the pens and pieces of paper lying on the floor and the nightstand by her bed.

As much as she wanted to keep writing, Miranda felt that she needed to evolve her process in a way that would keep this new habit exciting and perhaps even conducive to her professional development somehow.

Miranda took the heavy stack of white paper to her desk and sat in front of her laptop. She once again pondered what Leo had said to her about considering being laid off as something positive.

After glancing at the pages before her and combining what Leo said with what her old writing teacher used to say, Miranda went online and found a free website where she could write blog posts.

Since she had already diligently edited all her written work, Miranda typed out the best snippets that she'd come up with during the past weeks and created a blog post to share her feelings regarding being fired and struggling to find work.

Every morning after that, Miranda would sit down and transcribe the thoughts she'd jotted down on scrap paper into a new blog post. After completing five posts, Miranda finally mustered the courage to share links to her blog posts online—asking people to read, share, and comment with their thoughts.

The next day, Miranda woke up to find she had several new emails from businesses that wanted to get in touch with her about her blog posts.

Miranda responded to the emails and discovered that more than one company wanted her to be a freelance journalist or content writer after how popular her blog posts had become shortly after they were posted.

Before deciding what path to take, Miranda once again went for a walk to clear her head. Once outside and surrounded by the verdant landscape she loved so much, she struggled to do anything other than think about whether she should accept the writing job.

Miranda removed a white, pocket-sized notebook from the pocket of her green raincoat and began to write down her thoughts to try and organize them into anything that resembled a coherent thought. Before she could even read through what she had written, she realized how simple things really were. Miranda replaced the small notebook inside her coat and sprinted home.

Once she was sitting in front of her laptop, Miranda wrote the company that interested her the most to inform them that she accepted the job offer.

It was years before Miranda ever looked inside the white notebook to see what she had written that day as she walked through the forest by her apartment trying to clear her busy mind. The day she found the notebook, she was putting all her things into boxes to finally move into a bigger house in the city as a result of her success as a full-time journalist.

Miranda sat down on the bedroom floor of the apartment that would soon belong to someone else. She smiled as she read the last thing she had written before making the best decision of her life.

The last entry read: *I am writing because I need to, and without it, I will feel lost.*

THE DONATION

Pete looked at the watercolor painting he had been working on for the past hour and winced. He contorted his neck and squinted to try and see something that disappointed him less, but to no avail.

Why do I bother? Pete asked himself as he aggressively threw the paintbrushes down on the floor and slumped over, deeply dejected. He eyed his attempt at painting a boat sailing through a storm and realized that it was nowhere near as good as he had imagined it to be in his head.

Pete had spent several weeks deciding what to do and which voice he should listen to, his own or his father's, after graduating from college. Pete had studied marketing because his father, Carl, had always wanted him to go into business like him. However, Pete was a very different person from his father. Carl was a very analytical man who never understood Pete's desire to become a painter.

Although he encouraged Pete to follow his passion, he also advised him to be thoughtful about what career path he chose to pursue.

"There will always be signs that will help guide you down the right path," Carl would tell his son right after Pete received good grades in math or brochures inviting him to apply to study business at top universities.

Pete had been getting job offers to work for various marketing firms ever since leaving school, which he tried to tell himself were not actually signs that he should pursue a business career like his father. However, after being so disappointed by his first attempt at painting what was on his mind, Pete began to accept that perhaps it was time to accept that the world was clearly telling him that he was not destined to become a famous painter.

Pete started pacing frantically in his room as he tried to decide what he should do next. After a while, he opened his computer and began responding to the emails he had received inviting him for an interview. Almost immediately, Pete received responses from all but one company saying that the positions had been filled. Pete looked at the company that said they were still willing to give him an interview and saw that the position was for a door-to-door fundraising position.

Frustrated at himself for having wasted so much time painting something that did little more than simply prove that Pete was not cut out to be an artist, he begrudgingly responded that he would attend the interview.

It was only a few minutes before he got an email back to confirm the interview time. The email also explained that as part of the interview process, he would go door-to-door with an experienced team of salesmen to ask for charitable donations. Pete closed his laptop and walked over to the painting of the boat in a storm that he had done.

For a brief moment Pete contemplated continuing to paint, but then looked out the window and noticed that the large, steel trash can on the street was, for the first time, completely empty and not overflowing with trash.

This is a sign, Pete reasoned.

Driven by anger and disappointment, Pete dragged his painting down the flight of stairs onto the street and threw it inside the trash can. The painting didn't really fit, but that wasn't his concern anymore.

Once back inside, Pete laid down in bed and stared at the white ceiling above him. His racing thoughts kept him from falling asleep. Pete knew that his inability to control his emotions was one of his greatest weaknesses.

What if I just made the wrong choice? Pete pondered. Exhausted by his overthinking, Pete eventually fell asleep and didn't wake up until the sun had come up the following morning.

Upon waking, Pete wondered if it had all been a dream. Then, he wondered if the painting was still where he had left it, awkwardly placed inside the steel trash can on the street just outside his window.

Pete leaped out of bed and almost slammed his face against the glass window in his hurry to look outside. The painting was gone.

***

It was one of the coldest nights of the year, and Pete was not dressed for the weather. The email had warned about the cold, but Pete thought he would be alright with just a cotton sweater and a blue corduroy blazer. Even if he had wanted to dress in a way that ensured he wouldn't feel the cold, Pete was used to dressing formally for interviews and felt it would have been strange to show up dressed as if he were going skiing.

However, the interview part of the recruitment process took only about ten minutes. Afterward, Pete was quickly assigned a fundraising team to follow, shadow, and learn from during his interview day.

Pete hated every moment of shadowing the team. He disliked how the people on the team spoke to each other as if they all belonged to a cult and then suddenly acted all cheerful and disingenuous the second they stood before a homeowner and asked for a charitable donation.

It was late, and Pete had been to more houses than he ever believed possible in a single day. He had met people of all ages and temperaments. Most people did not seem as frustrated with the fundraisers knocking at their door as Pete felt having to be one of them.

After stopping for a short break to eat something, Pete sat down with the rest of the fundraisers and drank his coffee as slowly as possible to try to thaw himself out.

Damien, the team leader, noticed how cold Pete was getting.

"Do you want to make a quick visit to the store so we can get you some gloves and a scarf, Pete?"Damien asked, looking slightly annoyed.

Pete had already decided that he would quit after getting dinner and before embarking on the next run of houses. As much as he wanted to find a suitable business job, and as confident as he was that he could ace the interview and become a full-time door-to-door fundraiser if he wanted, he felt that he would not get anywhere doing this type of work. However, he had also realized that he had no idea where he was and that he was indeed very cold. Rather than try to find whatever store Damien was referring to by himself, he decided to let Damien show him and then he'd leave the interview right after.

"Sure, thanks a lot," Pete replied as he took another generous swig of black coffee. He didn't usually drink coffee late in the evening, but he already knew that his mind was going to be racing this evening and, therefore, he would not be getting the quality sleep he needed.

Once everyone on the team finished their food and drinks, they all got up and were told by Damien that they would be making a quick pit stop at the nearest shopping center so that Pete could get a scarf and some gloves. Pete made sure to look away to avoid any potential glares from the rest of the team, who surely wanted to go home as much as Pete did but still had a few more houses to visit.

Feeling slightly guilty and very cold, Pete and the rest of the team followed Damien to one of the largest shopping centers Pete had ever seen.

Not wanting to delay the group too much, Pete grabbed the nearest pair of gloves and scarf he could find and informed Damien that he was ready to pay. The entire team followed Pete and Damien to the cashier, where they encountered a seemingly endless line of people.

"Wow, that's a big line…" Pete said nervously, feeling very awkward and hating that he hadn't dressed appropriately for the weather. Damien didn't respond; he simply sighed and looked at his watch.

"I just hope the team gets to visit the five houses that need to be checked off the list before returning to the office," Damien said in a frustrated tone.

"I hope so too! Surely the queue will move quickly," Pete responded. The more he tried to think of a way to inform Damien that he would be quitting and not visiting any more houses, the more he realized there was no way of doing so without potentially making the other team members hate him even more than they probably already did.

After about twenty-five minutes, Pete finally arrived at the cashier and paid for his scarf and gloves.

"Well, now that Pete is appropriately dressed, we can continue. The unfortunate news is that we will not have time to visit all the houses we were supposed to. Looking at the time, it seems we only have enough time left to visit one," Damien explained. He purposefully avoided eye contact with Pete, who was hoping a hole would open up in the cement under his feet and swallow him whole. Everyone on the team was muttering things between each other that Pete wholeheartedly believed they were about him.

"Actually, Damien... I..." Pete began thinking of a way to quit that would allow him to avoid being lynched by the fundraisers.

"Yes, Pete?" Damien asked.

"Never mind... sorry for the delay," Pete said, ultimately deciding to preserve his integrity and follow the team to just one more house before going home and sending an email to the company thanking them for their consideration but informing them that he would not be continuing in the hiring process.

Damien ushered the team toward the last house of the day.

***

Damien knocked loudly on the door once and then retreated a couple of steps back. The house was very small and surrounded by luscious shrubbery; it seemed more like a cottage than a house. Pete half expected a wizard to answer Damien's knock. Instead, a large man in his late thirties opened the door. This man was wearing a holey T-shirt emblazoned with a band's logo along with a patchy beard that was in desperate need of grooming.

Before the man could ask who the group was, Damien once again explained that they were a team of fundraisers asking homeowners in the neighborhood for charitable donations. Pete kept thinking about how in a few seconds, this man would tell Damien to leave and Pete would no longer be subjected to Damien's fake fundraising voice.

"Alright, come in. It's cold. My name is Michael," the large man said as he stepped back and ushered the team inside his home.

Pete smiled, but inside, he was furious as he was desperate to go home.

Once inside, Pete noticed the soothing and welcoming scent of some sort of beef stew being cooked. The place was very cluttered, with books, bags, and small sculptures scattered all over the floor. That made the house seem even smaller than it already was.

"I live here with my wife, but she's not home yet. She's in an art expo, but she'll be home soon," Michael explained with a smile, seemingly happy to have visitors at his place.

As Damien explained the purpose of the charitable donation, Pete looked aimlessly around the house, as he had already done several times that day.

Almost immediately, he noticed something on the floor that caught his eye. His heart skipped a beat. Pete rushed forward and picked up the painting of the boat crossing a storm he had thrown away just a few days ago.

"Where did you get this?" Pete asked. Damien shot a look of disapproval at Pete, as he was not allowed to speak during these visits.

"My wife found it on the street one day while visiting a friend. She said it was beautiful and that she couldn't believe someone would just throw it away," Michael responded. "I don't know anything about art, but she's an expert, so I believe her. It's strange because no one signed it, though…"

Pete looked at the painting as if its colors were moving and speaking to him. Although the entire fundraising team was looking at Pete in utter confusion and disbelief, Michael once again seemed amused.

"It's funny because the last time I brought something home off the street, my wife got mad at me. It was a traffic sign just lying on the street that I thought would look funny in the living room. So, when she brought this home, I asked her why I wasn't allowed to bring things in off the street and she could. Of course, she explained that this wasn't just a street sign but a work of art…"

With every word Michael spoke, Pete's smile grew larger.

"You're wrong," Pete said. "It most definitely is a sign, and one that I will never ignore again."

Chapter 7

Five Stories About Adventure

The Flight

Eleanor had never been on a plane in her life. On the other hand, I had already lived in seven different countries before turning thirty. I had probably flown to visit my parents in Spain during my school breaks more times than Eleanor had driven across the country to visit her parents.

As we got ready and prepared to leave the apartment, I was excited to give Eleanor a positive first flying experience.

"I could get us to Spain with my eyes closed," I said, trying to assuage her nervousness.

"But I know I'm going to get nervous. You have to hold my hand when we take off!" Eleanor demanded.

"With pleasure!" I responded enthusiastically.

It had been years since I'd seen someone so nervous about flying, especially over a flight that was less than two hours long. Luckily, I knew what I was doing and found Eleanor's trepidation very sweet.

As we got on the express train that took us directly to the airport, I realized I had left my Spanish ID in the apartment.

"Does that mean we can't fly?" Eleanor asked nervously.

"No, it's ok. We can still make it. I'll take the train back home once we get to the airport," I replied. Luckily, I always arrived exceptionally early for flights. This time, I had planned to arrive three hours before takeoff just to make sure everything went smoothly and so I could show Eleanor around the airport that I had come to know so well.

Upon arriving at the station, we noticed black smoke emerging from the nose of the train. Shortly after, a woman came on the PA system and said that the train was on fire and everyone needed to deboard quickly, which we did.

"It's ok; I'll take a taxi!" I said hastily as Eleanor and I rushed into the airport and away from the black smoke.

Even though it was rush hour and it would take me two hours to get to the apartment and back, I got in the taxi. Eleanor stayed behind with the luggage in a café near where we had to check in, and I tried not to think about how much money the taxi ride was going to cost me.

I had been in the taxi for about thirty minutes when I realized that I had left the keys to the apartment in the luggage that was at the airport with Eleanor. When I informed the taxi driver, he took me back to the airport but still charged me the entire fee for the original trip.

When Eleanor saw me rushing toward her madly, she stood up in bewilderment.

"What happened?" she asked, clearly confused.

"The keys to the apartment are in the suitcase…" I replied despondently.

Eventually, we found a train that was not on fire and made it to the apartment, where I retrieved my Spanish ID. By the time we arrived back at the airport, we had already missed our flight and had to take a later one.

***

As the plane began to move, I reached toward Eleanor so that she could grab my hand tightly when her nerves kicked in. However, Eleanor turned to me with a relaxed smile and gently began caressing my hand.

"Aren't you nervous?" I asked.

"I would have been. But today was so hectic that now I have no energy left to be scared..." Eleanor replied before kissing me on the cheek and laughing.

DETOUR

It had been a long time since Marcus had gotten so drunk. The taxi driver had been giving him dirty looks ever since his friends poured him into the backseat and told the driver where to drop him off.

"I need to stop, please!" Marcus exclaimed. "I'm gonna throw up!"

The taxi driver did not hesitate to let Marcus out by the side of the road, where he sprinted toward the forest. At this time of night, the woods were completely dark and silent except for the sound of Marcus stumbling through the branches and twigs trying to find a place to vomit.

Once Marcus had rid himself of a small percentage of the alcohol currently coursing through his system, he could not find his way back to where the taxi had dropped him off. Regardless of where he turned, he just seemed to be going deeper and deeper into the woods—and since he'd only ever seen them from the road while driving past in the car, he didn't have a good sense of which way to go.

Eventually, Marcus returned to the road, but the taxi was no longer there. Instead, a garbage truck passed by and, seeing Marcus's disheveled state, offered him a ride to the nearest train station.

"I've never been in a garbage truck before!" Marcus mused, slurring his words so much that the two men driving him to the station couldn't help but laugh.

Once they dropped him off, Marcus ran to catch the train but missed it by a few seconds. He peered at the screen and finally managed to make out that this was the last train of the night. Determined to find the sanitation workers again and wanting to get as far away as possible from the strange men dressed in all-black hoodies at the other end of the station, Marcus ran back into the street and eventually ended up back in the woods.

Marcus stumbled through the woods again until he finally saw a chain-link fence that he recognized. It was the fence that separated the forest from the highway.

Marcus ran up the muddy hill and climbed the fence. Before jumping onto the highway, his jacket got stuck and ripped, leaving a massive hole on the left side of the coat.

A toll collector saw Marcus wandering next to the highway and allowed him inside the toll booth, then called a taxi to come pick Marcus up.

Once the taxi arrived, Marcus stumbled inside and fell asleep on the seat immediately.

"Do you know where you live, boy?" the man at the toll booth asked.

The taxi driver smiled and said, "I just had this guy in my cab, but he ran off into the woods! Don't worry. I'll get him home!"

Marcus woke up partway through the drive and tried to think of what he would tell his mother when she saw the state he was in.

"Just tell her a dog or something attacked you," the taxi driver suggested.

"And what about the smell of alcohol on me?" Marcus asked.

"Tell her the dog was Irish!"

BUSKING

Anna and I watched the busker perform fantastic music on his old, beat-up, acoustic guitar on the side of the street for what felt like an hour before he began talking to us and asking us about our lives.

"He plays guitar too!" Anna yelled, enthusiastically pointing at me—as if it wasn't clear who she was referring to.

"Is that so?" the busker asked as he handed me his guitar. He introduced himself as Morten and invited me to play.

Nervously, I accepted Morten's guitar and took his place on the little wooden seat he had been sitting on. Morten took a cigarette break and watched curiously to see what I could do on his instrument.

After about ten minutes of playing the songs I knew, Morten was impressed.

"I'm going to play at a bar in ten minutes. You guys should come with me!" he invited.

"Yes, we'd love to!" Anna replied. I was slightly nervous that he would ask me to play at this bar, but I agreed anyway. The three of us walked through the busy streets of Anna's hometown, which was filled with young people and older adults alike enjoying their Saturday night out on the town.

Once we arrived at the bar, Morten was greeted by many people who seemed bohemian and musical like him.

"You're on in five minutes!" Morten said as he handed me his guitar with a smile.

Anna once again leaped in excitement, but I was crippled with fear. The bar was not packed, but there was a table right next to the stage where a huge family was having a meal and some drinks.

Once I got on stage and connected the guitar to the amplifier, I told several jokes before getting started to loosen the tension I was feeling. Everyone looked at me as if they were worried that I would try to be a comedian all night instead of providing them with some live music.

After a deep breath, I began playing all the songs I knew, and in no time, everyone in the bar got up on their feet and started dancing and singing along.

It was one of the most exciting moments of my life, and although I probably played four or five songs, I felt like I had been playing for only a moment when Morten came up to me and asked for his guitar back.

I involuntarily hesitated to return the guitar to Morten, wanting to play longer, and he laughed.

"You got it now, huh?" he asked.

"Got what?" I queried.

"The performing bug!" he crowed.

I smiled and said, "Yeah, I guess I do. That was amazing!"

I sang and danced to every song Morten played, and when he was done, I asked if I could play a few more. He told me that he was going on tour in a week and asked if wanted to join him as he traveled through the country.

I looked at Anna, who, this time, did not jump up and down in excitement. That was the sign I needed to bring me back down to earth.

After that day, I began busking on the street every weekend. I eventually returned to the bar where I had played with Morten, and I'm there every Sunday night to this day.

BIRTHDAY

Andrea had fallen in love with Barcelona from the moment she and her dog, Bailey, landed in Spain. After living in Germany her whole life, she immediately appreciated the warm climate and the feeling that if she lived in Barcelona, she would never need to go on vacation again.

Andrea had studied Spanish for most of her life, and this trip was aimed at completing the certification she needed to become an English teacher and to finally become fluent in Spanish. However, she found that she was too nervous to speak Spanish with the locals, so she constantly resorted to speaking English very slowly and using hand gestures.

When Andrea's friend Sophie wrote that she was going to visit Andrea for her birthday in a week, Andrea became ebullient. She would be able to speak German, or even English at a normal pace.

Andrea told her aunt Carina, who lived in Barcelona and was giving Andrea a place to stay, about Sophie's visit. "You must be so happy that your best friend is coming to visit you!" Carina exclaimed.

Andrea smiled. "Sophie is not my best friend, but maybe after this, she will be. It's lovely of her to come all the way here for a visit when she knows that I've been struggling with the language!"

A couple of days before Sophie was due to arrive, Andrea received a text saying that Sophie would be visiting Barcelona with her new boyfriend.

Andrea was unaware that Sophie even had a boyfriend and was unexcited about spending her birthday with a stranger, but she wrote back saying she was excited to meet him.

The night that Sophie landed, she, her boyfriend, and Andrea were meant to have dinner in a restaurant by the hotel where Sophie was staying.

Knowing that Bailey needed to be walked, Andrea decided to walk to the restaurant instead of taking the train even though it meant she would need to leave an hour earlier to arrive on time.

During their walk, Andrea surveyed everything around her as if taking mental photographs. The way people walked, talked, and did everything was different from what she was used to. The fact that she was minutes away from being reunited with someone who reminded her so much of home made her heart more open and receptive to everything this new city had to offer.

When Andrea was walking along the ocean, less than ten minutes away from arriving at the restaurant, she heard her phone beep to indicate a new text message had come in.

Sophie: Hi. Sorry, we are so tired after the flight. I think we are just going to go right to sleep. Can we meet up tomorrow instead? Thank you!

Andrea felt her heart sink. She wanted to throw the phone into the ocean on her left but instead replied that everything was OK. Except everything wasn't OK. Tomorrow was her birthday, and Andrea didn't want to feel this way on her last day of being 23.

Feeling too exhausted to walk back to her aunt's place, Andrea got on the metro despite her aunt's exhortation to never take the train late at night by herself. She had never used the metro before, but was convinced nothing could make her more upset than she already was.

Although she did not feel unsafe, she felt incredibly uncomfortable—like a sardine stuffed in a can. Many young and rowdy teenagers appeared to be using the metro as a jungle gym.

Bailey usually did not take kindly to loud strangers, but even he was too exhausted to protest. Andrea made herself as small as possible and glued her eyes to the map on the metro's wall that showed how many stops were left before she got off.

Andrea could hear her phone buzzing in her pocket with the specific ringtone she had designated for her parents. Unable to answer because doing so would mean elbowing someone, Andrea let it ring.

A large group of teenagers began aggressively shouting and taunting one another. Bailey started to growl, which prompted Andrea to put her hand on his muzzle. The last thing she needed was Bailey trying to participate in the hostilities.

It did not take long for the enraged youths to begin fighting each other in front of everyone. Even people who were just sitting quietly, like Andrea, got sucked into the chaos as they tried to get up from their seats to move away from the violence.

Andrea could not move because Bailey was now trying to free himself from her grip and it took all of her concentration to hang onto him. The metro doors opened. It still wasn't Andrea's stop, but she decided to get off anyway.

Just as she was almost entirely off the metro, Andrea felt someone accidentally shove her forward. Because she was cradling Bailey with both hands, Andrea couldn't grab on to anything or even brace for impact on the way down. She hit her head hard on the concrete floor.

If it hadn't been for Bailey barking manically, Andrea might have remained unconscious on the floor for much longer.

When she came to, she was flat on the floor and heard a male voice above her asking, "Can you stand up?"

Andrea looked up to see a boy roughly around her age, with kind brown eyes and messy black and gray hair.

Andrea slowly got up with the help of the kind stranger.

She did her best to answer his questions, but her mind was too fuzzy to comprehend what was happening.

"I'll take you to a hospital!" the boy said.

"No, I'm OK!" Andrea insisted.

"I think you might have a concussion!" he told her firmly.

"I'm fine, thank you." Andrea just wanted to go home and cry.

"At least take my number in case you need help with anything…" he persisted.

Andrea agreed to take the boy's number.

"What's your name?" she asked.

"José!"

***

The next morning, Andrea did end up going to the hospital with her aunt. It turned out that she did have a concussion, but she was allowed to go home later that evening.

Once she was out of the hospital, Andrea took Bailey to the vet to ensure nothing had happened to him in the altercation the night before.

"Andrea!" a somewhat familiar voice bellowed.

Andrea turned around to see the face of the boy who had helped her get off the floor after she fell in the metro station.

"José?" she said tentatively.

"You remember my name! Are you OK?" he asked.

José was wearing white scrubs and was holding a clipboard. He was a vet.

"Yeah, I'm OK. I'm here for Bailey!" Andrea responded, belatedly realizing it was clear that she would not go to a veterinary clinic to get herself checked.

José offered to take a look at Bailey himself.

In the meantime, Andrea was getting texts from Sophie asking Andrea if they could just celebrate her birthday in their hotel room since both Sophie and her boyfriend were still tired from the flight from Germany.

"My brother is opening a bar this evening in Alicante. It's a few hours away by car, and I'm driving alone. If you want, I could take you there for dinner, and then I'll drive you back home. Don't worry; I won't be drinking…" José offered.

Andrea smiled and replied that she would get back to him once she got home.

"OK, get home safe. Goodbye, Bailey!"

***

"But didn't you already buy a ticket to fly back to Germany in two days?" Carina asked Andrea after hearing about José's proposition. Andrea was strongly considering the trip; after all, he was very handsome.

"Yeah, I know," Andrea said with a shrug.

"Does José know?" her aunt pestered.

"No," admitted Andrea.

"And what about Sophie? Would you rather go visit her, even despite how she is treating you?" continued Carina.

Everything Carina was asking was valid.

Andrea sat in her room and looked at her phone, as if waiting for someone to call her and let her know what to do.

José is very handsome, she thought.

Andrea smiled as she picked up her phone to type out a text.

> Andrea: José, I'd love to join you for the drive to Alicante tonight.

Sophie never texted again asking what happened or even to wish her a happy birthday, and anyway, Andrea was too excited and happy to feel bothered about her friend's indifference.

The Road Trip

"I don't understand. Why did you say no to seeing her again if you like her?" Natalie questioned her best friend José.

That is a good question, José thought.

"We had an amazing first date. We kissed and said we'd see each other again soon. When I woke up the next morning and saw the message from her telling me that she had been too scared to confess that she was leaving for Germany in two days, I knew this was my terrible luck ruining my life again!" José admitted.

"But if she was too scared to tell you, it's because she liked you! Especially if she said that she was willing to postpone her trip and stay here for you!" Natalie argued.

The more José tried to think of a counterargument, the more he realized how right his best friend was.

"Well, it's too late now anyways. She's back in Germany, and even if I wanted to fly there, I can't go because of Harley," José protested.

Harley was José's cocker spaniel. She was two years old and could not go on airplanes due to her short nose, which could cause breathing problems on the flight.

Natalia grinned at José as she put her coffee down on the circular wooden table between them and looked at him, satisfied.

"You have a car… and one you've been meaning to take on a road trip for some time now…" she coaxed.

Once again, she was right.

***

The drive from Spain to Germany was about eleven hours—and even longer with Harley in the backseat.

"So she has no idea you're coming. How do you even know where she lives?" asked Natalie.

"On our first date, we realized that she lived next door to a cousin of mine. My cousin already said he'd let me stay with him in case Andrea does not want to see me when I surprise her!" shared José.

Natalie helped José pack his things into the backseat of his blue SUV and settled Harley onto her favorite brown bed in the spacious cargo area.

"Ready?" Natalie asked as she looked at José through the passenger seat's open window.

José nodded and drove off to tell Andrea that he had changed his mind and understood why she had been nervous to tell him about her return flight to Germany.

***

As José and Harley left Spain and entered France, the sun was finally starting to rise over the horizon. It illuminated the intimidating trucks zooming past them and the verdant greenery in the surrounding fields.

José felt bad for Harley, who had no choice but to endure his terrible and impassioned singing for the entire journey. Luckily, Harley was very quiet for the first couple of hours, probably sleeping, which made him jealous.

José knew that driving tired was more dangerous than driving drunk, but he had started packing his bags late in the afternoon and only managed to get a few hours of sleep. He also wanted to arrive in Germany before Andrea went to sleep for the night.

Once the sun was completely out and the road no longer seemed like a new and exciting prospect, Harley and José began to feel exhaustion set in.

After enduring Harley's whining for about an hour, which was probably payback for having had to endure José's awful singing, the two of them stopped at a gas station in France.

He hadn't felt so foolish and powerless for a very long time as he did that morning trying to figure out how to put gas in his car in a foreign language. At one point, José may as well have been playing Tetris on the touch screen at the pump for all the good it was doing.

Finally, a kind, elderly man who was fueling up his car at the next pump came over to help, as he spoke English. He was surprisingly chatty, but José took advantage of the conversation as he thought about the hours of driving ahead of him.

"Why didn't you just call and tell the girl how you feel?" Idris, the elderly man, asked.

"I thought this would be more romantic," admitted José.

"That might be true, but I think you jumped a couple of steps ahead. Are you sure she feels the same way?" Idris asked.

Regardless of how much José tried to forget Idris's question, he found it hard to think about anything else for the rest of the drive.

The second stop happened once Harley began barking in the back. José parked the car in a gas station in Lyon and walked Harley through an expansive forest that was unfortunately filled with litter.

Harley was pulling on the leash so much that he decided to unleash her and let her run around the woods to burn off her extra energy. Almost immediately after unleashing his dog, José learned why Harley had been so interested in being set free.

"Leave the squirrel!" José screamed as he summoned the little energy he had acquired from the bitter yet expensive gas station espressos.

José ran through the woods, hoping that Harley wouldn't chase the squirrel in front of an oncoming truck. Eventually, he caught up with Harley, picked her up, and carried her back to the car, where he placed her in the trunk and informed her that because of her bad behavior, he would now sing the entire rest of the trip to Germany.

The rest of the trip was nowhere near as exciting as the first few hours, which made finally arriving at Andrea's place all the more thrilling. The entire trip, José had been worrying about what Andrea would think when seeing José. What if Idris was right? What if his recent behavior had made her lose interest in him and, therefore, she would not appreciate the romantic gesture he was about to complete?

José parked the car in front of Andrea's house and looked at his phone. He had several missed calls from Natalie, but he would have to reply to them some other time.

José got out of the car, leaving Harley and his luggage in the trunk. He couldn't remember feeling this nervous in a very long time. Continuing to ignore his phone buzzing inside his jeans pocket, José rang the doorbell and took a couple of tentative steps back.

A man in his late 40s answered the door and said something in German.

"Excuse me, is Andrea home?" José asked uncertainly.

The man continued to speak in German, so José took out his phone to translate when he received yet another call from Natalie.

"Nat, I can't speak right now. I need to translate something into German!" José exclaimed.

"Well, I have someone here who can probably help!" Natalie said as she turned her phone camera to show a very embarrassed-looking Andrea.

José's jaw dropped.

"Hi, José, is that my father behind you?" Andrea asked.

Judging by the man's ebullient smile when he saw Andrea on José's phone, it was clear that this man was obviously her father.

"So, I guess we were both thinking of the same way to surprise each other. Only, I stayed a few more days without telling you so that I could surprise you…" Andrea explained.

José looked at the picture on his phone in disbelief, then smiled.

"So, you're not angry at me?" he asked.

"Of course not. I wanted to show you that I liked you and that I was sorry I didn't tell you about my flight home, which I canceled for you!" exclaimed Andrea.

As Andrea's dad took the phone and began speaking to his daughter, Jose let out a deep sigh of relief. Now the only question was how to get back to Spain.

Chapter 8

Five Stories About the Golden Years

Photo Album

Nathan sat on his black leather couch, perusing the photo album his son had made for him for his 80th birthday a few days ago. The day had been very hectic with everyone running around the house and bringing Nathan presents before his big birthday dinner.

Things had quieted down now, and it was the time in the afternoon when Nathan usually sat on his old sofa that he'd had for over twenty years and rested his feet. Originally, the sofa had been placed in front of the big window where Nathan could look out over the large, carefully maintained front yard and the quiet street beyond.

A few years ago, though, Nathan decided to turn the couch around to face away from the window. He had started to feel self-conscious about falling asleep and having the neighborhood children see him with his eyes closed and mouth open.

As Nathan opened the impressively heavy photo album, he noticed the noise he detested hearing when sitting on his couch: the booming and obnoxious sound of children playing surprisingly close to his window.

Rather than turning around to see exactly what was going on, Nathan continued flipping the pages of his photo album. It did not take long for him to become fully immersed in the photographs. As he looked through them, the photos took him back to every memory they showed.

Nathan had one son—William. William was the father of three rowdy, lively young boys who had spent the entire birthday weekend running up and down Nathan's house as if it were the most exciting theme park they had ever seen. One of the main reasons why Nathan was so happy to be sitting on his sofa was that he hadn't managed to have a quiet moment to himself ever since William and the children had been home. However, the noise outside was starting to break Nathan's concentration.

Turning the album's pages, Nathan saw photos of himself when he was about thirty years younger—before William was even dating the woman who would later become his wife and the mother of his three energetic children.

The more Nathan perused the album, the quieter everything around him became and the more he smiled. Nathan stopped turning the pages and started to reminisce about the past.

Nathan remembered how there used to be a time when William was even more willful and defiant than his three boys. Nathan smiled when he realized that he, himself, had probably been the worst of all as a child.

As Nathan reached the last page of the album, he felt his heart ache. He wished that the album was longer or that there was another one for him to look through so that he could continue reminiscing about moments from the past that he'd forgotten about.

Nathan closed the album and gently ran his fingers across the beige leather as if the album was a living thing. As if still looking through the pictures, Nathan's mind began running through very vivid memories of his time with William as a child and with William's children when they were too young to walk, much less sprint and leap the way they currently did. His thoughts made the sounds outside his window disappear completely, until he heard someone call his name.

Nathan slowly got up from his sofa and walked over to the window. William and his three boys were outside in his yard, running around like they usually did.

"Hey, Dad! The boys wanted to see you again. They said they missed you! I just know they can be a lot, so we decided to play outside in your yard to burn off some energy before we come inside. I hope that's ok." William cried as his three children ran circles around his legs.

Nathan smiled broadly and waved at his son to let him know everything was fine.

All three boys waved at Nathan excitedly, as if it had been years since they'd seen him rather than a day.

Still smiling, Nathan returned to his sofa. But instead of sitting down, he turned it around to face the window. For the first time in many years, he could look out into the front yard of his house from his seat on the black leather sofa. Although he'd already looked through the whole photo album, now he could look out over the memories he was making that very moment by watching his son and his three rowdy grandchildren, who were genuinely excited to see him every day, playing outside his window.

THE BREAKFAST ORDER

Nathan and his oldest grandchild, Jake, who was six years old at the time, were sitting opposite each other at a diner just a couple blocks away from Nathan's apartment.

Jake loved visiting the US because it meant he and his family could stay at Nathan's apartment there. Nathan didn't live in the United States either, but he had a small apartment that he mainly visited during the summer. This year, Nathan had invited his son William and the rest of William's family to join him at the apartment and spend a couple of weeks there during the summer holidays.

Jake had been woken up by his grandfather, who asked Jake if he wanted to go to breakfast at the diner nearby. Jake loved his grandfather a lot, and his grandfather often played together with Jake as if they were the same age, but the two of them rarely spent time alone together.

Finding no reason to say no, Jake got up and dressed as quickly as possible. The two of them walked over to the diner Jake always saw when visiting his grandfather's apartment, but had yet to eat in. Jake's father William had become overly fastidious about what Jake could eat and drink, and he primarily ate vegetables and drank water— maybe sometimes milk if he was lucky. Therefore, sitting in a classic American diner with his grandfather filled Jake with excitement as he pondered all the possible things he would be allowed to eat.

Jake laughed just looking at the menu, which was almost too big for him to even hold. The menu was laminated in plastic and covered in ketchup and other mysterious, food-looking stains, which made Jake all the more excited to eat there. The menu also had big pictures of some of the foods, which Jake focused on exclusively without even reading what the dishes actually were.

A red-haired waitress with large, round glasses and a nametag that read "Janet" came up to their table and spoke to them in a very enthusiastic tone. She greeted Nathan and Jake as if they were guests of honor and asked what they wanted to eat.

Nathan ordered first, and Janet repeated his choice as she scribbled on her notepad.

"Thank you. That sounds great," Nathan confirmed.

"And what can I get you, young man?" Janet inquired.

"I'll have the XL breakfast platter!" Jake exclaimed excitedly.

Janet and Nathan looked at each other with similar expressions of mild concern.

"That is a very big platter. Are you sure you can eat it? It has pancakes with—" Janet began.

"Yes, I'm sure!" Jake enthused.

"Jake, your dad says sometimes you order more than you can eat. Maybe we should ask Janet if there are other options more suited to you. Why don't you look at the menu and read everything you're ordering?" suggested Nathan.

Janet smiled and was about to recommend other dishes to Jake when she was interrupted again.

"No, that's what I want, and I don't want anything else!" Jake demanded.

Nathan looked at his grandchild, surprised at his mild outburst. Janet smiled again and made her way to the kitchen.

"You know, sometimes it's good to listen to people. Even if we think we are right, it does not always mean we are…" Nathan tried to explain to his grandchild, who shrugged and seemed disinterested.

"I'm gonna eat all of it!" insisted Jake.

"And what if you don't?" prompted Nathan.

Jake looked at all the delicious food around him and was convinced that he would have no problem putting away the XL breakfast platter.

"Then I'll go and clean the kitchen of the diner!" Jake finally suggested, to which Nathan chuckled quietly.

When the food finally arrived, Nathan and Jake marveled at how Janet masterfully balanced the enormous platter of pancakes, bacon, eggs, and toast.

"This is for you, young man," Janet said as she very slowly lowered the meal that seemed large enough to feed an entire family.

Jake eyed the enormous meal enthusiastically, especially the creamy sphere on top of his towering stack of pancakes.

"Ice cream!" Jake cried as he looked at the puffy scoop.

Nathan smiled. "Jake, can I give you some advice about what you're about to eat?"

Jake shot his grandfather a frustrated look and shook his head emphatically. Nathan kept silent, but couldn't help continuing to smile.

After contemplating the massive breakfast as if it were some trophy that had just been awarded to him, Jake grabbed a spoon and took a big scoop of the "ice cream" on top of his pancakes.

Almost immediately after putting the scoop in his mouth, Jake made a face like he had just tasted something much worse than the vegetables his father encouraged him to eat on a daily basis.

"Already figured out that it's pure butter and not ice cream?" Nathan asked, trying very hard not to laugh.

Jake spat out the butter onto his plate and took a big gulp of his drink.

***

"Thank you for not making me clean the kitchen," Jake said as he and his grandfather walked home from the diner.

Nathan was carrying pretty much everything Jake had been served for breakfast in a plastic takeout container.

"It's OK. As long as you learned an important lesson then it's completely fine," Nathan reassured him.

"I did. Next time, spread the butter on something first!" Jake exclaimed as he put his arm around his grandfather and headed home.

DISCIPLINE

Grandpa Albert was waiting in line with his son and grandson Nathan at the Italian restaurant in the airport. Nathan and Albert had a very special connection where they were constantly playing pranks on people and telling silly jokes that no one else found as funny as they did.

Much to Nathan's dismay, his winter break was over and it was time to go home, which meant he had to say goodbye to his grandfather. Grandpa Albert had accompanied them to the airport to wish Nathan and the rest of the family goodbye.

During the entire car ride to the airport, Nathan and Grandpa Albert were reminiscing about all the fun stuff they did together and all the fun things they wanted to do next time Nathan and his family were in town.

Once the entire family had ordered their food, they all took their trays and sat together at a table close to the TV screen that would announce when their flight would begin boarding.

"Nate," Nathan's dad Mike said as he nudged his oldest son, "can you give a slice of pizza to your little brother?"

Nathan's little brother, Zach, who was only a couple of years younger than he was, reached out to grab a slice from Nathan, who immediately pulled his pizza away in anger.

"No!" Nathan declared.

Grandpa Albert smiled. "C'mon, Nate. He's hungry and you know that you got the last pizza they had…"

Zach slammed his small fists against the wooden table in frustration.

"He can't have any of my pizza!" Nathan exclaimed angrily as he took another bite of his margherita pizza.

Even Grandpa Albert looked unimpressed this time.

Normally, Grandpa Albert always sided with Nathan and ensured he got what he wanted at all times due to the strong bond they had. However, this time, he was visibly frustrated at Nate's reluctance to share his pizza with his younger brother.

Grandpa Albert almost said something to his grandson, but then realized he didn't want to create trouble. Albert lived a pretty solitary life, and he always got a lot of grief from his children about how he had to be more conscious of his health and many other things. However, with his grandson Nate, there was nothing to worry about other than having fun—and that made him reluctant to ruin their relationship by trying to discipline Nathan in any way.

Nate ate the pizza so enthusiastically that it seemed as if he was eating just to keep the food away from his little brother rather than to satiate his own hunger.

Grandpa Albert became so troubled by Nathan's behavior that he had to stand up and go for a quick walk. Albert had never felt like his grandson had done anything wrong before, and would often come to his defense whenever Nate's parents were angry at him about something. This made his disappointment all the more frustrating.

"Grandpa!" Nathan called out as he ran up behind Albert.

"Yes?" answered Albert.

"I need your advice!" Nate explained.

"What is it?" asked Albert.

"I wanted to give my little brother a slice of pizza, but I didn't like the way he just tried to take it without me even answering him. I wanted Dad to tell Zach not to be rude but instead he got angry at me! I don't want Zach to be hungry, but I didn't like how Dad got angry at me and not at Zach for trying to take my pizza before I could even say if he could have some. What should I do?"

Grandpa Albert smiled as he felt a heavy weight fall off his shoulders. Suddenly, everything became clear to him. His role was not to discipline; instead, it was one that he felt a lot more excited about—to advise.

Looking at his grandson, Albert knew that Nathan would never have confided this information to his father and that he ran to ask his grandfather for advice because of the trust they shared.

Albert put his hand on his grandson's shoulder. The two of them walked through the airport and conversed about the situation. Grandpa Albert never disciplined Nate but merely advised him, which was endlessly more gratifying to him.

HUMBERTO

Nathan had always preferred his Grandpa Albert to his Grandpa Humberto. Albert was his father's father, and Nathan loved playing games with him so much that Nathan even preferred spending time with his grandpa rather than with his own friends from school.

Humberto was his mother's father. Humberto was slightly older and was a much more stoic and stern man. Nathan had never seen him angry, but had also never seen him express any emotion.

Nathan sat down to watch his favorite film with the entire family one day, which happened to be a particularly emotional film that always made everyone cry, and noticed that Humberto hadn't shed a single tear. After that moment, Nathan considered his grandfather Humberto utterly devoid of emotion, which was the complete opposite from Grandpa Albert.

One day, Humberto's small cocker spaniel got really sick and had to be taken immediately to the vet, where the doctor said that the dog was very ill and also too old to survive the surgery he needed to get.

Nathan and his parents were at the vet with Humberto when the doctor presented this horrible news. Nathan looked at Grandpa Humberto and was shocked to see that he didn't shed a single tear over the fate of his lifelong companion.

"I can't believe Grandpa didn't even cry about his dog's diagnosis," Nathan said once he got home and was alone with his parents.

"Nathan, your grandfather cannot cry. He has dry eye syndrome," Nathan's mother explained.

"What?" Nathan cried, never having heard of such a thing.

"It's true," Nathan's dad added, "but he cries inside every time you leave his house after visiting."

Nathan pondered the news he had just been given.

***

The next day, Nathan walked all the way to visit Grandpa Humberto by himself. Once he was inside, Nathan sat with him all day and listened to his grandpa talk about his cocker spaniel and how he was afraid the dog would have to be put down.

Although Grandpa Humberto did not shed a tear, this time Nathan knew what he was feeling inside.

BOXED FEELINGS

George had been living with his grandfather, Harold, for several years. The house they lived in was small, but since George's parents could no longer look after him, this was the best alternative.

The house was situated in a semirural part of town filled with trees, neatly maintained lawns, and people mostly over the age of 60. George spent most of his free time trying to find work to afford his own place, but he was in his last year of high school, which meant that he had to divide his time between studying for his exams and trying to find a suitable university to attend.

Lately, George had been finding it challenging not to feel overwhelmed by everything— something Harold had noticed immediately. Harold came from a generation of people who did not speak about their feelings, and George found it hard to contain his emotions.

Wanting to help his grandson feel better, Harold approached George one day after George got home from school with an idea for how to handle his frustrations.

George entered the house with a solemn expression on his face.

"George, I have an idea," Harold declared. He was wearing his usual flannel shirt and oversized jeans as he looked excitedly at George.

"Hi, Grandad; what is it?" George asked.

Harold extended his left hand to point out a cardboard box resting on a small wooden table by the front door to George.

"What is that?" George questioned.

"That is the box where you are to drop off all your frustrations when you walk through this door," Harold explained as he pointed to the yellow legal pad resting by the box. "You grab a piece of paper, and you write down your frustrations and put them in the box. That way, you leave all your worries behind when you come into this house. You are not to open the box at any point because that would mean you are allowing your frustrations back into your heart. Once the box gets filled up, we empty everything inside and start from scratch!"

Harold was very proud of his idea. He had been struggling to devise ways to help rid his grandson of his worries to no avail. The more he hoped George would discover how to feel better on his own, the worse George seemed to become. Harold knew George needed help, but he hadn't been exactly sure what to do.

"You really think that's going to help me?" George asked, somewhat bemused.

"I really do! It's something my parents used to do with me. No one is ever allowed to open it; we only empty it once it is full," said Harold.

Looking nonplussed, George agreed to use the box. He immediately wrote something down on a sheet of yellow paper, folded it, opened the cardboard lid, and placed the paper inside the box.

"Perfect!" Harold exclaimed, convinced that this would help put a smile on his grandson's face again. "Now, just leave your troubles inside that box and focus on the things that you need to do. I'll give you your space."

For the next few days, George's mood did not seem to improve. Harold was disappointed his idea hadn't worked and unsure about what to do next. He sat in his room and wondered what to do to help his grandson, but no matter how hard he tried to think of something, he failed to come up with a new idea that he felt would work.

After a couple of weeks of watching George become increasingly frustrated with his workload, Harold decided to open the box and see what George had written and put inside—even though that was something that was against the rules of the box.

The note read:

I am frustrated because I wish my grandad would ask me about my worries and talk to me, other than require that I ignore them completely. And if you are reading this, then you are breaking your own rules, grandad.

Less than five minutes after Harold opened the box, George walked through the front door and saw his granddad reading his note.

"You're cheating..." George said with a mocking half-smile.

"And you're right about what you wrote. I'm sorry," Harold apologized.

That evening, Harold and George sat down to talk for the first time in many years. George confessed that he felt lonely and isolated living in Harold's house, and Harold admitted that he recognized that he should have been more communicative with George.

After Harold and George came to an understanding, the box was put in the recycling bin, but the legal pad and pen were left where they were by the door.

"It seems that writing down our thoughts wasn't such a bad thing; maybe we just need to leave them out in the open instead of putting them in a box," suggested George.

Harold smiled and agreed.

***

The next day, Harold came downstairs to have breakfast and saw something written on the legal pad by the door. He bent over to read it:

Went to buy eggs. Writing notes that aren't part of a secret plan is not as fun as the ones that are, but I still like this idea. Maybe I'll become a writer or a negotiator after this. Thank you for caring about me. Love, George.

CHAPTER 9

FIVE FUNNY AND UPLIFTING STORIES

THE FROG BOY

Stevie was sitting in the hotel lobby next to his parents with a giant smile on his face. It was the third and final day of the family's visit to his favorite theme park. He had already gone on all his favorite rides at least twice and eaten more hot dogs and pizzas than he had ever consumed at any other point in his life.

His parents had also enjoyed the experience, but it was time to drive back home. As Stevie sat on the red sofa decorated with imaginary, fantastical characters from the movies he loved watching, he reflected on all the fun he'd had at the park.

"What was your favorite part?" Stevie's mother asked him.

"I loved the show! The one where the prince saves the princess from the dragon and the castle!" enthused Stevie.

At night, once most of the rides had closed, there was a spectacle in the middle of the theme park where actors dressed as knights, princes, and monsters put on an open-air show filled with music and lights that made it feel as if everyone was inside a fantasy movie.

The more Stevie talked about it, the more excited he got about coming back next year.

Stevie didn't share with his mother how infatuated he had become with the actress who played the princess. When he watched the show over the past two nights, Stevie's heart had fluttered when she appeared in the castle window and pleaded for a prince to come and save her, which inevitably happened at the end of each show.

Before Stevie could say more about how much he loved the theme park, he saw a young girl about his age walk into the hotel reception area with her parents and a slightly older boy dressed all in black with gel in his hair—something Stevie thought only adults could wear.

The girl was blonde and looked a little like the princess from the evening shows. Stevie and the girl exchanged a glance before Stevie's father mentioned one of the very few things that could have distracted Stevie from the girl he had already deemed "the young princess" in his head.

"Stevie, would you like to go to the souvenir shop?"

As it happened, Stevie had been eyeing a plastic sword since the day they'd arrived at the hotel and passed the gift shop.

Sprinting past his father, who followed at a more sedate pace, Stevie raced to the store and found only one sword left.

"The last one..." Stevie said ominously to himself as he admired the sword and ran his finger carefully across the plastic blade as if it could cut him.

Stifling a laugh, Stevie's father took the sword and walked over to the cashier.

Waiting patiently by his father's side, Stevie noticed that he could still see the young princess in the lobby. When the older boy in black noticed them looking at each other, he stuck his tongue out at Stevie defiantly. Once again, the girl and Stevie exchanged glances.

Stevie shot a concerned look at his father to see if he had noticed this surprising interaction, but he hadn't.

Once the entire family was reunited on the sofa, Stevie began brandishing his sword bravely at the boy in black, who he had now mentally deemed "the dragon."

As Stevie's parents talked quietly, Stevie's imagination ran wild. He recalled all the amazing scenes from the nightly show and how appreciative the princess had been when the prince rescued her.

Stevie looked at his new sword and realized that it was up to him to recreate the fantastic story acted out the past three nights in the show.

Stevie swallowed his fear and gripped the sword tightly and courageously before making his way to stand before the dragon boy and challenge him for the right to save the princess.

As if the little girl and the boy in black knew precisely what was occurring, the princess looked worriedly at the boy in black, who began squaring up to Stevie.

He doesn't have a weapon; he has no chance against me, Stevie thought. However, the dragon boy did not seem bothered by the fact that Stevie was slashing the air in front of him with his sword as he approached.

The dragon boy quickly stepped in front of Stevie and began speaking loudly in a foreign language. Although Stevie could not understand what the dragon boy was saying, his tone communicated that it was hostile.

As Stevie brandished his sword, the dragon boy took out a toy laser that he had probably purchased at the park.

Intimidated by the weapon, Stevie looked at the princess and noticed she was looking on worriedly. Stevie knew this was his chance to impress her and prove that he was not scared of the laser he had contemplated asking his father to buy him before opting for the sword instead.

The dragon boy smiled and pointed the toy laser at Stevie. The toy weapon made sounds and lit up with different colors, making it clear that lasers were being fired.

Stevie jumped up in the air as far as he could each time the dragon boy shot a laser beam at him, making it clear that he was dodging each laser with his athletic prowess—something the young princess would surely admire.

Upon seeing Stevie's strategy for evading the imaginary laser shots, the dragon boy began laughing as loud as he could while pointing at him.

"Frog boy!" the boy exclaimed in a strange accent.

Stevie felt embarrassed. Before he could say anything back, the dragon boy walked off with the little blonde girl and left Stevie standing by himself with his sword.

"What was that about?" Stevie's mother asked him as he sat back down on the red sofa with his parents.

"I don't want to talk about it," Stevie replied.

A few moments later, Stevie got up and followed his parents to the restaurant they had been waiting to get into so they could have dinner as a family after a long day of enjoying rides at the park.

Throughout dinner, Stevie kept eyeing his sword, questioning if it were as powerful as he believed it would be.

"You don't like it?" Stevie's father asked as he lifted a slice of pepperoni pizza to his mouth.

"I do. I just don't know if I should have it. It's supposed to be used by a prince, and I couldn't even defeat a dragon," mumbled Stevie.

Whether they understood what he was talking about and knew things were not as grave as Stevie believed or were simply too confused to ask, Stevie's parents resumed their dinner after assuring him that if he wanted to be a prince, then he was a prince.

Although he appreciated the sentiment, Stevie felt disappointed after being mocked by the dragon boy and failing to be the prince he thought the little blonde girl needed.

Once dinner was over, Stevie and his parents exited the Italian restaurant and headed to the elevator to go up to their room and grab their luggage.

"Stevie, where is your sword?" his mother asked.

"I left it in the restaurant. I don't deserve it," replied Stevie.

"Of course you do. Go and get it before someone takes it!" his mother admonished.

Feeling disheartened, Stevie reluctantly returned to the restaurant and walked over to the booth he had been sitting in with his family, where he had forced down some spaghetti—Stevie always struggled to eat when he was upset.

Upon returning to the booth, he found his sword still on the floor. Strangely, he had been hoping someone had taken it.

Stevie lifted the sword and turned around to leave the restaurant.

In front of him stood the little blonde girl he'd seen earlier, but without the boy with the laser toy this time.

"I thought you were amazing," she said before kissing him on the cheek.

Before Stevie could say anything, the little girl smiled, turned around, and left.

Stevie stood in shock for a moment, then ran as fast as he could to meet his parents.

When they asked him what had excited him, Stevie held up the sword proudly before them as if the confrontation from earlier had never happened.

"The dragon boy was right. I was a frog before, but now I am a prince because the princess kissed me!" he exclaimed.

As if this declaration was all the explanation his parents needed, Stevie jumped in the air with his sword. He knew he would never leave it behind again now that he had been transformed from a frog to a prince because of the kiss he could still feel on his cheek.

LATE-NIGHT MOVIE

Joseph Sr. was coming home from a long day at the office. Although it had been a particularly trying day, filled with laboriously long meetings that seemingly culminated in nothing productive, he smiled.

As Joseph Sr. stopped the car at a red light, he looked down at the empty passenger seat and gleefully contemplated the reason for his good mood. On the seat next to him was a DVD box set with all of the films starring his eight-year-old son's favorite comedic actor. During his lunch break, Joseph Sr. had walked past an entertainment store and saw the box set. He immediately realized that this would be something his son would very much appreciate having, so he walked in and purchased it, excited to see what kind of reception he would have at home once he arrived with one of the best gifts he could imagine giving his son Joseph Jr.

Joseph Sr. had been working a lot lately and felt very disconnected from his family, especially his son. Every night he arrived home late from work, Joseph Jr. was already in bed. In the morning, Joseph didn't get to spend time with his son because, according to his wife, Joseph Jr. was having trouble sleeping at night. That meant he struggled to get up on time for school and usually lay in bed for longer than he was supposed to.

Joseph wanted to find a way to help his son get the rest he needed, but he was too busy with work to focus on his son's issue. What worried him most was wondering if his son was struggling to sleep because of Joseph Sr.'s absence most of the week, even on weekends, due to his heavy workload.

Once Joseph got home, he entered the house and immediately presented his son with the box set.

Joseph Jr. bounced around the house and screamed excitedly at the top of his lungs.

"Can we watch it now?! Please?!" Joseph Jr. begged his parents, holding onto the box so tightly it looked like he was scared a gust of wind would blow it away.

Joseph Sr. looked at his wife to see her look of disapproval.

"I would love to, but you need to get some sleep. You have school tomorrow, and it's not good to show up tired," Joseph declared, wondering if perhaps it had not been a wise choice to bring home the box set on a school night.

After a few more attempts to convince his parents to let him watch the DVDs, Joseph seemed to finally acquiesce to their wishes and disappeared to his room.

Less than ten minutes after running upstairs to his room without the box set, Joseph Jr. sprinted back down the stairs into the kitchen with unprecedented resolve. Seeing his son so keyed up made Joseph Sr. understand why it was hard for his son to sleep at night. In fact, it did not take long for Joseph Sr. to seriously contemplate the notion that the set of DVDs had only served to exacerbate the issue severely.

Joseph Sr. sat down at his desk and began to look through his emails before going to bed.

"I brought you a whiskey!" Joseph Jr. exclaimed as he suddenly emerged from behind his father, holding up a glass much too big for whiskey and filled to the brim as if it were apple juice.

"What is this for?" wondered Joseph Sr.

"I thought you might want some whiskey!" Joseph Jr. exclaimed. Joseph bewilderedly looked at his son, unsure of how he even knew where the whiskey was kept. It had been months since he had had a drink after work, but he felt oddly guilty refusing to take the glass from his son considering how he had wanted to reconnect with Joseph Jr. for so long.

"Thank you…" Joseph Sr. replied as he carefully took the overfilled glass and gingerly lowered it onto the desk.

As the night progressed, Joseph Jr. continued to perform small gestures seemingly aimed at making his father's evening more comfortable.

"Hi, dad; I brought you some slippers so you can keep your socks clean!" Joseph exclaimed as he proudly dangled some fluffy, pink slippers before his father. "Those belong to your mother!" Joseph Sr. responded, trying to stifle a laugh. Ultimately, he decided to wear them to humor his son, who was clearly trying to bribe his way into being able to watch the DVDs that evening.

As Joseph Sr. turned off his laptop and headed downstairs to eat something, wearing his pink, fluffy slippers and carrying a now-empty glass of whiskey, he arrived at the kitchen table to see a tall glass of beer and a cheese sandwich waiting for him.

Joseph Sr. had intended to heat up the dinner his wife had left him in the fridge, so he was surprised to see two slices of bread with an excessive amount of cheese in between resting on his wife's fine china, which she only used when they entertained very high-profile guests.

"Is that your mother's fine china?" asked Joseph Sr.

"Yes, and that is the finest sliced bread with cheese, just for you!" replied Joseph Jr. proudly.

Joseph Sr. eyed the tall glass of beer and worried that if the evening continued this way, a cheese sandwich would not be enough to soak up all the alcohol his son was presenting him with.

This time, he left the drink untouched, but he did eat the sandwich, which was the first thing he had ever seen Joseph Jr. make. Joseph Sr. winced when he realized there was a thick layer of ketchup over each slice of cheese.

After cleaning up his plate and putting the beer in the fridge, Joseph Sr. began to head upstairs to the bedroom when his son jumped in front of him, blocking the way.

"I put your pajamas in the washer so you can sleep with fresh clothes!" he enthused.

"In the washer?" Joseph Sr. inquired.

"Yes, mom showed me how. They should be ready in three hours," crowed Joseph Jr.

Joseph Sr. could not help but smile.

"I was kind of hoping to go to bed now, son..." he said gently.

"It's OK. I'll ask mom if you can borrow hers, so stay right here!" his son enthused.

"Son!" Joseph Sr. exclaimed.

"Yes?" he said.

"Let's watch one of those DVDs," Joseph Sr. said with a smile.

If his son was willing to go through all of this hard work, he at least deserved to watch one comedy.

Joseph Jr. bellowed with joy and quickly ran to the TV room to get ready.

***

Joseph Sr. put on the DVD and sat on the sofa with his arm around his son. He knew he would probably get reprimanded by his wife for turning on the movie, so he hoped after one film, Joseph Jr. would be too tired to ask to watch another.

Still wearing his fluffy pink slippers and feeling slightly light-headed from the whiskey, Joseph Sr. watched the first 10 minutes of the film before looking at his son, wondering why he wasn't laughing yet.

Joseph Jr. was fast asleep. His head was nestled on his father's chest, and his mouth was wide open. Although this was not what he thought would happen, Joseph Sr. smiled and continued watching the film. He kissed his son on the top of his head and rejoiced that his son was finally getting the sleep he needed after tiring himself out trying to bribe his father into watching the film.

Once the film finished, Joseph Sr. carried his son, who remained sound asleep, up to bed. Joseph Sr. arrived at his bedroom worried about what his wife might say but noticed that she was smiling just as much as he was.

"You're not mad?" he asked tentatively.

"No," his wife replied, "but you might be after you see what your pajamas look like now…"

"What happened?" he asked.

"Your son washed something red with your white pajamas, so now everything is bright pink," she explained.

Joseph Sr. laughed. "Well, at least now they match my fluffy slippers."

GDSF

Jake had never been to the youth club where everyone from his school hung out on the weekends. He'd always heard people talking about the club and the fun stuff they did there over the weekend, though.

Jake was very introverted and generally didn't like social settings, but one day after school, a couple of his friends said they would play cards at the social club on Saturday.

"Aren't there, like, teachers there and stuff?" Jake asked as he waited for his mom to pick him up at the school entrance.

"Yeah, but they don't care about anything. I think the teachers just go to get away from their significant others. They don't have to teach us anything, and there are some parents there too, so it's not like they are responsible for us either," Zachary responded, one hand gripping the padded strap of his red backpack.

"I heard that Ms. Thomas showed up drunk and told Doug about all the guys she's dated. It gets pretty wild there," Dean added excitedly.

"Are you serious?" Zachary asked incredulously.

"Yeah. She just sat there and listed all the men I hate for being lucky enough to date her."

"So that's your idea of a fun Saturday night? Sitting around with your geography teacher, hearing about her love life?" Jake inquired.

"Yeah! You got anything better to do?" Zachary responded.

The truth was, Jake had no plans other than staying home and sleeping. Jake was unconvinced that things would be as enjoyable as his friends made them out to be, but he had no plans, and if there were teachers around, then it couldn't be that intimidating.

***

The youth center was busier than any of the bars Jake and his friends had snuck into occasionally during weekends. There was music playing, but you couldn't hear the words of the song because everyone was talking so loudly at the same time.

There were people of all ages engaged in different activities. There was a round table filled with students playing cards with teachers, three large red sofas creating a semicircle around a large TV screen showing age-appropriate films, and a bar where you could order any soft drink you wanted (but no alcohol).

"I told you this would be awesome, didn't I?" Zachary asked with a satisfied grin on his face as he wiped his round glasses on his white, button-down shirt.

"It looks like every Thanksgiving I've ever had rolled into one place," Jake replied, unsure of how he felt about it.

Jake looked around and saw some people from his high school laughing and genuinely seeming to have a good time. It didn't take long before people started coming up to him and engaging him in conversation. After about an hour, Jake realized that, shockingly, he was having a good time.

For most of the evening, Jake sat on the sofa and watched movies, since he was an avid cinephile. Zachary and Dean were following Ms. Thomas around and asking her about her life before becoming a teacher, which was obviously making her somewhat uncomfortable.

After a couple of hours, Jake was ready to find his friends and say goodbye before heading home. Before he could begin searching for them, though, they found him.

"Jakey! We're playing GDSF! Come join us!" Zachary exclaimed.

"You're playing what?" asked Jake.

"Garbage Dump Skateboard Football, of course!" retorted Zachary.

Jake was now even more confused than before.

Rather than explain, Zachary and Dean dragged Jake outside to the building's driveway. There was a pretty steep slope, and at the bottom were two garbage dumpsters a couple of feet from each other.

"The idea is to release the skateboard and try to make it go between the dumpsters. If it goes through, then you get the point!" Dean exclaimed as Jake watched kids from his school release the skateboard and get frustrated when it smashed against one of the garbage dumpsters.

It took about ten minutes before it was finally Jake's turn.

As Jake was handed the skateboard, he noticed four of the most popular kids from his school walk up.

"What are they doing here?" Dean asked, frustrated.

"I heard they have to come at least once a month as a requirement for being on the basketball team. What are the chances they would come today!" muttered Zachary.

"OK, I'm pretty sure we shouldn't be playing this game, and I'm not gonna do this in front of the popular kids!" Jake said and started to hand the skateboard to someone else. Before he could escape from the game, Bash, one of the new arrivals and arguably the most popular guy in his school, approached. He asked Jake why he was bailing from the game, to which Jake had no response.

"Then let's do it, because I ain't going back inside to play cards with the teachers or to order an orange juice from the bar," Bash said as he stood directly in front of Jake.

Jake turned around and began aiming the skateboard at the gap between the dumpsters.

"He should sit on the board!" one of Bash's friends exclaimed. To Jake's dismay, Dean and Zachary eagerly agreed.

Jake shot a look of disapproval at his friends.

Zachary ran over to him.

"Dude, if you go through the garbage dumpsters sitting on the board, these guys will think you're awesome, consequently making us awesome too. You gotta do it!" he whispered.

Jake begrudgingly sat down on the skateboard, and after a couple of minutes of assessing the situation, he rolled himself down the slope and silently prayed that he would slip between the dumpsters. Instead, he crashed directly into one of them, which flipped over and spilled garbage all over the driveway—not to mention all over Jake, who was lying on the hard ground listening to everyone laugh hysterically.

It did not take long for a teacher and some parents to show up and start yelling at Jake as if he had orchestrated the entire thing.

***

The next day at school, Jake was practically quivering with fear as he wondered what possible nicknames the popular kids were going to give him after the antics he had reluctantly taken part in at the youth center.

Jake and everyone playing GDSF had been banned from ever going back to the youth center.

"Dude, whatever they call you, just remember that you are a pioneer for riding that skateboard down the slope into that dumpster," Zachary said as he rested his hand on Jake's shoulder.

"I didn't even want to play that stupid game, and now I'm probably going to get a beating or a new nickname," grumbled Jake.

"If it's any consolation, I did manage to get Ms. Thomas to confess that she dated a lot before becoming a teacher..." Zachary said hopefully.

Jake finished his lunch and stood up to return his tray when he noticed Bash and his friends approaching.

Jake considered running away, but he knew that would only make matters worse.

"Jake!" Bash called out.

"Yeah?" he replied.

"That's your name, right?" Bash said with a swagger.

"Yes..." Jake responded, relishing the last few moments he had before surely received a new, less-favorable name.

"You're a genius," Bash said.

"What?" sputtered Jake.

"You got me and the guys kicked out of the youth center with your GDSF idea. We hated going to that place. Nice work," congratulated Bash.

"Thanks," Jake replied.

"Since you're probably not allowed to go back, maybe we can hang out next weekend. Cool?" said Bash.

"Cool," Jake responded as Bash and his goons walked away.

Jake put his tray down and returned to sit with Zachary and Dean. He explained what had happened.

"See, I told you it would be fine!" Zachary exclaimed.

Jake sighed with relief. "I don't think I'll hang out with them, though."

"What? Why not?" Dean inquired incredulously.

"If that's what they like doing, getting kicked out of fun places and seeing things get trashed—literally—then I think I'm better off just hanging out with you guys," Jake responded as he smiled at Zachary and Dean.

"Can we hang out with Bash and his gang?" Zachary asked. "After all, we're the ones who created GDSF…"

Jake scoffed, then smiled.

THE ESCAPE

Jimmi was furious that at the last minute, his mother had canceled her plans to drive him over to his best friend's house. Jimmi was supposed to go hang out at Sam's house on Saturday night, and his mother had agreed to drive him. However, at the last minute, Jimmi's mother remembered that she had an online yoga class that she didn't want to miss.

"It's not fair!" Jimmi vehemently protested. "You said you would drive me. Why did you forget about your class?"

"I didn't plan on forgetting, Jim. Just reschedule it for next weekend," she said calmly.

The more Jimmi tried to reason with his mother, the more furious he got. He wasn't making any progress, and it was becoming increasingly evident that he would not be seeing his friend Sam.

"Fine, have it your way. I tried to reason with you!" Jimmi yelled as he ran to his room and began packing his things.

Jimmi had always wondered where he would go if he ever decided to leave home. Although he had never managed to come up with an answer, he decided that he was about to find out.

Jimmi packed a banana, a water bottle, a map, and some clean underwear into his backpack before putting his wallet in his jeans pocket and opening his bedroom window.

It was late, but there was still light outside. Jimmi climbed out his bedroom window just so his mother would not find out until later that he was gone. He scrambled over the wooden fence around his home and began walking toward the bus station.

Once he got to the bus station, he waited for the bus that dropped him off at school, as he planned to ride it to the end of the route. Although he had only been gone for a few minutes, he was already thinking about how his mother would react once she found out he was gone.

The bus finally arrived, and Jimmi jumped on. Things inside the bus were completely different on the weekend. On school mornings, he would always sit with other classmates and things on the bus were very quiet and subdued. However, the scene that was unfolding before him now was very different. The bus was packed with loud, obnoxious people much older than he was. Everyone looked at Jimmi as if he was in the wrong place.

Jimmi sat by himself against the window and looked outside, wondering if he had made the right decision. As time passed, more people crammed into the bus until an older man who appeared to be speaking to himself sat by Jimmi. The first thing Jimmi noticed was the bad smell emanating from the stranger next to him.

As the bus approached his usual stop, Jimmi decided the best thing to do would be to get off, which he did.

Once outside, Jimmi relaxed and, for the first time in his life, felt content to be standing so close to his school. He looked at the closed gate and realized he had no idea where to go. Before he could decide where to go next, Jimi suddenly remembered his backpack, which he was no longer holding on to.

Jimmi watched the bus leave with his backpack still there, lying next to the smelly old man who was probably helping himself to Jimmi's banana or a fresh pair of underwear.

Jimmi sat down on the grass and again began imagining how his mother would react once she found out he was gone. Surely by now, she had found out. Jimmi had turned his phone off so she could not call him and beg him to come home.

As the minutes passed and Jimmi just sat and watched cars go by, he began to feel guilty about what he was putting his mother through, but not guilty enough to do anything about it. After about twenty minutes, Jimmi decided to walk in the direction the bus went and hopefully find the shopping center, which he knew was close to the school.

Suddenly, Jimmi realized what would be the best revenge. There was a video game store in the shopping center that he loved going to, and there was a specific game that he wanted his parents to buy him. However, every time he asked, they would tell him it was too violent. Jimmi decided to go into the store and buy it himself—something he had been told he could not do.

Before Jimmi could start toward the shopping center, a car stopped right in front of him and rolled down the window. It was his math teacher, Mr. McMillan.

"Hey, Jimmi! What are you doing here?" asked Mr. McMillan.

"Hi, Mr. McMillan. I had just left something at school, but I'm going home now!" replied Jimmi.

"It's late. How are you getting home?" he asked.

"The bus," replied Jimmi.

"At this time, it's not safe. I'll drive you home," offered Mr. McMillan.

Jimmi protested, but eventually accepted his math teacher's offer.

Fifteen minutes later, Jimmi was right back where he had started.

"Say hi to your parents for me!" Mr. McMillan said as he waved and drove off.

There was no way Jimmi would take the bus or walk all the way back to the shopping center, so he just walked circles around the neighborhood until it was completely dark.

Once there was no more light in the sky, Jimmi walked through the door.

"Hey honey, dinner's almost ready. Can you come down?" he heard his mother call.

"What?!" he sputtered to himself.

"Dinner is almost ready. Please come out of your room and have dinner with us," she continued.

Jimmi couldn't believe it. His mother hadn't even noticed he had left.

Jimmi walked into his room and sat down on his bed. The first thing he realized was that he wasn't even mad. He was too exhausted from walking circles around the house to be angry.

After laughing about the whole situation, Jimmi walked down to join his family for dinner.

"Why didn't you answer your phone?" Jimmi's mother asked.

"I had it turned off so I could sleep," he answered.

"That's what I thought. I didn't want to disturb you, but my yoga thing was canceled, so I could've taken you to your friend's place after all..." she shared.

I'm never escaping again, Jimmi thought, still not mad and finding the entire situation funny. At the end of the day, he decided he preferred being home and eating a warm meal than eating a cold banana by his school on a Saturday night.

Halloween Egging

"So, what is this guy's name?" Mitchell asked.

"I'm not sure. Philippe or something. He's French, I think…" David replied.

David was strolling through the forest by his house with his best friend Mitchell, as he did most Sundays before going home and preparing for school the next day. It was a particularly cold afternoon, and the sun would be going down very soon, so the friends were making their way back home.

"Have you met him already?" Mitchell inquired.

"Yeah, my mother dragged me to their house. My mom and his mom were friends in school or something, which means I am forced to be his friend too," answered David.

"How is he?" asked Mitchell.

David shrugged and frowned as he kicked a few branches off the leafy path that led him back to his parent's house.

"He's alright; a bit loud and obnoxious..." admitted David.

Mitchell scoffed and ran his fingers through his messy, auburn hair.

"Oh, he's gonna fit right in here then," Mitchell said.

"C'mon. Not everyone is so bad here," answered David.

"The Harleys are..." Mitchell responded passionately.

David smiled in agreement. "Yeah, I guess the Harleys are pretty awful..."

"The Harleys" was the moniker David and Mitchell had assigned to a group of five kids, all slightly older than them, who lived in the same gated community and were always up to no good. These five boys hung out in the country club at night, playing pool or terrorizing little children and adults alike with their rebellious antics.

Everyone in the gated community rode bicycles, since it was the easiest way to get around the neighborhood. These boys were nicknamed the Harleys because their bikes always seemed to be the biggest and most impressive, with bright stickers and shiny paint, making it seem as if this motley crew of boys was riding around on motorcycles.

David and Mitchell had become best friends several years ago for many reasons. One of the things they always agreed on was their dislike of the Harleys. Although none of the five Harleys members had ever done anything to David or Mitchell, none of the slightly older but much more confident boys had ever even said hi to them or acknowledged their presence in all their years of living in the same gated community.

David zipped up his father's oversized, suede jacket as the day began to get colder.

"Is Philipe already at your place with his mom?" asked Mitchell.

"Yeah, I think so. I should probably hurry; I was supposed to be there by now…" David replied. "See you later, Mitch!"

***

"I thought we were only going for a quick walk close to the house?" David asked as he followed Philippe down the road that led to the country club, which would be filled with grown-ups and older kids at this time.

"I'm just meeting up with some guys I met yesterday at the country club. They were there last night playing pool and they invited me to hang out. Maybe you know them?" asked Philippe.

"What are their names?" David asked apprehensively, pinching the inside of his father's jacket.

As Philipe listed the five names David expected but regretted hearing, he began bracing himself for the meeting he was about to have with Harleys.

***

The country club was very different at night. It was a lot louder, and all the food usually served during the day had been replaced by the smell of beer and popcorn.

David had seen the five large and shiny bicycles parked outside the country club and was already feeling overwhelmed.

One of the Harleys greeted Philippe enthusiastically, as if they had been friends for as long as David and Mitchell had been.

Philippe introduced David to the Harleys. Each of the boys was significantly taller than David, but they all waved to him and greeted him in a much more amicable way than David had expected.

"Yeah, we know this kid. He's always hanging out with the little runt. What's your buddy's name, the really short one?" Axl, one of the Harleys, asked David.

"Mitchell?" he answered.

"Yeah, that one. How come you never hang out with us?" Dennis, another Harley member, asked.

Unsure of what to say, David simply shrugged.

"You look like a runt yourself with that jacket. It's three sizes too big for you!" Axl commented.

Before David could respond, Philippe and the rest of the Harleys began playing pool. David had never played pool, so he just watched.

After about half an hour, Philippe told the other kids that he and David had to get back home before their parents started to worry.

"Are we good for tomorrow?" Axl asked.

"Yeah, of course," Philippe replied.

"You wanna join us, little boy?" Dennis asked David.

"You guys going trick-or-treating?" David asked, knowing that the next day was Halloween.

All the other boys laughed.

"Not exactly," Axl started. "We're gonna egg every house in the neighborhood. It's our Halloween tradition. You wanna join?"

David looked up at the older boys, who all had their eyes locked on David awaiting his response.

"Yeah, I'd love to," David replied.

"That's my guy!" Philippe said as he patted David on the back a little too aggressively.

***

"Are you crazy?" Mitchell asked. "You can't go around egging houses. That's a crime!"

"It's not a crime!" David protested.

The two friends were walking home from school. David had told Mitchell there was some exciting news he had to share, but he had to wait to explain until school was over.

"Yes, it is. You'll go to jail…" warned Mitchell.

"You're just jealous that I'm gonna be hanging out with the Harleys, and you won't!" argued David.

"Of course not. I don't want to hang out with them. They're losers, and if you are friends with them, then you're a loser too!" sputtered Mitchell.

"Well, I'd rather be friends with them than be friends with you!" David exclaimed as he sprinted the last couple of blocks home by himself, leaving his best friend behind.

Once David got home, his mother asked him why he was so excited and if he wanted to start getting his costume ready.

"Mom, I have great news!" David exclaimed.

"What is it, honey?" she asked.

"I'm part of the Harleys now!" he announced.

"The what?" she said.

"And I'm going to be egging houses with them tonight. I'm going to do what cool kids do!" David said proudly.

"You're going to do WHAT?!" David's mother demanded.

**

In retrospect, I probably should not have told Mom about the egging, David pondered as he sat in his bedroom by himself. She'd grounded him immediately.

He had been so excited about being part of the Harleys that he hadn't been able to contain his plans.

Desperate to find a way to still participate in the egging ritual, David snuck down into the kitchen and stole as many eggs as he could from the fridge without his mother noticing before running back upstairs to his room.

David sat down on his bed, laid out two dozen eggs on the blue bedsheet, and started devising his plan. If he couldn't go out egging houses, at least he could egg the only house he still had access to and prove to the Harleys that he was worthy of their friendship despite having failed to show up at the country club at the specified time.

They're all probably riding around on their awesome bikes, having fun wondering why I'm not there, David thought, trying not to accidentally crack an egg in frustration

Determined to prove himself and make up for not showing up at the country club, David opened the window of his room and began dropping eggs on his own house. The first two simply rolled down the roof and broke on the pavement in front of the house.

David shot the next few eggs directly downward as violently as he could and smiled as he saw the front porch begin to take a yellowish hue. Luckily, the eggs did not make too much noise as they rolled down so David felt confident that he could continue launching eggs without his parents immediately finding out.

As David tossed the last few eggs, he failed to hear the front door open or see his dad walk out onto the front porch to investigate what the strange sound was.

David yelped as he saw an egg fall directly on his father's head.

Oh no, David thought as he stood, frozen, in front of the window. He considered retreating and shutting the window quietly but then realized it would be tough to convince his parents that it had suddenly started raining eggs, or that a flying chicken had been circling their home from the skies. Therefore, he could only watch helplessly as his father glared at him angrily.

***

The next morning, David was once again cleaning the front porch since his parents had deemed his efforts to rid it of eggshells and stains from the night before unsatisfactory.

Mitchell passed by on his little green bicycle and saw David on his knees, scrubbing the wooden tiles of his front porch as hard as possible.

"What happened here?" he asked curiously.

"Someone egged my house..." David replied, too embarrassed to tell the truth at first.

"No way! They only egged your house, though. No one else's!" Mitchell exclaimed.

"Yup, no other house was egged, apparently..." David grunted as he tried as hard as he could to remove the yellow residue off the floor.

"Do you need some help?" Mitchell asked.

David looked up at his friend and smiled tentatively.

Mitchell parked his bike by the house and helped David continue cleaning up the mess.

After about five minutes, David confessed what had happened to Mitchell. Mitchell laughed so hard that he started rolling around on the floor getting some eggshell fragments on his white T-shirt.

"I'm sorry for what I said…" David said once Mitchell regained his composure.

"Me too," Mitchell replied.

The friends fist-bumped each other and continued cleaning.

"I don't want to be one of the Harleys. I just wanna be who I am," David finally confessed.

"And who is that?" asked Mitchell

"Someone who eggs his own house and father and then cleans it up the next morning…" David replied. Mitchell once again burst out laughing.

Chapter 10

Five Stories About the Simple Things in Life

The Underground Song

The moment I walked into the small underground apartment, I immediately knew that I would not be staying there that night. There was barely any space for me to put my things and the decor was very bleak. There was a window with a view of a cement wall and the garbage bins. If you got close enough to the window, you could look up and see people's feet passing by.

My girlfriend Carole lived about two hours away by train, but at least it was a big house where I would feel comfortable. Carole normally lived in the city, but was staying at her parents' place for the weekend. I sent her a quick message saying that I would be staying over at her parents' place with her because I hated the apartment I had rented.

Carole was overwhelmed with joy when she heard the news. I quickly got my stuff packed and headed over to the train station. Luckily, it was so late at night that the trip was not as long as I had predicted it to be.

Carole picked me up from the train station and drove me to her parents' home. Once inside, her parents questioned me about what had been so terrible about the apartment.

"It simply isn't what was advertised. I expected something much bigger and more modern," I explained.

As I described the apartment, Carole grew concerned and felt bad for me.

"Tomorrow, I will go sleep there with you if you want," she offered.

I agreed, considering I had only brought clothes to stay the one night at her parents' house.

The next morning, Carole and I spent the day together in her hometown just walking around and visiting the shops. She could tell that I was anxious about going back to stay in the underground apartment, but it was all I could afford at the time.

Once the sun went down, Carole joined me on the train ride back to the city so she could keep me company in the small apartment. On the trip there, Carole kept thinking of ways to make the apartment look nice and feel less depressing.

When we arrived at the place, there was a large group of drunk old men standing by the door. Carole and I both did our best to ignore them as we entered the building.

"Which floor is it?" Carole asked.

"It's underground…" I answered gloomily.

We both made our way down to the basement and I opened the door for Carole. I flinched at the fact that I could still hear the drunk old men yelling above our heads.

Carole could see the worry and discomfort on my face. She surveyed the apartment as if trying to find a hidden corpse.

"Has this place been renovated since last night?" Carole inquired.

"No, why?" I asked.

"Because it's not bad at all..." she commented.

I turned to look at Carole incredulously.

"Not bad? It's so small and you can hear all the cars passing by over our heads, not to mention the drunk people talking!" I retorted.

Upon hearing my response, Carole looked at me in the way only someone who had known me for years could. She was not surprised by my reaction, but it was clear that she felt differently about the place we were standing in.

"I think you are just focusing on the negative," she gently chided.

"That's because there is no positive to speak of, and even if there was, we wouldn't be able to see it because the noise from outside is driving me crazy!" I replied.

Carole smiled and began wandering around the apartment looking for something. Once she found what she was looking for, she walked over to my backpack and removed my small, portable speakers.

"What are you doing?" I asked.

"Fixing your problems," she answered.

"How?" I challenged.

"I'll show you," she replied calmly.

"Unless you pull out a plane ticket out of here, I don't see how I'm gonna feel better," I grumbled.

Despite my frustrated tone, Carole remained calm and confident about what she was doing. She connected the speakers to one of the wall outlets and then began playing music. She scrolled through her phone until she found the right song and then looked up at me with a beaming smile.

As soon as I heard my favorite song start playing, I felt all my worries and trepidations leave my body, as if I'd been transported back to my childhood home. Upon seeing me visibly relax, Carole walked over to me and took both my hands.

"I know it's not a song to dance to, but maybe we can try," she murmured.

Without saying anything, I began slow dancing to a song that I had heard during some of the best moments of my entire life. I closed my eyes and held Carole tightly in my arms. The moment was so pleasant that I completely forgot about the things that had been bothering me up to that point.

"How did you know to do this?" I asked.

"Sometimes all it takes is a small change in perspective. The problem in our minds can often be larger than the problem outside in the real world, so we need something to tear down the walls we create for ourselves," she whispered.

I looked at Carole and knew that she was right.

That night, Carole and I slept peacefully. I enjoyed being in the little underground apartment; it felt like we had our own little cocoon where no one could bother us and where we had the chance to create a lasting memory for the rest of our lives.

Although we are not together anymore, I still carry the lesson she taught me that night in the underground apartment. Whenever things get a bit too stressful or I am feeling like I am losing my way in life, I just sit down and play the song Carole played for me that night. Even though I have heard it more times than I can count, it still manages to transport me back to the night when we slow danced to that song while a few drunk old men conversed above our heads.

The weight of managing an entire company and supporting a large family can sometimes overwhelm me. When it does, and I feel like I need to escape to the place that Carole showed me I can always go to in moments of stress, I close my eyes and play that song. Even all these years later, that song manages to put a smile on my face and make everything around me disappear just for a couple of minutes.

THE DATE

I met Fabienne in a bar in London a couple of months ago. We had been trying to meet up ever since that night, but something always got in the way. However, in a few hours I would finally be going on a date with the beautiful blonde girl I had met on a night I initially hadn't even wanted to go out.

Fabienne worked at Chanel and had a master's degree from one of the most prestigious universities in London. I had just arrived home from the mall, where I had spent most of the money I had made that month on a new and elegant outfit that I felt would impress Fabienne and not turn her off because I was not as wealthy or successful as she was.

As I waited for Fabienne to arrive, I zipped my coat up to my neck to avoid getting too cold, even though I was eager to show off my new shirt.

Fabienne arrived late but was very apologetic about her tardiness.

We went upstairs and sat down in one of the fanciest restaurants I had ever seen in my life, which I tried very hard not to make too apparent.

Throughout dinner, I talked about all my job prospects and how I had been diligently studying the stock market to start making a very high income. I also talked a lot about luxury cars in a way that made it seem like I could afford one. The truth was, I just loved reading car magazines while I sat in the waiting room at the doctor's or dentist's office.

However, Fabienne seemed uninterested in all the things I had to say.

"I like your shirt," she said.

"Oh, thank you. Yeah, I rarely wear it," I said nonchalantly.

Finally glad to see Fabienne smiling, I removed my coat entirely and stood up to show her the shirt from all angles.

Fabienne immediately started laughing when she saw the price tag still attached.

"What?!" I cried as I sat down and stared at the tag in disbelief.

As embarrassing as that moment was, Fabienne found it highly endearing.

"So the truth is you bought that shirt for this date?" Fabienne asked.

"Yes. I'm sorry I lied," I replied dejectedly.

Fabienne smiled and, for the first time, seemed genuinely interested in me.

After that moment, the conversation flowed much more smoothly. Once the date was over and

I had walked her home, I asked Fabienne out on a second date.

"I would love to!" she replied, "but on one condition!"

"What is that?" I asked nervously.

"No more trying to impress me with boring stories about the stock market, and you bring that shirt with the security tag still attached!" she said with a laugh.

I smiled. "You've got a deal!"

LOST

Julian had been working harder than ever before. Being an entrepreneur was even more demanding than he had initially thought it would be. However, he knew he would have to do everything he could to succeed. Julian had recently quit his high-paying, senior management job at a bank so he could pursue his dream of starting his own business.

After a string of sleepless nights and many back-to-back meetings, Julian wondered if this was too much for him and if he should just ask for his old job back.

One Monday morning, Julian sat in front of his computer and began printing some documents that he urgently needed to sign that day. Due to exhaustion, Julian fell asleep with his head on the laptop's keyboard and didn't wake up until an hour later.

When he woke up, Julian realized not only had he missed a call he was supposed to take, but his documents had not been printed because his printer was out of paper.

Julian shot up from his chair, almost knocking his laptop over, and ran out of the house to find the nearest office supply store. He knew there was one a few blocks away, but he was so exhausted that he couldn't remember how to get there.

Julian wandered through the streets of his neighborhood for so long that all sense of urgency and stress eventually subsided. Finally, Julian remembered where the office supply store was.

After getting his documents printed, Julian walked back home, sat down at his laptop, and contemplated what had just happened. Even though he still had a mountain of work to do, he somehow felt a lot more relaxed than he'd been a few hours ago.

Julian grabbed a sheet of white paper from the sheaf he had just purchased and wrote:

Go on walks.

Julian then grabbed some scissors, cut out that sentence, and taped it on his laptop so he would never forget how getting lost taught him one of the best things he could do to clear his head even in the most stressful situations.

To this day, even as busy as Julian is running a highly successful company, he never forgets to go on walks early in the morning and late in the evening to clear his head and make him as productive as possible.

OUT OF PLACE

It had been a while since I had hung out with Gustav and the gang. Ever since I had met Emma, I'd stopped partying and living the wild life I used to lead before she entered my world and tethered me down to earth.

With Emma in my life, I had replaced drinking with exercising. Instead of spending money, I spent time with someone who truly made me happy. However, Gustav had been my best friend since high school, and he'd organized a party in London that I felt compelled to attend, considering it had been months since I hung out with him and the guys.

At the club, I saw everything with new eyes. What I used to think was sophisticated and exciting now seemed shallow and vain. Very wealthy people were showcasing their riches, and tall, beautiful women looked at everyone condescendingly.

Gustav talked to me endlessly about all the parties he had lined up for the coming week, but all I could think about was how uncomfortable Emma looked. None of the girls in our group were speaking to her, and all she was doing was waiting for me to finish talking so she wouldn't be bored.

At that moment, I realized what was important to me. I told Gustav that Emma and I had to go outside for a minute to talk, but instead we proceeded to sneak away from the club and head to the nearest burger joint so we could talk uninterruptedly.

It was one of the best nights of my life because it was the night I realized what was truly important to me and what was just superfluous and superficial.

THE SHIRT

Although it had been over ten years since I'd seen Fabienne, I still kept her in a very special place in my heart. Our first and, sadly, last date had been memorable; I'd accidentally shown up on the date with the price tag still on the shirt I had purchased specifically for that night.

Fabienne was still very successful, but luckily now I was too. There was no need to waste my monthly salary on a nice outfit this time.

Fabienne and I were both recently single, and we had reconnected through a mutual friend of ours from many years ago. Not in my wildest dreams would I have imagined that Fabienne and I would finally go on our long-awaited second date so many years later, both of us having just finished a serious and long-term relationship.

I looked at my closet and tried on several elegant shirts but could not decide on the right one. I couldn't believe that even after all these years, I was still nervous about seeing her.

I looked at my watch and realized that it would be me who was going to be late this time, because

I could not make up my mind about what shirt to wear.

After another ten minutes of trying to decide on my outfit, I remembered what I had learned from the last time I had been on a date with Fabienne: not to try and impress her and just to allow myself to be the silly person she enjoyed being around.

I rummaged through old boxes of clothes I rarely wore until I found the shirt I had purchased for our first date many years ago. Instead of a price tag on it, now there was a hole from where the tag had been ripped out.

Smiling, I put on the shirt and was pleasantly surprised to discover that it still fit me. This outfit, with the massive hole in the seam, was ultimately the opposite of what I had had in mind to wear to the date, but I knew Fabienne would appreciate the hilarity.

When I arrived just on time for the date and Fabienne saw the shirt with the hole, she immediately laughed and gave me the strongest, most endearing embrace I'd ever felt in my life. I was glad I had remembered my lesson from our last date to appreciate how critical little moments and gestures can be.

BONUS

A STORY ABOUT CHERISHING WHAT YOU HAVE

GREEN EYES

David had met Eleanor while working as a waiter in a small café next to the apartment he lived in with four other people. Eleanor was in culinary school at the time and juggled working as a waitress, her schoolwork, and taking care of her sick mother. However, despite all of her daily responsibilities, she always remained positive and enthusiastic about life.

The hours at the café were long and arduous, but ever since Eleanor had started working, the job felt less demanding and more enjoyable to David. Eleanor had auburn hair and a very fair complexion. Her eyes were a striking shade of green.

One evening, during an impromptu after-work trip to the bar for some drinks with a few people who worked at the café, David mustered up the courage to ask Eleanor out on a date. To his surprise and chagrin, Eleanor seemed reluctant.

"I'm sorry; I hope I didn't make you uncomfortable," David said as he sat next to Eleanor in a leather booth at the bar close to the café where they worked that the staff frequented on Friday nights.

"No, it's not that. You're a great guy, and I would love to go out on a date with you…" said Eleanor hesitantly.

David expected her to keep talking and braced for a rejection that did not come. After a few minutes had passed since Eleanor's seemingly troubled answer, David smiled and arranged for them to go out for dinner the next night.

During dinner, Eleanor confessed that she was having trouble accepting dates because of the bad experience she had had with her previous boyfriend. David decided not to pry and leave the issue alone. Still, Eleanor seemed compelled to explain, perhaps due to a sense of guilt for reacting so unenthusiastically to David's invitation to dinner the night before.

"I was dating this guy who I liked. We were very serious, but one day he just disappeared," shared Eleanor.

"Like, completely?" David asked, feeling somewhat foolish about the nature of his question.

"He wrote to me a month later explaining why he left me in such a devastating way. He said that he felt I was holding him back because I wasn't as successful as he was and that he wanted to find

someone with the same aspirations as him…"
whispered Eleanor.

"What a jerk!'"" David exclaimed.

Eleanor went on to elaborate that ever since that moment, she felt a little nervous about going on dates and that she liked David, so she did not want to ruin their friendship if things did not go well.

David assured her that she had nothing to worry about, and he meant it when he said that he would never do anything as malicious as what her ex-boyfriend had done to her.

"I suppose he felt the grass was greener without me," Eleanor said dejectedly.

"How could anyone want any green that's different from the one in your eyes?" David asked, knowing full well he had just recited a cheesy pickup line that would put the margarita pizza before him to shame. However, Eleanor smiled, which made David smile too.

After a couple more dates and introducing Eleanor to his minuscule apartment and the many people living there at the time, David finally asked Eleanor to be his girlfriend, to which she said yes—this time without any hesitation.

***

David and Eleanor had been dating for almost two years when he received a letter informing him that he had been accepted to attend one of the most prestigious universities in the country on a full scholarship.

After running around his cramped kitchen and accidentally knocking over several unwashed pots and pans, David called Eleanor and almost cried when he told her the news. Eleanor did cry with excitement.

That night, they went to dinner at a particularly fancy restaurant that they had always said they would go to one day when they either had the funds or a special enough reason to dine there.

David put on the one suit he had, which he had worn only once for his high school graduation about four years ago, even though it was now two sizes too small. Eleanor put on a green dress that David loved because it made her green eyes pop.

"Here is to an amazing new future," Eleanor said as she raised a glass to David's new opportunity.

"Which, don't forget, involves the new apartment we will be getting next year! Hopefully we'll find something good!" David added before raising his glass next to Eleanor's.

"Do you still want to do that? I've been meaning to start looking but I haven't been sure if it's the right thing to do yet," she said slowly.

"Of course, I want to. I will help you search and I'm sure we'll find something right for the both of us!" enthused David.

Just like when David had asked Eleanor out on their first date, she seemed hesitant and troubled.

David lowered his glass of champagne back onto the white tablecloth.

"Do you not want to live together anymore? Did something change?" he asked gently.

"Nothing changed for me. Something changed for you, and I'm scared that you're going to surprise me with more changes," she confessed.

David looked at her as if she had just said something very foolish.

"Have I not proven to you that I am not going to leave or run away? Trust me. This is good for both of us, not just me," he promised.

Eleanor smiled—the same gorgeous smile that made David become interested in her in the first place. Eleanor lifted her glass to finish the toast with David, who downed his glass of champagne almost entirely in one swallow.

Eleanor continued to smile, but it was clear that something was still on her mind. However, for the rest of the evening, she did her best to make the night entirely about David and the fantastic future that surely awaited.

***

Although David was only in his fourth month of college, he already seemed like a completely different person. At first, Eleanor loved seeing him so motivated and enthusiastic. However, as time passed, it became increasingly difficult to get in touch with him during the day or to talk about anything other than the new friends David had made and all the things they got up to during the week.

Eleanor was always supportive and was wary about mentioning how she felt David was drifting farther and farther away from her as time passed.

During dinner one night, Eleanor decided to bring up something that had been bothering her in hopes of getting an answer from David that would assuage her worries.

"I found a nice apartment today. I think it would be perfect for us. Have you found anything?" Eleanor said as she put down her glass of wine.

David kept his gaze focused on his food, which made Eleanor think he didn't hear her.

"I've been meaning to talk to you about that," he mumbled.

"What is it?"

"I've been talking to the guys at school. We're thinking of living together on campus next year; that way, we can be close to the student bar and hang out every day. I was going to bring this up earlier, but you know how busy I've been..." he trailed off.

Eleanor did not respond. She felt a knot in her stomach, and it was not because of the food she was eating.

David explained the situation further, but Eleanor struggled to pay attention.

"When would you be moving in with them?" she finally asked.

"We were thinking in a couple of weeks," David said, oblivious to her discomfort.

Rather than air her grievances, Eleanor remained quiet the rest of the evening in the hope that David would notice that she was upset. But he never did. Instead, he continued talking about how he and his friends would form a fine watch collectors society and recruit as many members as possible to meet wealthy people from campus. Eleanor did her best to smile.

***

After about six months, Eleanor stopped hearing from David. They were still together, but he often complained that he was too busy to visit her at her parents' place, where she now lived.

David spent all his time with his friends in the dormitory. One day, during one of the meetings of the fine watch society they'd started, one of the other students began talking about the importance of having the right shade of green on a particular type of watch. The student passed the watch around, and when it got to David, he couldn't take his eyes off it. The shade of green on the watch was exactly the same shade of green as Eleanor's eyes.

Like a man in a dream, David returned the watch and shot up from his chair. David ran up to his room and called Eleanor, who did not answer her phone.

David then called Eleanor's parents' house. Eleanor's mother picked up.

"Mrs. Mayne? It's David. Is Eleanor there?" he asked frantically.

There was a long pause from Eleanor's mother.

"No, she always works at this time. She has been for several months now…" she finally said.

"Work? Where?" David demanded.

After another uncomfortable silence, Eleanor's mother continued. "Eleanor has been working a night shift at the café where you two met. It's about two hours away from here, so we barely ever see her..."

David had no idea Eleanor had gone back to working at the café and was pulling a night shift. What he did know was that her parents' house was two hours away from the café, which meant that she was getting very little sleep.

David hung up the phone and ran to the café where he and Eleanor had met.

There she was, looking tired but still smiling.

David ran up to her and hugged her as hard as he could.

"I'm so sorry; I am so sorry for forgetting you. That will never happen again!" he promised.

Eleanor finally could no longer contain her emotions and started crying too.

A month later, David returned to his job at the café and moved in with Eleanor in the apartment where they were initially supposed to live.

After that strange moment in his dormitory lounge where he saw the same shade of green on a watch as in his girlfriend's eyes, he never forgot to remember that it is not only the simplest of things that can remind you of what is most important in life, but also that the simplest things are usually the most important things.

MANUSCRIPT 2
SHORT STORIES FOR ELDERLY

50 Funny Tales for Stimulating Memory, Cognition, and Relieving Stress

INTRODUCTION

Everyone has a memory that makes them laugh and lifts their spirits. Sometimes, however, these memories need a little help surfacing in our consciousness as we forget some of the moments that have made us smile in life.

This book offers 51 short stories that will make you see the funny side of life while reminding you of the joy it is to be alive and to share experiences with people who, over time, have proven to be indispensable architects of who we are today.

Every person we meet and every place we discover holds within it the ability to add a new dimension of joy and experience to our lives. Not all of our experiences are pleasant, but memories often act as a subconscious editor of the defining moments in our lives, highlighting the lesson and eschewing the hardship so that we may see the purpose behind the challenges everyone must endure.

This is to say that even in the darkest of times, say when we experience loss, as this book will show in five hilarious short stories in Chapter Four, or when we are simply going about our jobs, like in Chapter Six, there is hidden magic in the seemingly banal or mundane that we can look back at several years in the future and appreciate the weight of those moments.

Regardless of where we are from or where our paths have taken us, we are all connected by the gift of storytelling. Everyone has a story to tell, and none is more important than the other. Sometimes, the best way to relate to others and with ourselves is to listen to the stories of others so that the embers of our past may be rekindled as we find connective tissue between our shared experiences.

Everyone has a family; whether your family involves a house filled with boisterous aunts, uncles, and nephews or just a group of friends you made that you trust so much, you consider them family. In the first chapter of this book, you are sure to not only chuckle at the relatable yet astoundingly comical stories but also find some common ground between the trials and tribulations that we all go through when dealing with those closest to us.

Beyond family, this book also presents short stories related to love, childhood, adventure, and more! Every story is independent of each other, but they are all connected by the fact that they are funny, and sometimes the best thing to do when presented with the adversities of life is to find the humor in it all and just laugh, which is precisely what you will be doing with every story and every chapter.

You may read one of the stories in Chapter Nine and connect with characters feeling out of their element as they are introduced to new cultures but still find a way to make themselves feel at home and establish their unique presence. Alternatively, there might be stories in Chapter Four that remind you of the time you tried to make friends with the kids from the neighborhood and ended up ruining your mother's Halloween plans. You might even find your past reflected when reading Chapter Seven about the man who thought he wouldn't have any trouble going jogging with his dog to impress a girl. Regardless of where life has taken you and continues to take you, this book invites you to laugh along with everyone else who enjoys these invigorating stories that are written for everyone willing to sit down and reflect upon their own lives and experiences while seeing the funny side of it all, even in the most challenging of times.

It is not always easy to see the humor in our lives while we are going through it, which is why hindsight is a great narrator and an even better comedian! You can read this book by yourself by a warm fire, get together with your friends and read your favorite stories together, or let someone you trust and care for read these stories for you. At the same time, you can note down on a piece of paper what characters and storylines you can't wait to share with people from your own life because they are so reminiscent of your past experiences.

Regardless of where these stories take place and the situations they revolve around, you are invited to smile and rejoice as you are presented with moments that will surely hold a mirror to your own life and perhaps the lives of people who still keep ample space in your heart and mind. We are all storytellers, whether we know it or not, as we are all characters in the stories of others.

Sit back and let these stories put a smile on your face as you see your own life reflected in the funny and uplifting tales of others. Although there will be stories that challenge their characters and put them in sometimes unfavorable situations, every story will eventually shine a light on the joy and occasionally hilarious ordeal that it is to live and compile memories that can serve as the bridge that brings people together through laughter and storytelling.

Chapter 1

Five Stories About Family

Ernie

Donald was constantly mocked by his wife, Jennifer, for being entirely out of touch with anything that didn't revolve around his job.

"Your son could spend an entire day getting up to date on the world, and he still wouldn't be finished," Jennifer quipped as she leaned in toward the oval mirror and continued removing her makeup.

"I know what's going on in the world! It's my job to know what's going on in the world," Donald responded from the double bed as he removed his black dress shoes and sighed after a long day at the office.

"I mean things about the world that aren't related to politics. When was the last time you went to the cinema or put on a new song?"

"You know I don't have time for the cinema or to go buying CDs."

"The fact that you just mentioned buying CDs shows how out of touch you are."

"Why are you bringing this up now?" Donald protested.

Jennifer walked out of the bathroom and onto the beige nylon carpet of the bedroom.

"Because the only time you spend with your son is when you tell him the same bedtime story every night, and even then, you constantly check your phone."

"I get emails every five minutes, you know that," Donald retorted.

"I want you to focus and be present when you are with your son," Jennifer explained. Before Donald could respond, Henry sprinted into their bedroom with his pajama onesie already on and an alarming amount of energy.

"I'm ready for a story!" Henry declared as he leaped onto the double bed where Donald was resting.

"Ok, let's go," Donald replied as he led his son toward his bedroom to tell him a goodnight story.

***

Henry was tucked in bed under his blue duvet filled with stars and spaceships, with Donald sitting beside him, checking his phone.

Donald always told his son a bedtime story about a made-up character named Ernie. Donald's father had done the same when Donald was a child, and he loved doing the same with his own son and imagining the tradition continuing for many years.

"Dad, can I ask you something?" Henry asked as he patiently waited for his dad to start telling him about yet another adventure that Ernie went on, which ultimately ended with a life lesson or moral that Henry was supposed to absorb.

"Yes?" Donald asked, his eyes still glued to his phone as he scrolled through emails.

"Is Ernie the puppet I saw today in that chocolate commercial?"

Donald didn't respond. Donald had his eyes squinted and lips pursed, which meant he was concentrating hard on one thing, and therefore, everything else around him disappeared.

"Dad!" Henry cried.

"What? Oh, yes, yes he is," Donald replied, breaking eye contact from his phone to rapidly glance at his son.

"Oh," Henry replied as he sunk deeper into his bed.

"I'll tell you a story in two minutes, son."

"No, it's ok. I'm pretty tired."

"Are you sure?" Donald asked, finally putting his phone away.

"Yes. Goodnight," Henry replied softly as he pulled the sheets up all the way to his ears and turned to face away from his father.

Donald felt terrible but decided to let his son sleep and listen to what his wife and son were telling him.

***

The next day at the office, Donald received a call from his wife. Luckily, he was not in a meeting, so he picked him up and leaned back in his chair as he allowed himself some respite from the over-abundance of work.

After less than a minute of conversation, Donald could tell something was off.

"What's wrong?" he asked.

"I am on my way to pick up Henry from school."

"Why?" Donald cried, shooting forward in his chair.

"Apparently, he has been sleeping through all his classes. Did anything happen last night? He was too tired to have breakfast this morning too!"

Donald explained Henry's question and how he hadn't told Henry a story because he was too tired.

Jennifer scoffed.

"You told Henry that the Ernie from your stories is the toy from the chocolate commercial?" Jennifer asked.

"Yes."

"Henry is terrified of that commercial. It has a ventriloquist dummy named Bernie or something that scares even me! Henry told me he saw it and that he didn't want to see that commercial ever again," Lauren explained.

Donald groaned.

"He didn't sleep because he was too scared. Why did you even say yes when he asked you if that character was Ernie?"

"I wasn't paying attention. I'll come home and speak to him."

"Now? What about your big meeting?"

"I'll cancel it," Donald declared decisively. It was time to start putting his son first.

***

It was the next day, and Donald was arriving at work with a smile. He had spent the entire day with Henry after leaving the office, which mostly involved just sitting by his side as Henry slept. At night, Donald told his son another story, but this time, he decided to change the character's name to one that wouldn't remind his son of a frightening doll.

Donald turned his black leather chair around to gaze at the cityscape through his pane glass window.

His phone rang. It was Jennifer.

"Hey sweetie, how are you? How's Henry?"

Once again, Jennifer was on her way to pick up Henry from school because he was falling asleep in all his classes.

"Did you tell him another story?" Jennifer asked.

"I did!"

"You know he's terrified of Ernie now; it makes him think of an evil toy now."

"I know, but that's why I changed the name to a completely different one."

"What did you change the name to?" Lauren asked as she drove to her son's school.

"Chucky!" Donald replied.

Lauren groaned in frustration.

"Donald, you really need to watch more movies…"

THE AGE DISCREPANCY

Rupert loved helping his son with his math homework, maybe a little too much. Dan, Rupert's nine-year-old son, on the other hand, detested asking his dad for help.

"Dad, can you just answer the question? I don't need to know all of this!" Dan protested as he sunk his head onto his hands and stared helplessly at the piece of paper on the desk in front of him.

Rupert knew the complaint. Dan protested that Rupert spoke too generally about mathematical concepts and lost sight of the specific problem that needed to be resolved.

"Ok, I'm sorry. I'll try and make it simple," Rupert replied. Having worked as a finance lecturer at a top university for most of his adult life, condensing his mathematical thoughts was challenging.

Although it was Friday evening and the homework wouldn't be due until Monday morning, the entire family would spend all of Saturday visiting Rupert's favorite theme park to celebrate his birthday. Dan had been very proud of his son for deciding to get his homework done early, which made him genuinely want to get it done as soon as possible, so Dan could get his sleep and be full of energy for the park the next day.

***

The next morning, the entire family leaped out of the minivan and raced to the park entrance.

Jenny, Dan's mother, walked slowly as he held the hand of her three-year-old son Michael, who was visiting a theme park for the first time in his life.

"Hurry up!" Dan beckoned as he signaled his family to join him.

Before finally arriving at the ticket counter, Rupert noticed a sign notifying park visitors that children under the age of three could enter for free. Upon seeing this, Rupert pointed to the sign and winked at his wife.

"Three tickets, please," Rupert requested at the counter.

"How old is your youngest boy?" the attendant asked.

"Two!" Dan replied with a satisfied smile.

The attendant gave little Michael a quick look and then proceeded to prepare three tickets.

"He's not two; he's three!" Dan protested loudly, which made everyone, including the attendant, turn to look at Dan in surprise.

Rupert shot his son an intense and disapproving glare.

"No, he's not; he's two!"

Dan looked confused.

"So you've been lying to me my whole life? Michael is really two years old?!" Dan complained.

Rupert sheepishly turned to face the attendant again, who eventually sold the family only three tickets but maintained a face of disapproval.

***

"I can't tell him it was a lie because then he will think it is ok to be dishonest!" Rupert argued with his wife later that evening in their bedroom as they discussed how to explain to Dan that Michael was indeed three and not two years old.

"Did he believe you when you told him that you had made a mistake?" Jenny asked.

"I think so. He probably thinks I'm crazy for getting my own son's age confused, but I didn't know what else to tell him."

"I'm sure he doesn't think you're crazy. You're making too much of this," Jenny suggested.

Regardless, Rupert left the room and ventured into Dan's bedroom.

Unsure of what he was going to say, he opened the door and entered to find Dan sitting in front of his desk with the light on, working away at something.

"Hey, buddy. What are you up to?" Rupert inquired.

"Just working on my math homework," Dan replied without taking his eyes off the assignment in front of him.

"You had another assignment?"

"No, it's the same one from last night," Dan replied.

Confused, Rupert walked up to his son's desk and noticed that all the answers they had worked out together the previous night had been erased.

"How come you're doing it again?" Rupert asked.

"Well, since you confused Michaels's age today, I'm worried that you are not very good with numbers, so I better do this on my own this time."

Before Rupert could react, he heard his wife Jenny laughing by herself just outside the door as he overheard the entire conversation.

CHILDISH BEHAVIOR

Tanya always felt nervous whenever she had to spend time with Ada, her somewhat pretentious and judgmental mother-in-law. Even though they had been acquainted for several years, Tanya was still unable to feel comfortable around Ada's imposing presence.

Ada had never been rude in any way to Tanya, but her demeanor was that of someone who was distrusting or who perhaps was of a superior social hierarchy.

Even though Robert, Tanya's husband, kept telling her that this was all in her head, Tanya still chose to dress as best she could to pick up her mother-in-law from the airport. It was Ada's 70th birthday, and Robert had flown her over to stay with them for the weekend.

Robert had to work that particular Saturday, so Tanya drove to the airport with her son, Ronald, early to meet up with Ada and bring her home.

***

The pickup went fine, and both Ada and Ronald were in the backseat of the car as Tanya drove home. Tanya never felt sure why her mother-in-law always insisted on sitting in the back; perhaps, it had something to do with wanting to feel like she was being chauffeured.

"So, how is everything back home?" Tanya asked as she merged onto the highway.

"Fine. I have a new girl helping me with the apartment, but I don't know if she's gonna stay long…" Ada responded as she looked out the car window as if disapproving of everything she saw.

Ada always complained about the maids she hired to help her with the house. Tanya managed to stifle a laugh. The funny thing was that every maid was perfectly professional and competent. Still, they either quit because of how exasperating it could be to work for Ada or were fired for ridiculous reasons.

"I'm sorry, Ada. I'm sure you'll find someone to do a good job!" Tanya responded cheerfully.

And when you do, you'll just fire them again! Tanya thought.

Next to Ada, Robert was excitedly playing with his new toys, aggressively smashing them against each other and making loud explosion noises with his lips.

"Ronald, please keep it down. Your grandmother just got off a long flight," Tanya beckoned.

"Why do you call me Ronald? You always call me Ron...."

"Just please keep it down."

Ronald started playing quieter for about five minutes before returning to his loud action noises.

"Oh shit!" Ronald screamed in the voice of one of his toy soldiers, which he had just killed in the imaginary war he was waging in his mind and in the backseat of the car.

"Ronald!" Tanya exclaimed, turning bright red, "We do not use that kind of language in this family!"

"Yes, we do..." Ronald replied.

"No, we do not!" Tanya insisted, worriedly looking at her mother-in-law from the rearview mirror, who was clutching her pearls as if someone were about to steal them.

"Yes, we do, and you say much worse!" Ronald declared before enthusiastically listing all the bad words that his mother used daily.

"That's enough!" Tanya said, bringing the laundry list of curse words to an abrupt end. Tanya had never wanted the ground to swallow her as much as she did at that moment.

The rest of the trip was spent in absolute silence. Even Ronald felt overwhelmed by the tension.

Once everyone entered the house, Ada said she needed to lie in the guest bedroom and get some rest. Tanya was unsure if she meant because of the flight or because of how indignant she was over the incident from earlier.

"Ok, Ada. Get all the rest you need; just let me know if you need anything!"

The door closed before Tanya could get a response.

Tanya took a couple of deep breaths and went upstairs to her son's room to have a conversation. Typically, she would have acquiesced to her fury and used some choice words when castigating her child, but that would only make matters worse.

Tanya entered Ronald's room, who was still playing with his toys, and sat next to him on the bed.

"Ron, you know how you say you want to be a grown-up?"

"Yes," Ronald replied, putting his toys down.

"Well, grown-ups don't use that kind of language. Only children do, so if you want to act like a grown-up, you cannot use those dirty words!"

"How come you used them?" Ronald inquired.

"I was behaving like a child, but I'm going to act like a grown-up now, and I hope you do too!"

***

Robert, Ronald, Tanya, and Ada were huddled around the fireplace opening presents. Ada had been left alone with Ronald for a couple of days before her birthday, but as far as Tanya was concerned, there had been no more incidents regarding dirty language.

"And this one… is from Ronald… who used his own pocket money to get this for you, Mom!" Robert said as he handed his mother a gift-wrapped box.

"Please open it. I'll break my nails," Ada replied as she waved the present away.

Robert smiled and opened the present. Everyone except Ronald looked at the gift in confusion.

Tanya once again went red.

"Ronald, why did you buy Grandma a Barbie?" Tanya inquired, looking at the bright pink plastic box housing a Barbie doll.

"Well, you said that only children use dirty words, and I heard grandma talking to grandpa on the phone, and she was using A LOT of dirty words because she was angry that grandpa couldn't come to her birthday! So grandma must be a child!"

Ada gasped and immediately exited the room.

This time, Tanya couldn't help but chuckle.

BERNARDINE

It was Saturday morning, and as usual, I was up early to work out at the gym by my apartment. As usual, the gym was packed with the morning regulars.

By the time I noticed the attractive girl with a face I somewhat recognized, she was approaching me—she was close enough for it to be obvious she was about to engage me in conversation.

"Hi!" she ebulliently saluted.

"Hi!"

"You don't remember me, do you?"

At that point, I realized I must have recognized her from somewhere other than the gym.

I squinted and looked at the dark hair, brown eyes, and freckled face of the girl before me.

"The barbecue!" I exclaimed, "Yes, I spoke to you at Nico's barbecue a couple of weeks ago!"

She smiled and nodded.

"Yes. Do you remember my name?"

I didn't.

"Bernardine!" she cried.

"Of course, I'm so sorry. How are you?"

Bernardine and I spoke and eventually decided to exchange numbers. If I had known what would follow after exchanging numbers and going on a date with Bernardine, I probably would've wished I never would have gone to the gym that day in the first place, or to Nico's barbecue, for that matter.

***

It had been a couple of weeks since my second date with Bernardine. The second one had gone even worse than the first. No matter how hard I tried, I could not help myself from feeling bored or overwhelmed by Bernardine's energy and constant maniacal laughing.

However, the most annoying thing about her was the constant texting. Bernardine would text me asking if everything was ok if I didn't text her every hour.

The worst part was when we would meet at the gym. No matter where I was at the gym, Bernardine would find me and stand by me as she repeatedly inquired when our next date would be.

Things got so bad that I decided to drink with a cousin of mine named Danny, who had just come from a long-term relationship with a similarly intense and obsessive girlfriend. I wanted to ask him how he managed to end things so that I could hopefully do the same with Bernardine.

***

Once I replied to Bernardine, telling her where I was and who I was meeting, I put my phone away and waited for my cousin to arrive at the café I was meeting him at. Once Danny arrived, I explained my situation to him but could not go into too much detail because Bernardine appeared a few minutes after.

"What are you doing here?" I asked.

"Well, I wanted to meet your cousin. Is that so bad?" Bernardine replied as she extended her hand to Danny and introduced herself.

I was never able to share exactly what I was trying to do because Bernardine and Danny kept talking the entire time about Danny's ex-girlfriend and how controlling and obsessive she had been.

All I wanted to do was jump in and say that Bernardine was the exact same way, but instead, I sat quietly and festered in my unresolved frustrations.

***

The next day, I woke up hesitant about going to the gym. I was angry that I could no longer feel safe doing what I enjoyed most Saturday mornings because I was tired of having to hide from Bernardine.

As I walked over to my kitchen to make myself some coffee, I received a call from Danny. I dreaded having to explain to him what had happened because he would surely laugh hysterically at how awful my situation was becoming.

However, when I picked up the phone, it sounded very much like he was the anxious one.

"What's wrong?" I asked.

"I don't even know how to say this. Bernardine and I have been talking since the three of us had coffee. I think I really like her, but I know she is with you. I wanted to ask her out on a date, but I felt guilty doing it without talking to you first," Danny explained.

Suddenly, it occurred to me. Danny clearly had a thing for obsessive women, which made their encounter spark something inside him that would resolve all my problems.

"Well, you owe me one because Bernardine and I had something going, but you have my blessing to take her out on a date."

Danny thanked me and continued to do so every time he and Bernardine went out on a date.

The only thing that didn't change, however, was Bernardine's fixation with coming up to me constantly at the gym.

"Tell me more about your cousin. What does he like? How can I make him happy?" Bernardine would constantly ask as she followed me around the gym.

"Danny loves girls who work out at home with him!" I replied.

THE FRIGHT

Margaret took a moment to close her eyes and breathe. She was standing in her new kitchen by herself after a heated argument with her seven-year-old son, Matthew.

Things were stressful enough because she was pregnant and had just moved into a new house in a completely new city by herself.

Matthew had been a great help with the move, but on this particular afternoon, he had tested her already waning patience.

The frustrating situation that had unfolded a few minutes ago began doing circles in her mind.

Matthew had already made new friends with the neighborhood boys and wanted to show them his Halloween costume. Margaret couldn't even remember what costume it was, but when she told Matthew "No" because there were more important things to unbox first and because she had no idea in which box that costume was, he became irate.

Margaret reacted by screaming at him and telling him that he would have to go to bed earlier that night because of his emotional outburst.

"Close your eyes and breathe," Margaret reminded herself. Her therapist back home always told her to close her eyes and breathe whenever things got a little too much. She had also advised Margaret to do something silly that would make her laugh to make a difficult situation seem less daunting and intense. Still, Margaret had never gotten herself to try that particular proposed solution.

After only a few seconds of being still and trying to quiet her mind, Margaret heard something outside the kitchen window. Margaret walked over to her sink and looked out the window to see Matthew sitting on the front stairs of their house with his new neighborhood friend Otto.

The window was slightly ajar, so she could hear what her son was saying. When she heard her name mentioned in conversation, Margaret leaned in even closer, feeling the sink faucet push against her stomach.

"You know, my mother isn't actually my mother; she is a woman who stole me when I was a baby and refuses to let me go. I'm her prisoner, but one day I'll find my real mom," Matthew explained to his friend.

Margaret knew her son had a proclivity for telling creative narratives that were not fully representative of the truth.

"Matthew!" Margaret called out through the open window.

Matthew jumped, as did his friend Otto, who noticed Margaret looking at him through the window and sprinted home in fear.

"Come inside right now!"

Dejected and looking at his new friend running home, Matthew reluctantly did as he was told.

***

Margaret was once again by herself. This time she was in her room reflecting on the second argument she had with her son.

After a lengthy discussion, Matthew apologized and agreed to explain to Otto that what he had said about his mother wasn't true.

Margaret realized that she had perhaps been a little too harsh on her son. The next thing she did was begin searching for the moving box with the entire family's Halloween costume so she could surprise her son when he came home after explaining things to Otto.

After about an hour of searching, she finally found the right box. Margaret enthusiastically opened the box and pulled out her son's costume. As she did, she found the witch costume that she hadn't worn for many years.

I wonder, Margaret thought. Wondering if the costume would fit her now that she was pregnant and remembering her therapist's advice, Margaret slipped into the witch costume, hoping that it wouldn't rip due to her size and put her in an even worse mood.

Luckily, the costume fit perfectly, which put a smile on her face. It seemed that her therapist was right.

The doorbell rang as Matthew arrived home.

Realizing that she wouldn't have enough time to remove the costume without potentially tumbling over on her pregnant belly, she decided to run down wearing the witch costume to put a smile on her son's face.

"I'm coming!" she cried.

Once she arrived at the door, she slowly opened it and put on her best scary face.

Matthew opened his eyes wide while Otto turned whiter than a ghost.

Oh no, Margaret thought.

"You said you made it up!" Otto screamed at his friend just before turning around and sprinting back home as fast as he possibly could once more.

Margaret couldn't help but laugh. At least she was now in better spirits.

Chapter 2

Five Stories About Friendship

Beet Juice

Dani and I were very different from each other, which is why I found it strange that we shared such identical feelings toward the same girl at school. Jessica had been in the same school as Dani and me since kindergarten, but only recently had Dani and I began considering attractive girls.

"She came back from summer vacation looking amazing! She finally got rid of her braces!" Dani exclaimed as we sat together at the cafeteria during lunch.

"I know, and I saw that she is going to be in my social studies class. I wonder if she'll notice that I don't have my stupid Disney backpack anymore..." I added, looking around the cafeteria to see if Jessica was around.

"Well, you have a Star Wars backpack now. That's still Disney," Dani added.

"Yeah, but that's cool, Disney, completely different."

"What is your favorite thing about her?" Dani asked.

"I like when she asks questions in class. I should ask more questions, then maybe she would notice me too," I replied. As I responded, I noticed a group of girls from my year walk by the table and look at Dani and me and laugh as if they knew exactly what we were talking about.

"Did they hear what we were talking about?" Dani asked, looking back at the group of girls who were still laughing amongst each other.

"We need a codename for Jessica; otherwise, she will hear about how much we like her," I suggested as I took a bite out of the ham and cheese sandwich my mother always made me on Thursdays.

"She probably already knows. We've been talking about her a lot!" Dani complained.

"We need a name so that no one would ever suspect what we're talking about."

"Something that we both hate!" Dani suggested.

"Beetroot juice!" I cried, stifling a laugh as I remembered the last time my mother offered Dani and me beetroot juice the last time he came over to the house.

"Oh yeah, that was awful. Let's use the codename beet juice, then!"

From that moment on, Dani and I only referred to Jessica as beet juice, which not only proved to be effective but always made us laugh whenever we spoke about our deep infatuation with a beverage that we both detested more than math class.

Once school was over, Dani and I went to our separate homes but called each other immediately to see how much we could make each other laugh by replacing Jessica with her new code name.

"I love beet juice more than you!" I exclaimed over the phone and laughed as I heard Dani come back with an equally funnier reply that made it sound like we were both passionate about vegetable juice.

"All I want for my birthday is beet juice!" I added before hearing the door to my room open and seeing my mother asking me to come down for dinner.

***

That weekend, Dani came over to the house. My mother loved Dani because of how nerdy and well-mannered he was. However, this time, she was busy in the kitchen preparing a surprise for us, so she was not there to greet him as he entered the house.

Dani and I ran into my bedroom and started preparing the video games. We had only been inside for a couple of minutes before my mother walked in, holding a tray of something that she was proudly bringing into the room with a smile.

"So I overheard you boys talking about my famous beetroot juice the other day, so guess what I made you two?" my mother asked with a jubilant smile as she approached Dani and me, holding a tray of two sanguine red glasses of beetroot juice. The smell alone was conjuring up awful memories.

"I promise I wasn't eavesdropping. I just passed by and couldn't help but smile to hear how much you two boys loved it!"

Dani and I looked at each other, both equally unsure if we should laugh, gag, or cry.

THE DEAL

It was the second week of my postgraduate studies, and the most overwhelming aspect of getting started in university again was the sheer amount of people.

Just when I thought I had an idea of who I would be seeing daily, a new influx of fresh faces would venture into the classroom.

Moreover, although I had already worked in an office for several years, I found some of the lessons to be very advanced. The class I was struggling with the most was accounting, considering I had never worked in that field. Luckily, I happened to sit next to the nerdiest-looking person in the entire class, who helped me understand the more confusing topics that didn't come naturally to me.

"I don't know why the professor explains it in such a complicated way; here, let me explain it better," Josh would say as he took my notes and wrote more precise explanations of what the professor was trying to convey.

I thanked Josh every time he helped me and asked him if he would be showing up to the welcome party on Friday, to which he responded yes.

I was already going with a group of people I had met from my marketing class, so I told him I would see him there.

***

At the party, I was able to recognize a lot of faces and approach many more people. One of the people I was excited to see was Miranda, a Slovenian girl I met the first week and with whom I had gotten along very well. I did not get to talk a lot to her due to her already impressive popularity with seemingly everyone in the university, which was not surprising considering her incandescent beauty.

Once Miranda and I stopped talking, I saw Josh with his rounded glasses and neatly arranged black hair.

I waved, and he approached me.

"Was that your girlfriend?" Josh asked me as he pointed at Miranda, who was talking to a big group of boys.

"No, my girlfriend doesn't go to this school," I replied.

"Is she your friend?"

"Yeah, we met last week. Why?"

"If you can introduce me to her, I will help you with all the accounting assignments we get!" Josh exclaimed.

I could tell he was joking, but there was a semblance of truth in his joke.

I was very thankful to Josh for helping me with accounting, so I felt obliged to help him meet Miranda.

"Well, she seems kinda busy now, but I was speaking to her about maybe doing a bbq at my house next weekend. You could come, and I could create scenarios for you two to be alone and talk," I suggested.

Josh's face brightened up with excitement.

***

Normally, my girlfriend, Anna, was the one who organized the barbecues, but since she was out of town for work, I took care of everything.

I told Miranda that a lot of people would be arriving so that she would come ready to have fun and not suspect that I was setting her up with my newly made friend.

Once Josh arrived with a couple of his friends, I explained to him how I was going to play some salsa music so that he could show off the dance skills he said he had with her and that I was going to make the evening as conducive to them hitting it off.

However, when Miranda arrived, Josh completely froze. When I put the salsa music on, Josh said that he wasn't very good and preferred not to dance.

To encourage Josh to dance, I got up and danced a little salsa with Miranda to get things going, but Josh was still reluctant.

As I served the food, I lit some candles and played some smooth jazz to set the tone, but Josh said he was too nervous to sit next to Miranda, so instead, I ended up sitting next to her.

Once the evening was over, Miranda and everyone else left, leaving Josh and me alone.

"What happened?!" I asked.

"This happens to me when I find someone attractive; I just freeze up. It's not in my nature to be outgoing," Josh explained dejectedly.

I was about to comfort Josh and tell him that he didn't need to worry when I got a text from Miranda. The text read:

Miranda: Hi Daniel. I enjoyed your barbecue a lot and thank you for inviting me. However, I feel it was really obvious what you were trying to do. I know that you have a girlfriend, and although she is not around, I still think it was a bit strange how you were clearly flirting with me in the way we danced and in the way you sat next to me and lit a bunch of candles. I also thought you had said that a lot of people would be attending, which didn't turn out to be true. I like you a lot as a friend, and I think you should consider your girlfriend's feelings in all of this.

I looked up from the text message to give Daniel a thinly veiled frown.

"What is it?" Josh asked.

"Well, it appears that it is now you who will have to repay me."

Seeing Josh's confused expression, I showed him the message I had just received from Miranda.

"Oh... I see."

"Well, look at it like this. You can clear my name of any wrongdoing while expressing your true feelings to Miranda all in one swift favor," I said with a satisfied grin.

THE CONFESSION

At this point, Natalie and I had become such close friends that it felt strange worrying about something as seemingly insignificant as reminding her of the first time we met.

Natalie and I first met when we were both very young, maybe around eleven or twelve because our parents were friends and one day, we were forced to play with each other during a dinner party as most children are forced to do while their parents spend time together.

This happened a couple of times and even at that age, I found her very pretty indeed. In fact, I once tried to kiss her on the lips, but she refused and ran to her parents to tell on me, as if I had committed some horrible crime.

Natalie and I had reconnected recently due to her attending the same university I was about to graduate from and from that shared experience we became best friends.

I had never mentioned the kissing incident because I felt it would make things awkward, but I always wondered if she remembered.

One day, while we were having lunch next to the university, I decided it was finally time to bring it up.

"Hey Nat, here's a question for you," I started.

"Yes?"

"Do you remember when we were kids, when we first met, and I tried to kiss you?" I asked, feeling strange just bringing it up in the first place.

Natalie's face went white, and for a short while, it seemed as if she were about to choke on the food she was eating.

"That was *you*?" Natalie asked incredulously.

"Yes…"

"Oh my gosh, I can't believe that. I had no idea that was you. I just thought it was some other crazy who really liked me!" Natalie cried as she continued eating her food while shaking her head in comical disbelief.

After that encounter, everything felt awkward. Hanging out with Natalie felt different as if I had changed everything by bringing up the past.

It was at the house party of a mutual friend that I decided to confront her and ask if anything had changed between us.

"I just feel like you act differently around me ever since I brought up what happened when we were literally just children. I don't see what should make us stop being friends," I explained.

Natalie looked at me confused but then grabbed my hand and pulled me aside.

"You're right. I want you to know that it's not your fault that things are different. It's mine. I have liked you for a long time and I haven't been able to share that with you. When you brought up the past, for some reason I thought my honest reaction would reveal my feelings for you so I just got really nervous."

"So you've always known it was me who tried to kiss you?" I asked.

"Yes."

"And you've liked me for all this time?"

Natalie nodded.

I had never considered Natalie anything more than a friend, but at that moment I felt her honesty highlight feelings of my own towards her that perhaps hadn't been ready to surface up until that moment.

After a couple of seconds of just looking at each other, we finally kissed, which made some of our friends who were watching start whooping and making loud celebratory noises.

"Well, it only took about ten years for me to try a second time," I said jokingly, trying to alleviate the awkward tension after the kiss.

Natalie and I started dating, moved in together, and eventually got married. I will never forget how I told our story during my vows to everyone who was present at the church where we got married because of how romantic it was and how I expected to make everyone turn their head and smile at the sheer romance.

However, what will be even harder to forget will be the rapturous laughter that occurred when Natalie interrupted me telling the story of how after ten years, I finally mustered the courage to try and kiss her again at our mutual friend's house party by asking: "Wait a minute, the guy who kissed me at the house party was you?!"

Even I couldn't contain the laughter.

THE CHANGE OF PLANS

Edmond looked at his friend Donnie with disappointment but not disbelief. This type of behavior was typical of his friend.

"You said we were going to work on the finance assignment together. It's due next week, and I don't think I should get kicked out of university so that you can have a fling with as many girls as possible!" Edmond protested.

Edmond and Donnie lived together in a small two-bedroom apartment a couple of blocks from where they both went to university.

Edmond had never approved of Donnie's indulgent and carefree lifestyle. Still, they had been friends since childhood, and when they were both accepted into the same university, they decided the best thing to do would be to live together.

"I know, but we can work on it tomorrow," Donnie insisted, "I only have tonight to go on a date with this girl because then she flies back to England!"

"If she leaves tomorrow, then why is it so important to see her tonight? Do you know what isn't going to disappear magically back to England? Our exams!" Edmond cried, "Besides, you went out with a girl two nights ago! You didn't come back till the morning after being with her, so why are you rushed to meet this other girl?"

"Because Hannah was nice and we had a great time, but now I want to meet Rosy! And Rosy said she will only go out with me if I bring a friend for her friend, so that's why this has to be tonight!"

The two friends continued to argue for a couple more minutes until Edmond relented as he usually did in these situations.

"Fine, but tomorrow we will work on the assignment!" Edmond declared.

Donnie jumped and hugged his friend in celebration.

"Thank you, Eddie!"

"And here I was thinking you and Hannah were going to become a thing…" Edmond added.

"We might; you never know; I just gotta meet Rosy first, and then I'll figure things out with Hannah. I told her I was out of town, so I have time to think about things."

"You're awful," Edmond declared as he walked over to his bedroom to get ready.

"C'mon, Eddie, you need to live a little! Don't always do the right thing, and just have fun!" Donnie cried.

Edmond grunted quietly to himself.

***

The hotel terrace bar was filled with people in fancy clothes drinking cocktails. It was hard to hear with that many different voices talking and the loud music.

"This place is great, isn't it?" Donnie asked as he moved to the rhythm of the music with a contented grin.

Edmond didn't even bother replying; this wasn't and never had been his scene.

"Where are these girls, Donnie?"

"There she is!" Donnie exclaimed as he stood up to wave but then froze as if someone had cast a spell that paralyzed his limbs.

"What is it?" Edmond asked.

"It's Hannah…"

Edmond scoffed, "You're terrible. The girl you're meeting up with is Rosy, not Hannah!"

"I know; what I'm saying is the friend Rosy brought along is Hannah."

Edmonds's eyes widened, and his jaw dropped. Hannah was a tall blonde girl with a bright yellow dress, and behind her was Rosy, who was significantly shorter but just as attractive.

"Donnie?!" Hannah asked as she walked up to him in disbelief.

As uncomfortable as this situation was, Edmond couldn't help but smile as he noticed Donnie struggle to make any sounds whatsoever.

"You two know each other?" Rosy asked.

"Yeah, he told me he was out of town, but he clearly just said that so he could go on a date with you!" Hannah responded.

Donnie did his best to salvage the situation but only ended up getting slapped by Hannah and ignored by Rosy before being left alone with Edmond.

"Wait, what about you? Are you going to stay friends with this guy?" a still visibly irate Hannah asked Edmond.

"Me?" Edmond asked.

"Yeah, I saw he ditched you too. Come have drinks with us!" Rosy declared.

Donnie chuckled but then turned white when he saw Edmond stand up and start walking away with the girls.

"Eddie, what are you doing?!" Donnie cried.

Eddie turned around and smiled at his friend, "What you told me to do, living a little! Great advice!"

THE NEW FRIEND

John and Susannah were unhappy about their son's new friend, Alexander. Alexander was the complete opposite of their son, Matthew, and of all the friends Matthew had throughout his school life.

"I have noticed that Matthew is spending a lot of time with Alexander," Matthew's teacher, Emma, said to John and Susannah during the parent-teacher conference.

"Should we be concerned?" John asked as he sat in a small, very colorful classroom.

"Well, Alexander is the most defiant student we have. But I don't think encouraging your son to stop being friends with Alexander is the right approach," Emma said.

"What should we do then? Every time we talk to Matthew about not being friends with Alexander, he gets mad at us. He's not even talking to us anymore! He isn't usually this defiant and angry, but we think it's Alexanders' influence!" Susannah cried.

"That's completely normal behavior so don't worry too much. I think the best thing you should do is put a mirror in front of Matthew and make him see just how unlikely his new friendship really is," Emma suggested.

"And how do we do that?" John asked as he leaned closer to the teacher.

"Invite Alexander home for dinner, and let your son see just how little he fits in. Be perfectly agreeable and nice to Alexander so that Matthew sees that there is a disconnect in manners," Emma explained.

John and Susannah looked at each other worriedly.

***

John, Susannah, and Matthew took Alexander to dinner at a little pizzeria by their house that they loved to go to.

Throughout the meal, Alexander proceeded to laugh maniacally in such a way that food went flying all over the place, and slam his hands down on the table, which almost made the glasses fall over and break.

As uncomfortable as John and Susannah were throughout the meal, they felt that they were accomplishing their ultimate goal because Matthew seemed quite uncomfortable himself.

***

The next day, however, Matthew still refused to speak to his parents, and when he returned from school, he ran to his room to be alone.

Finally, John ventured into his son's room to try and make peace.

"Listen, Matthew; I know you are upset because we told you that you couldn't be friends with Alexander anymore. I just want you to know that we are not forcing you to stop being friends with him," John explained.

"That's not why I'm angry!" Matthew interjected.

"Oh, then what's wrong?"

"Alexander keeps asking me when he can come back to play at the house, and I don't know what to tell him anymore! He's awful, and I'm tired of lying!" Matthew cried, "I don't even know if they'll allow me back into the pizzeria after what Alexander did. I love the pizza there! It is the best!" Matthew exclaimed.

John scootched next to his son and put his arm around him.

"Don't worry, son. I'm sure you're still very welcome over there."

Matthew rested his head on his father's shoulder.

"I can't believe you would invite that crazy boy to my favorite restaurant. What were you and Mom thinking?" Matthew asked incredulously.

Chapter 3

Five Stories About Love

Cider

I hadn't seen my younger brother, Neil, since before moving out to London. I had already been living in London for over five years, but he was only now coming to visit me since he had to travel for work and would be staying near my apartment.

My mother had insisted that he stay with me, so I called him up and told him that I had an extra room since my roommate was also gone for work and that he would be very welcome to stay with me.

As we sat opposite each other at the outdoor pub, I noticed that he was precisely the same person he had always been.

"Did you just hear a word I said?" I asked.

Neil looked up from his phone and scoffed.

"I'm so sorry, John. It's just work, I'm constantly getting messages, and I find it so hard to disconnect," Neil said as he finally replaced his phone in his back pocket.

"It's ok; I was just saying that I should have dinner ready by seven if that's ok with your schedule," I repeated.

Before Neil could say anything, his face lit up as he noticed the waiter arriving with his food.

"Finally, I'm starving!" Neil exclaimed as he leaned back and watched his cheeseburger get placed before him.

On the other hand, I was not as content when I realized that the waiter had brought me the wrong type of cider.

"I asked for apple cider; this is raspberry," I informed the waiter, who apologized but explained that there was no other type of cider available.

Once the waiter left, I turned to Neil to express how frustrating it was that the waiter brought me the one flavor of cider I hated the most, to which he replied by not acknowledging a single word. At the same time, he took an intimidatingly big bite of his burger.

He never listens, I thought.

***

It was half past seven in the evening, and there was no sign of Neil, who wasn't responding to any of my calls or texts.

I glowered at the no longer hot food on the table that I had spent an hour cooking for Neil and me and got so frustrated that I considered throwing it all out just to make a point.

I picked up my phone one more time and called Neil. Nothing.

I sprang from the dining room seat and began putting all the food away when I heard the doorbell ring.

I ran over to the entrance of my apartment and opened the door. It was Neil. Neil was sweaty and red as if he had spent the entire evening sprinting. He was cradling what looked like two six-packs of cider with both hands against his chest.

"I'm so sorry, I'm late!" Neil apologized, still trying to catch his breath.

"What happened?" I asked.

"I wanted to get you your favorite cider as a thank-you gift for everything you've been doing, but no shop had the specific flavor you like. I went to four stores, and they had every other flavor except for your favorite, but then I found it and bought you two six packs. The bag broke, so I had to carry it like this, which is why I couldn't answer my phone. I am so sorry!"

As touching as Neil's story was, I looked at the drinks he was holding against his chest suspiciously.

"What flavor did you get, Neil?"

"The one the waiter didn't have today, raspberry; that's your favorite, right?"

I couldn't help but laugh and let go of the anger building up inside me.

"You know what, Neil? You may live in your little world, which makes you oblivious to what's happening around you, but at least you care. Come inside," I said as I stood back and let a confused-looking Neil wobble his way inside the apartment.

SAYING GOODBYE

If it wouldn't have been because I was less than a year away from leaving home and moving to my own apartment to start university, my mother, Eva, would never have allowed a dog to live in her house. Even with the assurance that the dog would be gone in about nine months, she still struggled with the idea of an animal wandering around the home she worked so hard to keep pristine.

"Does this mean that you won't be crying hysterically when I leave because you'll be excited to get the dog out of the house?" I would routinely ask my mother.

"Don't be silly! Of course, I'll be glad to get a dog out of this house, but that will never stop me from crying over you leaving!" my mother responded.

The day I brought my chocolate Labrador puppy home, my mother did her best to ignore just how cute he was because she feared becoming complacent with the rules she had enforced.

"But look how cute he is!" I exclaimed as I held the chubby and fluffy puppy, which I named Ernie, up to her face.

"It doesn't matter how cute he is; there are rules you will need to abide by. Once you leave, you can let your puppy run around free as much as you like!" my mother said, immediately becoming teary-eyed at the prospect of me leaving.

If she was unable to acknowledge Ernie's cuteness at this stage, then it was clear to me that there would be a part of her celebrating me leaving the house, regardless of how upset she was at that moment.

As the weeks and months passed, I noticed my mother warming up to Ernie and even stroking him from time to time when I wasn't looking. One morning, a couple of weeks before I was due to leave, I saw my mother talking to Ernie and explaining to him why she had so many rules that she enforced around the house, but I never let her know that I caught her doing that.

Once the day when I was due to leave finally arrived, my mother acted completely stoically as she helped me load up my luggage in the car and Ernie in the backseat.

As I walked around the house, I noticed nothing left for me to organize, so I made my way back to the car. My mother walked with me, and before she could even hug me or say goodbye, she burst out hysterically, crying.

I knew it; even the joy she must be feeling over Ernie leaving wasn't enough to stop her from crying, I thought.

I smirked and opened my arms to receive a hug, but instead, my mother opened the car door and threw herself at Ernie, wrapping her arms around him as tightly as she could as she sobbed.

"I'm going to miss you so much, Ernie. I'm so sorry I didn't let you get on top of any of the couches. I want you to be happy and to visit me as much as you possibly can. This will always be your house, my sweet little boy!" my mother cried as she swung herself around Ernie's neck.

Once I got over my mild jealousy, I couldn't help but laugh.

"And any thoughts about me leaving, Mom?" I asked mockingly.

I like to think the reason she didn't hear me is because of Ernie's heavy breathing next to her ear, as opposed to her not caring as much.

PAJAMA DAY

Megan had already been on two dates with David, the boy who went to the British school a few meters down the road from where she went. The first date had been a blind date set up by mutual friends of them both, but the second date was the one where she felt that she could fall for this boy.

David was articulate, funny, humble, and very easy on the eyes. He was three years older than Megan and already spoke about the universities he was considering applying to.

Megan had just moved away from her hometown and was not expecting to meet someone so interesting in such a short amount of time, but she couldn't help but spend all her days thinking of seeing David again. Megan loved how grown up

David was, very different from the childish boys from her past and the school she was in.

When Megan got a text from David asking if he could pick her up after school on Friday, Megan almost fell out of her bed and immediately called her best friend Simone to tell her.

"Friday?" Simone asked over the phone.

"Yeah, in two days. What's the problem?" Megan inquired.

"Friday is pajama day in school. Are you going to let him pick you up from school in your pajamas?"

"Oh no! I completely forgot!" Megan exclaimed.

Megan quickly ended the conversation with Simone and ran to her mother to explain the situation and beg her to bring a fresh set of clothes to school the second it was over so that Megan could run into the bathroom and change.

Megan's mother chuckled and said that she would be there five minutes before school ended and assured her not to worry.

"It's just; it's bad enough he's already three years older than me. I don't want him to see me in my pajamas; I want him to take me seriously!" Megan explained.

"And what's wrong with pajamas? I bought you those as a Christmas present; there's no shame in that!" Megan's mother argued.

***

The bell finally rang, which meant school was over. Megan leaped off her seat and ran out of the classroom.

"Good luck!" Simone yelled from her desk as she packed her things into her backpack.

"Thanks!" Megan cried.

Megan ran to the school gate that was now open but couldn't find her mom; in fact, she couldn't see any cars.

Megan took out her phone and called her mother.

"Where are you?" Megan demanded.

"The street is closed! There was an accident. No cars can get by. You will need to come here to get your clothes!"

Megan hung up the phone and raced down the street.

Luckily, her mother was not too far away, so she would probably be able to get the clothes, run back to school, and change before David could see her this way.

Once Megan reached the street where her mother was parked, she saw that everything was chaos due to an accident that appeared to have only just happened.

Megan raced down the street but didn't see a person on their bike riding directly toward her and crashed right into the bike rider, sending both him and herself flying across the pavement.

Megan cried from the pain in her foot.

"I'm so sorry I didn't see you! I was trying to avoid the police cars!" a man in his late thirties exclaimed as he ran to Megan, who collapsed on the floor.

Within seconds, Megan's mother, who saw the entire thing from her car, ran to Megan to see if she was alright, completely abandoning her car.

"Meg, are you OK?" she asked.

"Yes, just bring me the clothes!"

"I'm not going to leave you like this! You can change in the car!"

Megan's mother squatted down, picked Megan's body up off the ground, and turned around to carry her to her car. Megan wrapped her arms around her mother and winced from the pain in her ankle.

"Megan?" a boy's familiar voice asked from not too far away.

Megan turned her head to see David standing a couple of feet away from where she was hovering.

"David! Hi!" Megan cried.

"Are you OK?" David exclaimed as he ran up to Megan.

"Yes, I'm fine!" Megan said.

"No, she's not. Here, you're a strong boy!" Megan's mother said as she handed Megan over to David, who grabbed Megan in his arms and carried her over to her mother's car.

"I don't always get carried around by my mother while I'm wearing pajamas in the middle of the afternoon!" Megan explained as she did her best to mask the overwhelming embarrassment she felt as David walked her to safety.

David laughed.

"And I don't always arrive just in time to save damsels in distress, and yet here we are!"

THE DOG HOUSE

Mitchell was tired of being mocked for his inability to be handy and build things with his hands. The last time Mitchell had attempted to build his wife a gazebo for their front garden, he had failed terribly and had to resort to asking his friends to come and help him, who were a lot more manually savvy than he was.

"Can you believe it, Django?" Mitchell asked his dog as he lay cross-legged on the grass of the front garden of the home he lived in with his wife and Django, "They keep making fun of me to this day. You don't think I'm terrible at building things, do you?"

Django licked Mitchell's face.

Just as Mitchell wiped the drool off his face, the dark clouds above him and Django started dropping heavy rain almost immediately on both of them.

Mitchell jumped to his feet and ran inside, leaving a reluctant Django behind to get soaked.

"Django, come inside!"

Django barked and refused to move as if he were enjoying getting wet in the rain.

Mitchell looked at his dog with confusion and then suddenly had a brilliant idea.

"That's it! Guess what, Django? I'm going to build you a doghouse!" Mitchell cried through the rain. Django lept in excitement as if he had understood everything his owner had just said.

Mitchell spent the following week researching how to build a doghouse and getting all the materials ready. He did not have a shed, so he compiled all the tools and wood he needed in the garage and got to work immediately.

After a few days, Mitchell felt he was a few hours away from completing the entire house.

"Just remember, you promised to pick me up from the cinema at seven. That gives you five hours! Are you sure you should do this now and not tomorrow? I know how you get when you become focused on something!" Mitchell's wife, Ariella, stated.

"You doubt me too?!" Mitchell quipped, "Don't worry. I'll have this done in a couple of hours, and I'll have plenty of time to come to pick you up!"

Ariella looked dubious.

"Trust me!" Mitchell insisted.

***

Once Ariella left for the cinema with her friends, Mitchell got to work on finally erecting the doghouse and assembling all the various pieces he had prepared.

As confident as he was, Mitchell almost immediately began fearing that he had made some miscalculations in his blueprint due to some of the pieces of wood he had cut not fitting with other parts.

"Oh no…" Mitchell lamented.

Starting over would be embarrassing, so he persisted in making things work.

After a couple of hours, Mitchell was covered in sweat and sores but refused to give up.

Django watched from a distance and would approach Mitchell and regard the house he was building.

"Yes, you will soon be able to use it, Django. I just need a little more time, but soon it will be all yours!" Mitchell assured his dog.

However, as time passed, it became more evident that Mitchell was going to need to go back to the drawing board.

"I am finishing this TODAY!" Mitchell declared to himself, prompting Django to jump and bark in excitement.

Mitchell ran back to his garage and meticulously reviewed the blueprints. He looked them over until he gave himself a headache.

"That's it!" Mitchell cried as he figured out a way of fixing his mistake without having to start over. Mitchell ran back to his garden and continued where he had left off.

After another hour of rebuilding, the house was finally finished and was fit for purpose.

"There you go, Django!" Mitchell said triumphantly.

Django raced into the doghouse and began barking with excitement.

Mitchell smiled and looked at his watch. He was supposed to have picked up his wife an hour ago.

"She's going to kill me," Mitchell said as he realized he'd left his phone in the garage.

At that moment, the front door of the house opened, and a very frustrated Ariella walked inside.

"Mitchell!" she cried but received no response.

Ariella looked around the house and was greeted by an exasperated Django.

"What's wrong, Django?" Ariella asked, wondering if perhaps something had happened to Mitchell, and that was why they hadn't picked her up.

Ariella was led into the garden by Django, who sat down next to the doghouse and proceeded to bark furiously.

Ariella knelt on the grass and peeked into the doghouse to see Mitchell cowering inside as he presented a sympathetic smile begging for leniency.

"I'm so sorry!" Mitchell cried from within the doghouse, "I will fix this! I will make this up to you!"

"No, no, don't move. Just relax," Ariella insisted.

"Relax?" Mitchell asked incredulously.

"Yes. In fact, I'll get your pillow and bed sheets. I wouldn't want you to have a bad night's sleep tonight, so start getting comfortable!" Ariella exclaimed.

THE PICKUP LINE

Nate was not only one of the very few single people at his cousin's wedding but probably the least happy looking one.

"C'mon brother, Eleanor broke up with you a month ago. You need to get over her! Let life surprise you!" Nate's brother, Carl, exclaimed as he put his arm around Nate and shook his entire body as if that would somehow cure his emotional woes.

"Easy for you to say; you're probably going to be getting married yourself in a couple of years," Nate replied.

A few of Nate's friends joined the conversation when they noticed Nate looking like he was at a funeral as opposed to a wedding.

After what seemed like endless speeches from all of his friends about the importance of being resilient and not losing faith in love, Nate had had enough.

"Guys, I just don't think it's going to happen anytime soon. I just need to be sad and mourn the death of a relationship that was very special to me."

"Nate, what was so special about you and Katie?" Dominic, one of Nate's best friends, asked before taking a sip of his beer.

"I loved our story and how we met," Nate replied.

"Didn't you pick her up at the beach one night when you were very drunk?" Carl asked.

"Yeah, but it was better than that. I saw her from a long way away, and I called her beautiful, and she walked over to me," Nate explained.

All the guys looked at each other confused.

"That doesn't exactly sound like Romeo and Juliet to me," Dominic jested.

"You had to be there. I'm not in the right headspace to do the story justice," Nate refuted.

"I think you're just building it to be more than it was in your head, little brother!" Carl suggested.

Nate became frustrated.

"No, I'm not! It was very romantic!" Nate exclaimed as he put his beer on the floor and appeared to be about to deliver a passionate monologue.

"Well, then, show us!" Dominic demanded.

"I saw her from across the beach, locked eyes with her, and cried out, hey beautiful! Do you want to dance with me?!"

At that moment, a tall and beautiful-looking blonde girl heard Nate and thought he was speaking to her.

"Sure, I'd love to!" she replied from across the room.

Nate look perplexed.

"Go to her, you dummy!" Carl cried as he pushed his brother forward.

Nate walked over to the blonde girl, and within seconds, they were deep in conversation.

The guys watched incredulously as Nate grabbed the girl by the hand and took her to the dancefloor with an excited smile.

"How's it going, Nate?!" Dominic called out.

"Life is full of surprises!" Nate cried out, beaming with joy.

Chapter 4

Five Stories About Loss

Pets

Donnie loved coming home from first grade to see his two dogs and two canary birds.

Donnie and his parents had the dogs for several years, but the two canaries had come with the new house he and his family had recently moved into.

Moving cities had been challenging, but Donnie's parents had decided to keep the two birds because of how happy they seemed to make Donnie and how much they helped him in adapting to a new city and school.

"So, what have you named them again?" George, Donnie's father, asked.

"Well, the orange-looking one is called Tangerine, and the yellow-looking one is called Lemon!" Donnie asserted as he pointed at the two caged birds hovering above him.

George listened to his son talk enthusiastically about the birds and knew that he had made the right choice in keeping them, even though the family knew nothing about keeping birds.

"Do you think Buster and Dodger like the birds?" George asked, referring to the two Labradors that were also part of the family.

"Yes, they are best friends, all four of them!"

***

One day, as Donnie was still asleep and George was enjoying a cup of coffee outside in the front garden of the new house he had just rented for himself and his family, he noticed that one of the birds kept pecking at the other one.

Upon closer inspection, George noticed that the yellow bird, which his son had named Lemon, was missing a lot of feathers and looked injured.

"Hey, Tangerine, leave your brother alone!" George cried as he pointed an angry finger at the orange canary.

The bird stopped, but later that evening, as George went to inspect the state of Lemon, he noticed that he was missing even more feathers and noticed Tangerine pecking at his brother once more.

Worried that the now almost featherless canary would not make it through the night, George decided to let the birds fly and go their own way.

Now what do I tell Donnie? George pondered. At that moment, he remembered how he had lectured his son about the importance of telling the truth and confronting difficult situations.

***

The following day, George told his son the truth.

"I know this is tough, but please remember that you still have Buster and Dodger and us, of course. Animals can sometimes be strange, but I did what I thought was the right thing to protect little Lemon," George explained.

Donnie looked concerned and troubled about the incident. Before George could speak anymore, Donnie darted into the house without saying a word.

I hope he's ok, George thought, as he allowed his son some time by himself.

***

It had been almost an hour since George informed his son about the loss of the two birds from their home, and he was beginning to worry about how Donnie was taking it.

George got up from the sunchair and went inside to look for his son. Almost immediately, George found Donnie in the kitchen with Buster. George looked bewildered as he noticed his son lathering the family Labrador retriever with half a slice of lemon.

"Son, what are you doing?! Why are you stroking Buster with a lemon?!" George demanded.

"Well, you said it's important to protect our pets. You know how both Buster and Dodger hate lemons, and they flinch every time they see one? So to avoid Dodger eating Buster, or the other way around, like Tangerine was trying to eat his brother, I am spreading lemon juice all over both dogs so they don't start eating each other!"

George looked at Buster, sitting patiently alongside Donnie with a confused look in his yellow eyes. Dodger was sitting outside the kitchen, looking horrified at what was happening to his brother and what would ultimately be done to him in a few minutes.

GOLF HOCKEY

Timothy enjoyed sitting on the roof of the new house he and his family had moved into when his parents weren't around to tell him it was dangerous for him to do so. He particularly enjoyed looking out into the neighborhood he was now a part of, even if it was late October and it got cold in the afternoons.

On his street, Timothy heard a group of boys gather on the street and begin playing floor hockey. Timothy had never played hockey, but as he watched the boys from his neighborhood play, he found the game very exciting.

Suddenly, Timothy almost slipped from the roof when he noticed the boys calling to him and waving to him to come and join them.

Timothy pointed to himself, asking if they were speaking to him, to which they nodded and yelled at him to join them for some floor hockey.

Timothy gave them a thumbs-up and entered the house. He had never played floor hockey before, but he imagined he needed to show up ready to play, or else his presence might make everyone quite uncomfortable if he wasn't prepared to participate in the sport.

Timothy rummaged through his bedroom, put on what he deemed appropriate attire, and ran out onto the street.

Once Timothy reached the boys, all four of his neighbors looked at him in comical bewilderment.

When Timothy asked what was wrong, the tallest boy in the group answered, "It's what you're wearing!"

"I wore this to play floor hockey! Is something wrong with it?"

The same boy responded, "Well, you showed up wearing a bicycle helmet, wielding a plastic golf club and a baseball. I don't know how many sports you think we are planning on playing, but you are definitely not dressed for floor hockey!"

Timothy felt dejected.

"Wait!" the shortest boy in the group cried, "Is this your Halloween costume for tonight?"

Timothy looked around and noticed the group of boys looked excited.

"Yes," Timothy asserted.

All four of the boys looked excited.

"That's so cool," the tallest boy exclaimed.

Eventually, the boys stopped playing hockey and began talking about their Halloween costumes and agreed to go trick-or-treating that evening, which filled Timothy with excitement.

As Timothy returned home and waited for his mother to come back from the grocery store, he pondered ways to tell her that he would no longer be wearing the hand-made costume she had spent the past three days sewing together in a way that wouldn't infuriate her.

TRADING CARDS

Since Joel convinced his mother to buy him the cartoon trading cards he had wanted to start collecting, it was all he could talk about with his friends.

Joel no longer had to feel left out when his neighborhood friends continuously spoke about the cards they had and how they were going to form a group of boys in the neighborhood to trade and play with each other's cards.

The moment Joel had his own set of cards, he immediately told all his friends and arranged to meet at the park by his parent's house to show them to his friends.

At school, there were a lot of people who collected cartoon trading cards, too. During recess, Dylan, one of Joel's friends, showed Joel his very impressive collection of cards that he had been compiling for several months.

"Oh, wow, you have the blue eagle?!" Dylan cried as he looked adoringly at one of Joel's cards.

"Yeah! It was in the very first set my mother got me!" Joel replied proudly.

"I'll trade you for it!" Dylan exclaimed excitedly.

Joel had not even thought about trading yet, and he had already been ruminating about how he was going to introduce each of his cards to his neighborhood friends, who would be meeting him after school to peruse his brand-new collection.

Dylan noticed Joel's hesitation.

"I'll give you two of my red eagles for your blue one!" Dylan offered.

Finally, Joel acquiesced to his friend's offer and made the trade.

For the rest of the school day, Joel was unsure about how he felt about the trade. If Dylan really wanted the blue eagle card so much, then it probably would have impressed his neighborhood friends a lot more than two red cards ever would.

I need to get it back, Joel decided.

A few minutes before school was over, Joel excused himself to the bathroom but really went to Dylan's cubby to furtively retrieve the card he had traded. However, the moment he began to unzip and look into his friend's backpack, a teacher walked out of the classroom and held the door open for her students to walk out and leave class a little early.

Noticing that the teacher was looking directly at Joel, Joel smiled and zipped his friend's backpack closed.

"Are you leaving early, Joel?" the teacher asked.

"Yup!" Joel lied, putting his friend's backpack on and heading down the hallway to wait for his mother to pick him up.

The teacher walked outside too with her students, so Joel was forced to wait for his mother while carrying someone else's backpack and leaving his own back inside the school building.

Once Joel's mother picked him up, Joel sat in the backseat, dejected.

"So, are you excited about showing your friends your new card collection?"

"I won't be able to..." Joel replied solemnly.

"Why?!"

"Because we have to go back to school now, so I won't be able to make it before they need to go home," Joel replied.

"We have to turn back? Why?" Joel's mother inquired.

"Because I have to go make one final trade."

"You want to trade cards now?!"

"Not cards, backpacks..." Joel replied.

THE ROLLER COASTER

Cameron and Peter had been best friends for many years. They always played together during recess, visited each other's houses during weekends, and played video games. Cameron and Peter rarely ever argued about anything, which made them inseparable. However, ever since Jessica, the new girl, had joined their class, a rift had formed in the friendship.

Both Cameron and Peter were deeply infatuated with the very pretty new girl. Peter was more confident than Cameron, and he would often speak to her during recess while Cameron watched dejectedly since he could not bring himself to talk to a girl he liked.

One day, Cameron was buying some snacks from the school cafeteria and realized that Jessica was right beside him, waiting to purchase something too.

"Oh, you like chocolate raisins too!" Jessica exclaimed as she looked at what Cameron was about to buy with the money his mother had given him.

"Yes, they're my favorite!" Cameron replied.

Cameron and Jessica spoke during the entire time they were queuing to pay for their food.

"I'm guessing you're going to Peter's birthday party tomorrow, right?" Jessica asked.

"Yes, are you?"

"Yes, he invited me yesterday. I'll see you there!" Jessica replied.

Cameron was mad that Peter hadn't told him that he had invited Jessica to his birthday party. The two conversed about the issue during recess. They decided to put the matter to rest during the birthday celebration, which would be taking part in an amusement park that both Cameron and Peter loved to visit.

"If she sits next to me on the rollercoaster, then that means she likes me, but if she sits next to you then that means she likes you more!" Peter asserted.

Cameron nodded in agreement.

***

It was the day of the party, and the amusement park was filled with families and friends.

Cameron forced himself to talk to Jessica so that she would be inclined to sit next to him on the rollercoaster, and Peter was doing the same.

Finally, it was time to get on the ride that would dictate who Jessica liked more between the two friends.

Peter sat down with an empty seat next to him, and Cameron did the same.

To Cameron's disappointment, Jessica chose to sit next to Peter.

Cameron had been excited to sit next to Jessica since he was not frightened by roller coasters and wanted to show her how brave he was. Instead, he was forced to sit behind his friend and Jessica as they joyfully talked about how good the food at the park was and how they wanted to go back to the hot dog stand once the ride was over.

Once the ride started, Cameron put his hands up and did his best to enjoy the ride.

A couple of minutes into the ride, he noticed that Jessica went super quiet and that Peter looked worried. A few seconds later, Cameron witnessed Jessica throw up all over Peter's lap.

Cameron luckily did not get hit with any debris and was still able to enjoy the ride.

Once the ride was over, Jessica ashamedly stepped out of her seat and ran to the nearest bathroom while Peter stood uncomfortably covered in vomit.

Cameron looked at his friend and smiled.

"To the victor, go the spoils!" Cameron exclaimed.

THE FLIGHT

Jacob was on his last stop for a very long business trip. He had never been to Japan but was glad to see that everyone in the hotel spoke English.

Once his work day was finished, and he had no more meetings to attend, Jacob took a taxi back to his hotel to start packing for his flight back home.

Jacob had been flying for over a week and was severely sleep deprived, which made him worried that he would not wake up on top for his early morning flight. Therefore, even though it was only four in the afternoon, Jacob decided to go to bed very early and get the sleep he needed to wake up early and take a long flight back to his family.

At the concierge, Jacob asked for an 8:00 a.m. wake-up call and stressed the urgency of that call.

"Don't worry, sir. We will not forget to give you your wake-up call at 6:00 a.m." the man behind the desk assured Jacob.

Jacob smiled and went up to his room. Luckily, he was already packed for the flight, so after taking a quick shower, Jacob collapsed on the bed and fell asleep immediately.

***

Jacob woke up after having a nightmare about missing his flight and looked at his clock. It was almost seven.

"What?!" Jacob cried out at the thought of having slept over 12 hours and not getting his wake-up call from reception.

Jacob got himself ready in a hurry and ran down with his luggage.

"You didn't wake me up!" Jacob exclaimed in anger as he ran past the front desk onto the street to find a taxi.

Jacob was inside a taxi and speeding to the airport before he could hear a reply from the people he had just yelled at.

Jacob had never missed a flight and was worried that he was about to break that streak.

The taxi finally arrived at the airport. Jacob ran into the terminal and looked at the departure screen. His flight wasn't even there.

Jacob was confused. He looked at his watch. It was 7:30, an hour before his flight was due to leave, yet he couldn't find it on the screen.

Suddenly, Joel looked outside the terminal and noticed that instead of getting lighter, it was getting darker.

Horrified, Joel checked his phone to check precisely what the time was.

It's nighttime, not morning, Joel realized; I've only slept for like two hours.

Joel dejectedly found another taxi and returned to the hotel, where he walked past the concierge full of shame.

"Are we still good for the 6:00 a.m. wake-up call?" the receptionist asked with a smug smile.

Joel nodded.

Chapter 5

Five Stories About Childhood

Recess

Michael ran out to recess as if schoolwork would catch him and pull him back into the classroom if he wasn't fast enough.

He had only been a student at his new elementary school for a couple of months, but he already felt at home. The courtyard where he went for recess was three times the size of the one where he used to live. A group of boys would race around the courtyard to find the fastest boy in the school. Michael loved racing and was determined to be the fastest.

On this day, however, he noticed one of his friends, Alexander, racing with a group of girls around the courtyard with no particular direction.

Alexander was much faster than the girls and would constantly look back as the group flailed behind him with a satisfied smile.

Once recess was over, Michael went up to Alexander and asked him what he was doing with the girls.

"I wasn't racing; they were chasing me! They said whoever catches me gives me a kiss, so I ran away from them!" Alexander explained.

Michael contemplated that answer.

Why would anyone run away from a kiss? He pondered.

The next day, Michael ran back out to recess only to find the girls who had been chasing his friend Alexander now walking up toward him.

"Where is your friend?" one of the girls asked.

"I don't know. Why?"

"We saw you talking to him. Are you guys best friends?"

"Yeah," Michael replied.

"I'm Samantha, and these are my friends," the girl with short black hair and sharp features declared.

After a couple more minutes, Samantha said that since Alexander wasn't in school that day, Michael would be the one who would get kissed.

Feeling excited about the prospect of being chased by a group of girls, Michael smiled.

"Not if you can't catch me first!" Michael cried before sprinting away from the girls, who immediately began to chase him.

At first, it was fun to run away and to have all the boys look at him being chased by a group of girls, but after a few minutes, it got tiring, and then it got scary.

***

It had been a week of girls chasing Michael every time he went out for recess. Alexander was back in school, but the girls were now more interested in Michael.

Michael would walk next to Alexander every time he went into recess, but the girls were set on chasing Michael only.

"I don't understand why they don't chase you anymore!" Michael said as he tried to catch his breath and walked back into the classroom, grateful that class was about to start and that he was protected by the room he was in.

"I thought you liked it. You were jealous when we talked about it!"

"Now I'm jealous that they don't chase you anymore. It's terrifying!" Michael exclaimed. "Why did you miss school that day? If you hadn't missed school, everything would be fine!"

"I was sick. My mother spoke to the teacher that I would be staying home..."

This response got Michael thinking.

That night, Michael went home, locked himself in his room, and devised a plan to no longer be terrorized by the group of girls chasing him every recess.

***

As people arrived at school early in the morning, Michael entered the classroom and raced to hand something over to his teacher.

"Ms. Patterson, I have to give you this!" Michael explained as he handed his teacher a note.

"What is this?" she asked as she took the note and unfolded it.

"It's from my mother!"

Ms. Patterson looked surprised. She squinted to try and make what she was reading:

Dear Michaels's teacher, Michael is sick and cannot go to recess. He should stay inside and do his work instead of having fun during recess. Thank you.

Ms. Patterson did her best to stifle a laugh and looked at Michael with a smile.

"Michael, are you sure your mother wrote this?"

"Yes! Why?" Michael asked, worried that his plan wasn't going to work.

"Well, first of all, it's signed by Michaels's mother!"

Michael eventually told the teacher the truth, who laughed and ensured that the girls would never chase him again.

That day, Michael went out to recess with trepidation but noticed that the girls were looking at him with disdain yet refrained from chasing him.

Excited about his regained freedom, Michael ran to the group of boys who were racing each other and continued to do what he always did during recess. Due to all the practice he had been having recently with the girls, Michael became the fastest runner out of all the boys.

THE KISSING ROOM

Albert had heard about the kissing room. At first, he heard about it in passing as a couple of people passed him by were speaking of it, but then he noticed that his friends were talking about it too.

"What is the kissing room?" Albert asked as he unwrapped the peanut butter and jelly sandwich his mother had wrapped in tinfoil for his school lunch. Albert's friends always envied what his parents made him for lunch.

"You don't know? Everybody talking about it!" Dean replied enthusiastically as he unwrapped a rye bread and turkey sandwich.

"Is it a room where people kiss?"

"No, it's a room where the band KISS performs their music; of course, it is!" Jared mocked. Jared's parents were vegan, so Albert never knew what his friend was eating. This time it appeared that Jared had a Tupperware filled with orange-colored pasta and broccoli.

"Have you been there? Where is it?" Albert asked excitedly.

"It's in the sports equipment room, the one where we get our basketballs and footballs from during PE. I heard that Anthony and that new girl went there to kiss. Apparently, no one goes through that hallway from 1 to 1:30," Dean explained.

Albert leaned in closer as if ensuring that no one else in the packed and loud cafeteria could hear.

"There's no need to be secretive about it, Albie. Everyone knows," Jared explained.

"Yeah. In fact, everyone's been there already and kissed a girl!" Dean added.

Albert straightened his back and glared skeptically at his two friends.

"Have you guys kissed a girl there?"

"Sure! Everyone has. I don't understand why you haven't gone!" Dean cried.

"Who have you kissed?" Albert demanded.

"A gentleman doesn't kiss and tell," Dean replied.

Albert scoffed dismissively and turned to Jared, who was smirking confidently.

"Emma."

"Emma?" Albert cried, "The new girl? She hasn't even been in school. And she's probably the best-looking girl in the world!"

"And a great kisser too!"

"Yeah, right!" Albert protested.

"Just because no girl would ever be interested in someone who's terrified of hamsters doesn't mean that they wouldn't be interested in me!" Jared declared.

"I'm not terrified… they're just weird looking," Albert clarified, trying to mask the shame he felt.

***

It was 1 p.m. Just as planned, Albert excused himself from Geography to go to the sports equipment room. As he did so and was allowed to go to the bathroom by the teacher, Jared and Dean turned their heads back and smiled at Albert approvingly.

Albert had no idea what to expect. He was dared by his two friends to go inside the kissing room and kiss whichever girl he found there waiting.

More than wanting to find someone to kiss, Albert didn't want his friends to think he was too scared to go into the kissing room, especially after the way they mocked him for being scared of hamsters.

As Albert went down into the basement of the school and approached the kissing room, he felt increasingly nervous. What if there really was a girl waiting?

Once he arrived at the sports equipment room, he looked around to ensure no one was looking and went inside. Albert closed the door immediately to ensure no one suspected someone was inside and ran deep into the room, dodging hockey sticks and orange cones in the process.

Albert investigated the room to ensure no one was around. He was not looking for anyone to kiss him, simply to ensure he was alone.

"Ok, ten seconds, and then I leave. That will show them. One, two, three, four..." Albert heard something behind him, which made him turn in fear.

Emma, a pretty blonde girl who had missed school for a couple of days, was sitting on the floor, in between some tennis rackets stroking something in her hand.

"Emma! What are you doing here?"

"I could ask you the same question..."

Albert struggled to produce a sensible answer.

"Were you looking for this, perhaps?" Emma asked as she raised the hamster in between her hands. "Someone opened the door a few minutes ago and let it inside. I'm not sure why, but it's scared."

My stupid friends set me up, Albert thought.

"No, it's not mine. But I know who it belongs to."

Albert explained the situation and the dare about going into the kissing room.

"That's very silly. So they bought a hamster just to scare you?"

"I guess so."

"Well, come here. I'll show you that they're not scary."

Albert apprehensively approached Emma and the hamster. Somehow, with her holding the animal and gently stroking it, it did not seem that scary.

After flinching his hand back a couple of times, Albert finally began stroking the animal confidently as Emma did the same and cradled it with her left hand.

"I'm not gonna kiss you…" Emma declared.

"I know. That's not why I'm here!"

"Then why are you here?"

"I guess I just fell for my friend's stupid prank. Why are you here?"

"My sister left for college last week, and I've been missing her a lot. Sometimes I just feel like crying, so I come here. I think some boys and some of them came here a few times and suddenly started a rumor about this being a kissing room. It's ridiculous."

"I know. My friends are quite stupid…"

"We should teach them a lesson," Emma suggested.

"Like what?"

"We should walk out together holding hands. Then they'll really think you kissed me."

Albert smiled. It was a great idea.

***

Dean and Jared looked from the corner of the hall at the sports equipment room.

"The doors opening!" Dean declared as he excitedly pulled on Jared's t-shirt.

"Five bucks says he runs out screaming," Jared added.

When both boys saw Albert emerge from the room, holding Emma's hand and brandishing a satisfied smile, they went white and completely speechless.

Emma was also smiling contentedly as she strutted forward with Alberts's hand on her left hand and her new little hamster on her right.

"You know, I think I'll keep this little guy," Emma said, referring to the hamster safely nestled between her hip and her hand, "he'll keep me company, so I don't miss my sister anymore," Emma whispered to Albert, who laughed and noticed that this was the most confident he had ever felt around a girl in school before.

Albert didn't get a kiss in the kissing room, but this was definitely the closest he ever felt to one day getting one. Albert had never felt more confident, and he would have continued to feel that way if Emma's new hamster hadn't accidentally escaped her grasp and suddenly leaped on Albert's shoulder, inadvertently causing him to run away screaming in fear.

Emma laughed and found it endearing.

THE TREE

Dennis returned to school excited to see his friends again, especially the ones in his art class. His art class was small; only five other students took part, but spending time with them was Dennis' favorite time of day.

"How was your summer?" Ms. Saunders asked her pupils as she got the materials, she needed for class ready.

Everyone seated around the circular wooden table went around sharing their summer holiday experiences.

"And you, Dennis? Did you have a nice summer?" Ms. Saunders asked.

Dennis had a proclivity to let his imagination run away from him. In truth, his holiday had not been as exciting as he had hoped, but the rest of his friends had told such compelling stories that he didn't want to feel left out.

"Yes! It was amazing!"

"Do you want to tell us about it?" Ms. Saunders asked.

Dennis looked around and noticed everyone in his art class staring at him intently and excitedly as if the best story had been purposefully reserved for last.

"Well, I went into the woods with my dad and walked the dog," Dennis began, "and then we found a magical blue tree that was shiny and gave people superpowers!"

Although the story had begun with the truth, Dennis felt compelled to not let his classmates down by ending the story by merely narrating the fact that the dog went to the bathroom, ran for a while, and then accompanied them back home.

After noticing that his friends didn't recoil at the sheer absurdity of his tale, Dennis felt motivated to keep going. He hadn't seen Ms. Saunders' look of bemused surprise.

"And my dad was too scared to touch the tree, but I touched it!"

"And what happened?" Reggie—the shortest kid in the class with rounded spectacles that made him look a little like a miniature Harry Potter—demanded.

"The tree gave me superpowers!" Dennis exclaimed, once more scanning the room to see if any of his classmates were looking at him with a similar expression to the one on Ms. Saunders. Everyone seemed highly intrigued.

"And do you still have them?" Nick, the tall blonde boy with freckles, asked.

"Yes, I do!"

***

It was break time, and all the kids were gathered around the thick oak tree that had always provided students with shade during recess but had apparently come crashing down onto the ground during the summer.

Dennis ran up to the tree and heard students speculating about what might have caused the tree to fall.

"Dennis!" called out Nick.

"Yeah?"

"You should lift the tree! You should show off your superpowers!" Nick responded excitedly.

Dennis turned red.

"Can you throw it over the fence?" Reggie asked.

Everyone had turned to look at Dennis, who felt overwhelmed by the situation and ran away as fast as he could.

***

The following day, Dennis was back in art class but felt too embarrassed to speak. Whenever Ms. Saunders asked him a question, he simply responded by moving either his hands or his head.

Dennis continued his reluctance to speak all day until it was time for him to be picked up by his mother.

"So, how was school?" Rachel, Dennis' mother, asked.

"Fine," Dennis responded dejectedly, finally speaking.

Once they got home, Dennis ran up to his room and decided to not leave until it was dinner time.

However, a couple of hours after being home, Rachel went up to her son's room and sat next to him as he took a nap on his bed.

"Can I ask you something?" Rachel asked Dennis as she put her hand on the blue duvet covering his shoulder.

"Yes."

"Did you not speak at all today in school?"

"How do you know?" Dennis asked.

"Because I got a call from all the mothers of the kids in your art class."

"You got a call?"

"Yeah, apparently, their children aren't speaking to their parents and are being completely silent like you."

"Really? Why?" Dennis asked, sitting upright on his bed.

"Apparently, they want to be just like you, so they are copying the things you do," Rachel explained.

Dennis smiled at this response.

"They want to be like me?"

"Yeah, so they're refusing to speak. Maybe tomorrow you could show up to school and talk again so your friends will talk to their parents again."

Dennis smiled, "Ok!" he asserted.

Rachel stood up front from her son's bed and headed out the door but then stopped as she remembered one last thing.

"Oh, by the way, would you happen to know why Reggie's parents found their son painting their tree bright blue?" Rachel asked as she stood by the open door.

"No idea!" Dennis cried.

FACE MASK

Marie felt strange putting on a sanitary face mask on her four-year-old son at the hairdresser, but she knew it was food for a good cause.

The last time she had taken her son John to the hairdresser, which was the first time she had ever done so, John had thrown up all over the place because a stray hair had fallen into his open mouth.

Marie had always known that John was very fastidious about his food and getting his hands dirty. Still, that day, as she stood in front of several other people getting their haircuts and watched in horror as her child threw up all over the white marble floor, she realized just how squeamish he was.

Luckily, the hairdresser recognized that it was an involuntary reaction on John's part and that he was a sweet child, despite the accident.

"Just bring him in next time with a face mask that he can use to cover his mouth, and there won't be a problem," the hairdresser had recommended.

Marie took that advice and purchased a bundle of sanitary face masks the following day.

This time, as Marie stood once again at the hairdresser's with her young boy, she was prepared.

"I see the face mask is on," the hairdresser said as he kneeled to be at eye level with John.

"I know you are a very sweet boy and that you don't want stray hairs going into your mouth. So don't worry, you have your mask, and I will be very careful!"

Marie smiled as John nodded with appreciation.

Once the appointment was over, John had his haircut. Marie left to meet her husband, Roger, at a nearby steakhouse.

Marie arrived at the steakhouse and saw Roger sitting on a bench by the restaurant's entrance. There was a long queue to get a table.

"How long have you been waiting?" Marie asked her husband.

"Twenty minutes. We should get our table soon," Roger replied as he picked up his son and admired his new haircut.

"No vomit this time?" Roger asked.

"Not this time!" John replied excitedly.

"No. He behaved wonderfully!" Marie responded, "I was worried that people would think he was a misbehaved child, but everyone was so lovely over there!"

"That's because he is a very good boy!" Roger said as he kissed his son on top of his head and ruffled his freshly cut hair.

There was an older woman in her late 70s who was dressed in all black sitting next to Roger, also waiting for a table, and was beaming a smile at John.

"I can tell that he is a very sweet boy. You're a sweet boy, aren't you?" the elderly woman asked as she rubbed a black mole on her impressively long nose.

John laughed cheerfully at the woman, and Roger thanked her for her kind words.

"I'm going to go to the bathroom quickly. I'll be right back!" Roger announced.

It seemed that no one listened to Roger because John was looking up lovingly at the old lady who was winking at John and making him laugh with her silly face.

Roger smiled and sprinted to the bathroom.

A few minutes later, Roger returned to see that the old lady was gone, which meant that he and his family would be getting their table at any moment. Roger also noticed that John was wearing his face mask again.

"Why is John wearing a face mask again?" Roger asked.

Marie looked upset.

"Don't even ask," Marie replied.

"What? Is he squeamish around stray pieces of steak too?" Roger inquired.

"John kept staring at the old lady, and then he turned to me with a big smile and asked me as loud as he could if the old lady next to him was a witch," Marie responded as she dug her face between her palms.

"So the face mask is to—"

"Keep him quiet, yes," Marie interjected.

THE SOUVENIR

Although it was Matt's birthday, and the entire family was celebrating by taking him to the planetarium, Matt was in one of his worst moods ever.

Matt's parents had promised him a trip to Disneyland but canceled last minute so they could spend time with some friends who were visiting town and wanted to see Matt on his birthday.

Julian was Matt's godfather and wanted to cheer his godson up by buying him an excellent souvenir from the planetarium they were all in.

"Do you think he would like this?" Julian asked as he showed Matt's father, Donald, a toy spaceship as everyone perused the planetarium's gift shop.

"I think he'll love it, but right now, it's best just to let him be mad for a little bit. Eventually, his mood subsides if you leave him be," Donald explained.

"Nonsense, watch me cheer him up!" Julian exclaimed.

"Julian, I'm telling you, it's best to leave that boy alone for a little bit."

"No way, Matty loves his godfather!" Julian insisted.

Donald shrugged his shoulders and let his friend go ahead and approach Matt.

"Hey Mattie, how you doing?" Julian asked.

"I'm ok, I guess," Matt replied.

"What do you think of this toy? Do you think it's cool enough to be in a toy store?"

"Yeah…" Matt replied.

"Do you think they used cool colors, or could they have improved on the design? I think it's one of the most exciting spaceships we saw today, don't you think?"

"I think it's fine," Matt answered.

Julian continued to ask Matt questions, hoping that Matt would eventually figure out that Julian was about to gift him the toy until he became exasperated.

"If you like it so much, then you buy it!" Matt yelled furiously at his godfather.

Julian jumped back and saw Donald laughing to himself.

Dejected, Julian walked back to where he found the toy spaceship and put it back in its place.

"You're not getting him the toy anymore?" Donald asked.

Julian did not answer but continued walking out of the store in disappointment.

"Should I buy you a toy or let you be by yourself for a while?!" Donald jested loudly from inside the gift shop.

Chapter 6

Five Stories About Work

New Job

Stuart had just started working as marketing manager for a new agency. Luckily, the new job was relatively close to his home, so he didn't have to relocate himself or his family anywhere.

The job was similar to what he had been doing before, but the environment was very different. Everyone was a lot more laid back and less formal than they were at his last job; in fact, he struggled to find anyone older than him in the office.

The atmosphere in the office seemed to make everyone very relaxed, but Stuart struggled to adapt to the more youthful and informal culture that he was now a part of.

"I doubt anyone will be at the office on a Sunday at this hour," Stuart asserted to his wife, Angela, as he slid his laptop into his satchel and pulled open his nightstand cupboard to retrieve his car keys.

"What about Ben?" Angela asked.

"What about him?"

"I have my dinner with the girls. He can't be left here alone."

Stuart had completely forgotten that his wife had dinner plans with her friends.

"OK, well, he can come with me to the office. He will probably fit in more with the people working there than I do!" Stuart decided.

"He's eight years old!" Angela cried.

***

It was late, and the office was empty. Stuart was in his office typing away on his computer as he prepared the presentation he would be delivering bright and early the next day.

Ben was running around the office and finally seemed to calm down once he entered the conference room, where Stuart would finally officially be meeting his team for the first time since joining the company.

"Ben, are you OK in there?" Stuart called from his office.

"Yes!" Ben cried.

"You know I have my big presentation tomorrow, right, and that's why I can't play with you right now?"

"Yes!" Ben responded.

Stuart looked at his watch and grunted as he realized he would return to the office in less than ten hours.

"OK, time to go!" Stuart declared as he slammed his laptop down and went to fetch his son.

***

The following day, Stuart arrived at the office slightly late but filled with copious amounts of caffeine. He briefly stopped at his office before racing to the conference room to present to his team.

Once inside, everyone smiled enthusiastically at Stuart.

"There he is!" Robert, Stuart's boss, cried, "The best person in the universe!"

"What?" Stuart asked as he looked around the room, feeling like he was missing the joke.

Robert stepped aside so that Stuart could see the drawing board where people wrote things down as they presented. The board was filled with colorful illustrations, and written in large black capital letters was the message: Stuart is the best person in the universe!

Stuart's complexion turned white.

"Oh, wow… I can explain…" Stuart began.

"Well, we like to see that you are getting into the swing of things here," Robert interjected. "We were worried this was going to be a boring meeting, but stuff like this shows that you know what this company is all about. The floor is yours!"

Robert looked around at the conference room and smiled.

Thank you, Ben.

THE CASTING

Mario, Tatiana, and David decided to have lunch together in their favorite salad bar a couple of blocks from the office. It was around 2 p.m., so the restaurant was quite empty and quiet.

Tatiana and David were close friends, but Mario worked for another account in the marketing agency, so they did not spend too much time with him.

"So, Mario, is your job as awesome as it seems?" David asked as he took a bite out of the chicken breast in his Caesar salad.

"What makes you think my job is awesome?" Mario asked incredulously.

"Oh, come on. I mean, we don't really know what you do with your account, but we know that every week you disappear for an entire day because you have to cast models for your product launch events. Surely there are worse ways to spend your Fridays than looking at a bunch of models," Tatiana responded.

"I suppose you're right, and at first, it's very fun looking at models for an entire day, but it's just part of my routine now. Anyways, tomorrow I won't be able to do it because I have something else I have to do."

"Ooh, so who's gonna do it tomorrow?" David asked as he leaned in closer to Mario.

"I don't know. The boss said that she will see who has the most available time tomorrow and ask them to do it," Mario explained as he got started on his cobb salad.

David's eyes widened, "Interesting."

"Well, it won't be either David or me. You have to finish your report tomorrow, right?" Tatiana asked.

"Yeah, but I can maybe get it done in time," David replied.

"You think you can do the entire report before the afternoon?" Tatiana inquired.

"Or I can get it done today after lunch."

"But I thought we were going to the cinema!" Tatiana cried.

David shot Tatiana a sheepish grin, "Any chance we can reschedule? I would really like to finish this report today if possible."

"You're unbelievable. Some friend you are," Tatiana scoffed as she leaned back in her chair and shook her head.

***

The following day, David arrived to work slightly sleep deprived but happy to no longer have to worry about turning in the report, which he had submitted that morning at around 1 a.m.

As expected, Davids's boss walked out of her office and announced that they needed someone who was not so busy that day to help with the model casting.

"I submitted my report so I could help!" David cried. Tatiana shook her head in disapproval once more.

"All of it? Already?" Davids's boss asked in shock.

"Yes," David replied with an expectant smile.

"Wow, well done. Ok, you can help out with the casting. Come into my office in an hour, and we'll do the casting together."

David waited till his boss was back in her office for him to shoot his arms in celebration.

After an hour of imagining the type of models he would be meeting, he got up from his desk and walked over to his boss's office to head downstairs and get started with the casting.

Tatiana was left to seethe by herself as she stared angrily at her computer screen.

Once it was time for lunch, Tatiana walked downstairs to have lunch with some colleagues and noticed that the door that led to the room where the casting was taking place was slightly ajar.

Tatiana decided to sneak a peek to see just how much David was enjoying his afternoon.

Upon leaning forward and looking into the room, all Tatiana managed to see was a room full of very handsome male models waiting their turn to speak and get their picture taken and a very solemn and dejected-looking David sitting next to his boss as she interviewed the male models.

David caught a glimpse of Tatiana and sunk even deeper into his chair as if wanting the ground to swallow him whole.

Tatiana beamed a satisfied smile at David and gamboled out of the office building to enjoy lunch with her other friends.

MEETING THE NEW HIRE

As interesting as it had been watching potential recruits come into the office day after day and get interviewed, John was relieved to hear that HR had finally chosen someone to work alongside him in the marketing department.

The past two weeks had been hectic with people coming in and out of the office, looking to join the company and begin work immediately.

John sat behind his computer and read the email his boss had sent to everyone late last night. John beamed when he saw that not only did the very beautiful woman he had noticed enter the office a couple of days ago get hired but that she would be coming into the office later that afternoon to talk to John about the role and getting her space set up.

Because John had been single for three years and all of his work colleagues loved teasing him about how they needed to help him find a mate, not to mention that everyone overheard John say how attractive he found Jennifer, the new recruit, he would surely be teased by everyone the moment she walked in and sat next to him.

However, John felt compelled to ensure that he looked good and that his appearance wasn't as disheveled as it usually was on early Monday mornings after a long weekend. Therefore, John devised a plan to use the upstairs bathroom, which technically belonged to another company altogether, to clean himself up a bit and comb his hair to avoid anyone from his office walking in and catching him, making himself presentable for Jennifer.

According to the email, Jennifer was due to arrive in ten minutes, which gave him enough time to go upstairs and give himself a quick look in the mirror without having to stand next to his coworkers who often visited the office bathroom to brush their teeth first thing before getting to work.

John furtively exited the office and took the stairs to the upper floor of the office building. Once he was safely sequestered from mockery in the upstairs bathroom, John began looking at his teeth and fixing his hair.

John had only been in the bathroom for a minute when someone from the office to which the bathroom belonged walked in and looked at John bewildered. John smiled at the man which he sometimes saw entering or exiting the building throughout the work week and pretended to be washing his hands.

If he asks why I'm not using my office bathroom, I'll just say that it's broken, John reasoned.

As the man left, he shot a displeased glare at John before shutting the door behind him.

What's his problem?

John finished surveying his appearance in the mirror and finally deemed himself ready to be seen by the beautiful Jennifer.

John walked over to exit the bathroom but noticed that it was locked. John pulled at the doorknob to no avail.

Oh no, I'm locked in.

Although John was not claustrophobic, his heart began to race when he noticed that he had left his phone down at the office. He did have his watch on him, however, which showed that he had to make his way down to the office immediately if he didn't want to miss Jennifer arriving, especially if she arrived early, which she probably would do, considering it was her first day.

John considered breaking down the door or screaming, but considering he was probably locked in on purpose by the guy who had just used the bathroom, screaming would likely prove to be a futile exercise.

John took a few steps back, folded his arms, and looked at the door angrily as if the door had personally slighted him. His only solution was to wait until someone walked in and let him out.

What are they all going to think? What is Jennifer going to think?

There had been other times in the past when John had used the upstairs bathroom as opposed to the one in front of his office due to suffering from bad stomach pains.

"Out of all the times I've used this bathroom, why now?!" John lamented.

John had now been stuck inside the bathroom for 15 minutes. He had no idea if no one had noticed his absence or if everyone was out searching for him so that he could begin talking to Jennifer about her new responsibilities.

I'm going to have to yell for help.

John took a few steps back and took a deep breath. Just as he was about to scream, the door finally opened.

John didn't bother looking to see who had stepped inside. Instead, John raced out of the bathroom and down the stairs into his office.

Once inside, he noticed everyone staring at him, including Jennifer, who was sitting next to his desk waiting for him.

"John, what happened to your hair?!" Damien, one of John's friends and colleagues, demanded, "And where have you been?"

John realized that he must have accidentally tousled his hair during the stressful moment inside the upstairs bathroom.

"In the bathroom, sorry."

John sat down next to Jennifer and shook her hand.

"Hi, I'm John. Sorry for the wait."

John and Jennifer began talking, but all John could think about was how strange it must have sounded to confess that he had been 15 minutes in the bathroom, and soon it was all he could think about.

"By the way, I was in the bathroom for so long because I was locked inside…" John said in a failed whisper.

Everyone in John's near vicinity began roaring with laughter, and even John couldn't help but laugh.

THE PRESENTATION

Eric was doing his best to assuage Miguel's nerves. Miguel was due to present for the first time in front of a big client. Although he wouldn't be presenting alone, he was feeling overwhelmed by the prospect of standing in front of a large group of people who had the potential to invest a lot of money into the company if the presentation went well.

"I don't know if I can do this," Miguel kept saying as Eric drove him out of the office and into the city where they were scheduled to present.

"How about this, Micky? I have to stop by my place first to get some papers. Once we're there, I'll make you a cup of tea, and we can sit down and go over the entire presentation to settle your nerves. How does that sound?"

Miguel nodded, his eyes clenched shut.

Once Eric and Miguel were at Eric's home, Miguel sat down on Eric's living room sofa and attempted to settle his nerves.

"Here, some snacks for you," Eric said as he put down some honey-roasted peanuts on the coffee table in front of Miguel.

Miguel proceeded to devour the peanuts and make it seem as if he hadn't eaten in days.

"You might want to take it easy on those," Eric advised, but Miguel was too preoccupied with his own thoughts to worry about pacing himself.

"The problem is, Eric, that I become too anxious and lose all my confidence. This is a lot of money at stake, and I don't know if I have the confidence to command the room. Why don't you present by yourself?"

"You heard the boss. He wants you to work on your presentation skills, and he believes in you. Surely that inspires confidence, doesn't it?" Eric asked his friend, whose mouth seemed like it would explode if he attempted to fit another honey-roasted peanut in there.

Eric attempted to say something but was too nervous to realize that his mouth was incapable of doing anything other than managing the excess of food inside it.

***

Eric and Miguel waited outside the conference room where they were due to present in a few minutes.

Miguel looked very nervous, even more than Eric had expected.

"Eric, we have a problem…"

"Mickey, just take a deep breath and don't worry. You're gonna do great!" Eric assured his friend.

"No, you don't understand," Miguel began.

"Look, we can't fall apart now. Just believe in yourself, and you will inspire confidence," Eric explained.

"Eric!" Miguel cried.

At that moment, the conference room door opened, and both Miguel and Eric were invited inside.

Miguel and Eric stood up from their chairs and entered the conference room.

***

The presentation went as Eric predicted. Miguel began to crumble under pressure and failed to speak confidently, prompting Eric to take control of the situation.

Once the presentation was over, the clients had an endless amount of questions, which was probably due to the incongruity of the presentation due to Miguel exuding a very different energy from Eric.

"Well, I just think we have a lot of unanswered questions that leave us feeling a little befuddled," one of the clients declared from across the long round wooden table.

"Look, there is no need for you to answer questions. It is very simple, we have all the tools to make your business grow, and we can do it better and for less than anyone else out there in the market. We have explained everything, and we are willing to enter into negotiations, but right now, you have to understand that you will not find a better alternative to our business. That should answer all your questions!" Miguel cried.

Everyone in the conference room looked aghast, including Eric.

Eric desperately wanted to remedy the situation but found himself lost for words.

"Well, I think that's exactly the confidence we were waiting for. Well done," the client responded.

Eric smiled and did his best to mask his nervousness. Miguel seemed like he was on the verge of yet another outburst.

"Ok, well, I think that's all we need to hear. We would love to take on your business!" the client exclaimed.

***

Miguel and Eric jumped into the car after the meeting and raced to Eric's home again.

"I can't believe that; where did that come from? You were great in the end!" Eric exclaimed.

"Drive faster!" Miguel demanded.

"What?"

"Drive faster!" Miguel repeated.

"Why?" Eric asked.

"You think I suddenly became a confident person in a matter of seconds? Drive faster!" The only reason I screamed at the clients was that all those peanuts burned a hole in my stomach, and if I stayed there a second longer, I would have gone to the bathroom right there in the conference room.

Eric did as he was told.

THE RIGHT PERSON

Pilar was a very sweet woman but also incredibly naive. She was one of the oldest people in the company and always struggled with understanding modern technology.

When Pilar came to Joe, the company's marketing manager, for advice on the best way to find potential candidates for a job opening, Joe looked at her confused.

"You're in HR, and you don't know how to post a job opening online?" Joe inquired.

"I do know. It's just that I already have a pretty comprehensive list of candidates, but the boss demands at least twenty," Pilar retorted.

"And how many do you have?"

"Fifteen. Do you know any other websites? I heard that Swiper is quite good!"

Joe stifled a laugh when he realized that Pilar was unaware that Swiper was a dating website as opposed to a platform for finding job candidates.

"Yeah, I heard that it's a great platform. In fact, that's how I got hired!" Joe cried.

"Really? Wow, I'm going to look into it!" Pilar responded.

Joe wished her luck and returned to his office, eager to share the hilarious news with the rest of his team.

***

The next day, Joe was eager to ask Pilar how the search had gone since his team had found the prank so funny and wanted to know if Pilar had actually gone through with using the dating website.

Joe knocked on Pilar's door and walked inside. Once he heard her usher him in.

"Hey, I just wanted to know how it went on Swiper?" Joe asked.

"Oh, it went great! I found lots of potential candidates for the position!" Pilar responded enthusiastically from behind her desk.

"That's great!" Joe responded, once again attempting to stifle a laugh.

"In fact, I found so many great candidates that I sent a mass email to the previous 15 candidates I already had in mind telling them that the position had been filled."

"What?!" Joe cried.

"Yeah, none of the previous fifteen were as friendly and responsive as the ones on Swiper!" Pilar explained.

Joe realized he was going to get in a lot of trouble once his boss found out about the prank.

"Pilar! I was only kidding! Swiper is a dating app! You need to find those 15 candidates again and tell them nothing is canceled!" Joe cried.

"Why did you tell me it was an app for finding job candidates?!" Pilar demanded.

"It was a prank!" Joe exclaimed as he covered his face in his hands, trying hard not to break down.

Pilar grinned at Joe.

"Calm down. I'm only messing with you now," Pilar confessed.

"What?" Joe asked.

"I found out what the app really was and realized you were messing with me. Don't worry; your job is safe for now. And for what it's worth, it was funny what you did," Pilar explained.

Joe caught his breath and regained his composure.

"Well, I guess I got what I deserved. Well played," Joe said. "I suppose I owe you an apology. How about we go for a drink after work?"

"I can't tonight," Pilar responded, still smiling.

"How come?"

"Well, I got a date. Swiper is quite good, as it turns out!" Pilar responded.

CHAPTER 7

FIVE STORIES ABOUT ADVENTURE

THE HOME VIDEO

Mitchell was looking forward to the holiday he and his family were about to embark on. He had been to Spain only once as a child and was excited to be going there again with his wife and son.

However, Mitchell was slightly nervous about being in the car for 12 hours with his family, considering after only a couple hours of driving, he would already be leaving the country that spoke his language.

Mitchell's wife, Denise, entered the bedroom holding the new video camera she had gotten for her birthday and that she was thoroughly excited to try out.

"You can finally put it to good use; no more recording Sunday breakfast or your drives to yoga class," Mitchell quipped.

Denise did not look amused.

"What's wrong?"

"I've been meaning to send my parents back home footage from our new life, and I want to record this trip so they can see how happy I am," Denise replied.

"Sounds great; what's the problem?"

"Every time I try to record something during one of our trips, you always say that there's no time and that we have to keep driving. I always end up recording flashes of things through the window as I drive 100 miles an hour. It would be nice if I could send something to my family that puts a smile on their face other than making them squint and lean closer to the screen."

Mitchell recognized that his impatience for arriving at places on time limited his wife's ability to document their time together.

"You're right; I'm sorry. I know how important it is for you to show your family how happy you are. I promise you that on this trip, we can stop as many times as you want for you to record," Mitchell declared.

Denise smiled and put down the camera on the nightstand table by the bed to embrace her husband.

"We should get some sleep," Mitchell asserted, "we have to get up in less than seven hours."

***

After six hours of driving and having already stopped twice, Mitchell was already passing through places he had never been to before but was eager to push forward. The family had left much later than they had planned due to Mitchell's son, Stu, not being able to find his favorite toy, only to finally discover it in one of the deepest crevices of the attic where he liked to sit alone and play.

"Wow, look at those hills! They're beautiful!" Denise exclaimed.

Mitchell knew what was coming.

"Can you slow down so I can film them?"

As much as Mitchell wanted to make up for lost time, he remembered the conversation he had with his wife the previous night and decided to do the right thing.

"No, I won't slow down," Mitchell began. Denise looked at her husband incredulously, "I'll come to a full stop so you can get out of the car and record everything you want."

Denise smiled excitedly and got her camera ready.

Mitchell parked the car by the side of the desolate road and let his wife jump out and run onto the verdant and bucolic countryside.

Mitchell turned around to look enviously at Stu, who was fast asleep in the back seat, holding on to his toy and getting the sleep that Mitchell desperately needed at that moment. Mitchell had been hoping that having four coffees would keep him awake during the drive, but as the minutes passed and the warm sun caressed his exhausted limbs, Mitchell couldn't help but join his son and fall asleep.

After hearing the door slam shut behind him, Mitchell jolted awake and realized that his wife had just gotten back in the car.

"Ok, ready? Let's keep going!" Mitchel asserted as he switched on the engine and continued the trajectory.

Forcing himself to speak and massaging his face with one hand to keep himself awake, Mitchell continued driving, hoping that his nap would prove effective in keeping him awake.

"Dad?" Stu asked from the backseat.

"Yes, son?"

"Where, Mom?"

"Right next to you!" Mitchell replied as he glanced up at the rearview mirror, only to discover to his great surprise and terror, that Stu was still the only person other than himself in the car.

Mitchell broke the car immediately, which created a loud screeching sound, and released a trail of smoke behind.

Mitchell turned his body around, and the small silhouette of his wife standing almost a mile behind them. Although she was very far away, her body posture made it abundantly clear that Mitchell would not be picking up a happy person once he returned to her position.

Mitchell reversed the car apprehensively and went over what he would say to assuage his wife's understandable irritation.

"How nice of you to come to get me," Denise smirked.

"I thought I heard the car door shut!"

"Yes, I realized I left it open and ran back to close it. If you want, I can show you; I got it all on tape, even you abandoning me..."

Once the entire family was back inside, the uncomfortable silence seemed to get progressively more prominent as the minutes passed until Mitchell heard his wife start to giggle in the backseat.

"What's so funny?" Mitchell asked.

Denise was looking down at the little screen on her camera with a grin that continued to grow the more she looked at it. Before she could answer, Denise let out an enthusiastic chuckle and finally put the camera away.

"I got everything on tape," Denise replied as she wiped tears from her eyes, "and my family is going to laugh so much when they hear all the names I called you as I filmed you slowly driving away and then suddenly stopping. This is exactly the type of footage I've been looking for."

TEJO

Anna had never been to Colombia, so Joe was very excited to introduce his new girlfriend to his home country.

Anna and Joe had been dating for almost two years, and they had booked tickets to fly together to Colombia, the country where Joe was born and where his extended family lived, a couple of months ago.

Joe had moved to Germany to live with Anna, so he was now excited to let Anna be immersed in someone else's culture.

"Oh, we have to play Tejo!" Joe exclaimed as he grabbed Anna's hand, who was sitting next to him on the plane to Colombia.

"What is Tejo?" Anna asked.

Joe loved how Anna was excited and curious about everything regarding Colombia. Although Joe had been born in Colombia and most of his family lived there, he had left at a very young age.

Then he pursued education and work in Europe, so the few things he actually knew about Colombia he wanted to share with Anna.

"Tejo is a national game in Colombia that is played by throwing little balls filled with gunpowder that you throw at targets on the floor. If you hit the targets, the gunpowder balls explode and make a loud sound!" Joe explained.

Anna looked skeptical.

"Is it deafening?" Anna asked.

"I don't know. I've never played it, but I've heard it's very fun!" Joe responded.

"Well, you know that I hate loud noises. I don't know if that's going to be right for me!"

"C'mon. You said you wanted to explore and experience as much of Colombia as possible. I've wanted to play this game for such a long time. I'm sure you'll like it!" Joe cried.

Anna smiled.

"Sure. I'd love to play!"

Joe clapped his hands in excitement.

***

Joe and Anna had been in Colombia for a week, and Anna had stayed true to her promise of immersing herself in as much culture and experiences as possible. However, it was the evening when they were due to play Tejo, and Anna was starting to feel nervous.

Right before going into the outdoor bar to play, Joe, Anna, and some of Joe's family gathered to have something to drink beforehand.

"You're just drinking lemonade?" Joe asked Anna.

"Yes! I don't feel alcohol and gunpowder are a wise combination!" Anna replied.

"Ok, but I wouldn't drink from that jug. It's pink and has clearly been passed around. I told you not to drink water here unless it's from a bottle!" Joe reminded Anna.

"I'll be fine!" Anna exclaimed as she served herself a large glass of the local pink lemonade.

Once everyone was finished with their drinks and snacks, they all went into the bar and began playing Tejo.

Almost immediately once, the first target exploded with a loud bang! Anna fled the scene and disappeared into the bathroom.

Joe went in to check on Anna but came back, explaining that she refused to come out.

Joe and his family played for twenty minutes and then called it a night.

Anna finally came out of the bathroom and looked pale.

"I'm so sorry! I had no idea the explosions would scare you so much!" Joe said.

"If explosions scared me, then I would've been terrified over what just happened to that bathroom!" Anna exclaimed.

"What?"

"Let's just say the real gunpowder in this place is that pink lemonade!" Anna exclaimed as she grabbed her stomach in pain and sprinted back into the bathroom.

THE TREEHOUSE

Joey and Michelle were excited about finally seeing each other again. The couple had been dating for a little under a year but had physically been together for only half of that time.

Joey and Michelle met in France, where Joey lived and where Michelle had spent the summer doing a language immersion course. Although Michelle had little time left in France before she had to return home to England, she ultimately accepted Joey's invitation to get coffee, which is where the mutual infatuation began.

Michelle ended up delaying her return flight home to spend a little more time with Joey, who became her boyfriend for a few days. She finally had to fly home and return to her studies.

Long distance was not easy on the relationship, and although they tried to make it work and to see each other as often as possible, things had been busy with Joey's work, and Michelle had been struggling with herself through her exams.

However, Joey and Michelle had recently decided that they needed to plan a short vacation for just the two of them before summer and were separately looking at intriguing destinations.

Despite Joey's aversion to leaving his comfort zone, he showed Michelle a village of treehouses in Spain where couples could stay in one of these treehouses and experience nature from above ground.

"You want to stay in one of these places?" Michelle asked incredulously.

"Yes, I think it could be fun!" Joey replied over the phone.

Michelle refrained from asking too many questions. She knew that if she pried too much, she would be liable to insert worrisome thoughts into Joey's mind that would make him apprehensive about going through with the short holiday.

"I want to show you that I am not as boring as you think I am. That I am capable of a little adventure!" Joey explained.

***

It was the week before Joey and Michelle were due to leave for their weekend away at the Spanish treehouse. Joey and Michelle were on the phone one day when Michelle happened to mention in passing that her mother was overly concerned about the cold weather that she saw would be taking place around the treehouse.

"She worries so much; she's a lot like you in that respect!" Michelle said over the phone.

There was silence on Joey's side.

"Joey?"

"Your mother's right. It's going to be freezing. I'm looking into it now; I hadn't even thought of that!" Joey responded.

Michelle signed. She had said too much.

"It's just a little cold. We'll, be fine!" Michelle asserted.

"I read that they don't have heating, and you know I have my big presentation right after we get back. I can't afford to get sick. I don't know if this trip is a good idea," Joey lamented.

Michelle managed to convince Joey not to cancel the trip, but she already knew that Joey's mind would be focused on the cold weather the entire time.

***

Just as she predicted, Joey complained about the cold the entire first hour they were there.

"If I get sick, I won't be able to work as hard on my presentation, and you know how important that presentation is!" Joey cried as he immersed himself in sweaters and jackets.

Michelle was too enchanted with the treehouse to care. She looked out at the wilderness surrounding her and smiled in contentment.

"Well, I'm feeling fine. I'm going to go downstairs to see the forest!" Michelle cried, paying no mind to Joey's concerns.

"Ok. It's colder outside than it is in here, at least. I'm staying here!"

Michelle put on her coat and walked over to the terrace to give the forest one last contemplative gaze. After about a minute of her looking at the bucolic scenery, she finally signed and returned inside.

"You know what. I understand what you're going through mentally. I know you're under a lot of pressure, so if you want to stay inside to ensure you don't get sick, I'll stay inside with you the entire trip," Michelle said.

Joey looked perplexed.

"Really?" he asked.

"Yes," Michelle replied with a smile.

The couple embraced and spent the entire weekend inside the treehouse, eating the food they had brought from home.

***

Once the weekend was over, Joey and Michelle got back in their car and began driving back home.

Joey had a triumphant smile on his face.

"You know what? I can't believe you did that for me. You literally stayed inside with me the entire time because of my silly fear of catching a cold," Joey began.

Michelle smiled from the passenger seat.

"You doing that for me showed me that I need to relax more and not be so worried about things. Especially if you are going to sacrifice what you want to do just to make me comfortable."

Michelle's smile grew, and suddenly, she started laughing.

"What's so funny?"

"I have to confess something," Michelle declared.

"What?"

"On the first day, just before I was about to go explore the forest, I looked outside, and I think I saw a wild boar roaming around. Well, that was enough to scare me into not wanting to leave the treehouse the entire weekend, not to mention that I didn't want you to know because then you were liable to make us drive home immediately!" Michelle confessed.

Joey laughed.

"A wild boar?" he asked.

"It might have been a deer, but I figured if you can have your irrational fears, so can I," Michelle asserted.

STUTTERING

James hadn't been on a date since he first moved to Australia. However, some of his work colleagues had set him up on a blind date that weekend, and he was very nervous.

James was born with a stutter that got worse during tense moments, such as the one he was experiencing now as he got ready to meet his date during dinner.

James confided in his roommate that he didn't understand why his colleagues set him up on a blind date if they were fully aware of his stutter and how bad it gets when he is nervous.

"Just be yourself, don't try to hide your stutter, and you will be fine!" Dominic, James's roommate, assured him.

***

Despite all the advice he received about not worrying about his stutter, James sat inside the coffee shop booth playing nervously with the napkin, which he had involuntarily torn to tiny shreds.

James chose a coffee shop he frequented and where he was friendly with the baristas to try and feel more comfortable.

"You feeling nervous?" Jane, one of James' barista friends, asked as she walked by his booth.

"Yes, very. I wish I felt as comfortable talking to dates as I do talking to you guys," James said.

James had only seen pictures of Stephanie, the girl he would be going on a date with, but he was able to recognize her once she walked inside immediately.

Stephanie looked even better in real life than in pictures, which assured James that he would be able to speak a single word fluently throughout their date.

"Hi," Stephanie said in a somewhat dismissive fashion as she sat down in the booth where James was waiting.

James tried to say hello back but nodded and presented Stephanie with a somewhat sheepish wave of the hand.

Throughout the date, Stephanie did most of the talking, and James just nodded or gave two or three-word answers.

At one point, Stephanie went to the bathroom, and James was left alone to wallow in disappointment.

"It's ok!" Jane assured James, "Just get out of your head, and you will be fine!"

James continued to speak to Jane until Stephanie returned.

At the end of the date, James and Stephanie went their separate ways, and James sprinted home, where he got under the bedsheets and went immediately to bed, feeling dejected.

The following morning, James woke up to a very long text from Stephanie that mentioned how refreshing she found it to be with someone who finally listened and didn't command every conversation.

Stephanie also mentioned that she saw how lovely James was to the barista and that she appreciated a man who chose his moments to talk and to listen.

James smiled and texted Stephanie enthusiastically.

If she wants a man who can listen, she is going to love me, James thought.

DOG JOGGING

Pete was on one of his usual morning jogs when he noticed the new waitress at the bar by his apartment.

He noticed her serving some of the elderly locals some coffee and was immediately stricken by her charming good looks and intoxicatingly lovely smile.

Pete stopped and propped his foot on a bench to tie his shoelace tighter, but he really just wanted to get a better look at the bar's new hire.

Once Pete arrived home from his morning exercise, he was greeted by his energetic Labrador retriever, Buckley, who leaped on Pete and ran excitedly around him in circles. Once Pete played with Buckley for a while, he told his roommate Joshua about the new waitress.

"So, are you gonna go talk to her?" Joshua asked.

"I don't know. Not yet, I think I want her to notice me first before I talk to her," Pete responded as he grabbed a drink of water from the fridge.

"Why? That makes no sense."

"I just want to see how she looks at me. If she looks at me like she's interested, then I will."

"That logic makes no sense," Joshua argued.

Buckley was running around the apartment as if Christmas were just around the corner.

"You still refuse to go jogging with Buckley? You know he has a lot more energy than you do," Joshua insisted.

Pete stopped himself before he provided Joshua with the same answer he always did as a thought occurred to him.

"You know what? That's not a bad idea! From now on, I'll go jogging with Buckley. Girls love dogs!" Pete exclaimed.

Joshua did not look impressed.

"Oh, that's great. You think it's fair that, finally, you decide to exercise your dog alongside you so you can impress a girl?"

"I'm sure Buckley doesn't mind what the reason is!" Pete retorted.

"Well, I think karma will take care of that mindset!" Joshua cried, "You don't even know how to jog alongside him! What if he sees another dog or something?"

Pete was too busy playing with Buckley to mind what his roommate was saying.

***

The following morning, Pete went jogging alongside Buckley by the beach. Pete slowed down his pace as he passed by the bar where the new waitress was serving coffee.

Pete jogged as close as he could to the bar so the waitress would see him and his dog.

There she was, serving some of the locals their breakfast when she noticed Buckley and Pete. The waitress smiled at Pete and looked adoringly at Buckley, who leapt in front of Pete at the wrong moment and caused him to fall over.

Pete fell on top of a table which went crashing onto the ground.

"Are you ok?!" the waitress cried as she ran over to Pete, who was on the ground being licked by Buckley, the culprit of the accident.

"I'm ok," Pete lied, ignoring the throbbing pain in his knee.

"Wait right here; I'll go get you some water!" the waitress cried as she shot up from the ground and ran into the bar.

Pete wanted to get up, but the pain wouldn't allow him, so he stayed on the floor and looked over at Buckley, who was brandishing what was unequivocally a satisfied smile.

"Yeah, ok, you're right. This is what I get!" Pete admitted.

CHAPTER 8

FIVE STORIES ABOUT THE GOLDEN YEARS

MASTERS

Orlando found it strange to be retired. He had spent all his life working, and although he had a great family and home to show for his work, he felt restless.

Orlando had eschewed anyone talking about his retirement leading up to the moment when he finally left his job of over 30 years, partly because of his reluctance to accept that it was happening.

Melinda, Orlando's wife, had spent months leading up to her husband's retirement sending him information on how to handle retirement gracefully and productively, to no avail.

Now that Orlando was no longer an employee and had a seemingly endless amount of free time, he wondered if his wife resented him for not having looked at all the information she had tried to provide him previously.

As the weeks and months passed, Orlando felt that perhaps his retirement would require him to forge a new kind of relationship with his wife, who he feared was unimpressed with how he was managing his spare time.

Orlando spent a lot of time at home just reading the paper and watching TV, which made him feel incredibly unproductive, but he was struggling to find ways to communicate and reconnect with his wife of two decades.

One afternoon, as Orlando was sitting watching TV by himself, worrying about the tension between him and his wife, Melinda called him into the kitchen for a talk.

"Yes?" Orlando asked as he sat down on the kitchen table.

"I know you've been frustrated and unsure of what to do with your time, so I went ahead and got this for you!" Melinda explained as she handed her husband a file filled with papers about a Master's degree course at a University near where they lived.

After perusing the documents, Orlando became visibly excited.

"This is amazing! I would love to take this course. You remembered talking about this years ago?" Orlando asked to which Melinda nodded proudly.

The couple embraced.

"You are amazing. Thank you so much for doing this. I was so worried about us. Thank you!" Orlando said.

Melinda smiled, but it was clear that something else was on her mind.

"What is it?" Orlando asked.

"Nothing!" Melinda replied, knowing she was a terrible liar.

Orlando smiled, pleading for his wife to divulge the truth.

"Ok, fine. I do want what's best for you, and I did this because I know that it would make you happy…" Melinda began.

"But…?" Orlando asked.

"But if I have to spend yet another week seeing you every second of every day from the moment I wake up to the moment I go to bed; I'm gonna go crazy!" Melinda cried, "We aren't used to this, and I think we both need a break!"

Orlando burst out laughing, which calmed Melinda's nerves about her confession.

"I understand," Orlando assured his wife as he pulled her in and kissed her on the forehead.

Things were good again.

DOGSITTING

When Carlos's friends canceled last minute on their availability to dog sit for him while he went on a two-week vacation with his girlfriend, Carlos became anxious about whether he could go on the holiday at all.

"Is there no one that can look after Elvis?" Joanne, Carlos's girlfriend, asked worriedly.

"No one else," Carlos replied, concerned that they were due to leave in three days, but they now had no idea what to do with their chocolate Labrador retriever, Elvis.

"What about your parents?" Joanne asked.

"My dad hates dogs; I don't think he'll want to do it."

"I don't think we have any other option. It wouldn't hurt to ask. Otherwise, we have to cancel our trip!" Joanne insisted.

As usual, Joanne was right.

Frank, Carlos's father, was not the warmest and most amiable of people, which made Carlos hesitant about asking him to take care of their dog, but as Joanne said, there were no other options.

When Carlos called, his mother, Silvia, picked up, she said she would ask Carlos's dad about dogsitting and called right back.

Carlos and Joanne waited for the call nervously. Luckily, Silvia called right back and said that Frank was willing, but only for a week and not two.

Not having any options left, Carlos and Joanne agreed to come back a week early.

***

After five days of enjoying their much-needed holiday, Carlos and Joanne decided to call home to check up on Elvis and see how the dog sitting was going.

As usual, Silvia picked up the phone.

"Hey, Mom, I just wanted to let you know that we are getting our stuff ready to head back home.

You can tell Dad that his time dealing with a dog is almost over," Carlos informed his mother over the phone.

"Well, actually, Frank wanted me to tell you that he is feeling a little sick and that he doesn't want to get your or Joanne sick, so you should stay on your holiday another week and enjoy your time together," Silvia explained to her son.

"What?" Carlos asked.

There was a brief silence during which Silvia sounded like she was speaking closer to the phone, "To be completely honest, sweetheart, your father has not stopped playing with Elvis since he got here. He instantly fell in love with him, and now they are best buds. He will never admit it, but I thought you should know the truth."

Carlos laughed and explained the truth to Joanne.

Silvia began talking in her normal voice again, which meant that Frank was nearby, "So yeah, if you want to stay an extra week while Frank recovers, that's completely fine!"

Carlos heard his father scream something in the background.

"Sorry, your dad says two extra weeks!" Silvia added.

The Application

Mark had been retired for a year and felt that now was the time to begin looking at postgraduate courses. His entire working life, he had wanted to go back to university but had been too busy to do so.

Now, with his newfound freedom, Mark was ready to start learning again.

Mark had unfortunately lost touch with his son over the past few years, primarily because of how busy both of them were with their jobs. However, Mark also wanted to use the spare time he now had on his hands to reconnect with his only son, Jared.

Unsure of how to reach out to Jared in the best way, Mark came up with an ingenious plan that would hopefully break the ice in an amicable and comedic way.

Jared had been a postgraduate business teacher for several years and had recently begun teaching artificial intelligence to young up-and-coming business people, a subject that Mark was also passionate about.

As a joke, Mark sent an email to his son with an application to start taking his artificial intelligence course as one of Jared's students.

This will surely make him laugh, Mark thought. However, as the day progressed, Mark began to worry that his son would not find it funny and that he would have preferred a different method of reconnecting.

Fortunately, the very next morning, Mark received an email from the university saying that his application had been sent in and that he would be considered and be sent a reply in the coming weeks.

Mark was astonished.

Jared must have sent in my application, Mark reasoned.

Mark wondered if his son had misunderstood the joke and thought that Mark had simply been using his son to secure his place in the postgraduate program.

Worrying that there had been a misunderstanding, Mark finally called his son.

Once Jared answered, Mark explained that he had sent in the application as a joke and that he was sorry if Jared had taken it literally and thought that Mark was just trying to take advantage of his son's position at the university.

"Oh no, don't worry, I got the joke completely, Dad," Jared responded with a satisfied chuckle.

"Good. And you still want me in the university?" Mark asked.

"Yes, so I can exact vengeance on you for all the times you had to explain every little math problem I had for homework in excruciatingly long and intricate detail to the point where I became terrified of asking you for help with my assignments," Jared confessed.

Mark laughed and rejoiced that his son hadn't lost his sense of humor, one of the personality traits that he and Jared had shared for many years when they were younger.

THE TRIP

Conan and Sonia had been wanting to go on a holiday for several years but had never made the time to actually go ahead and plan an extended vacation for the two of them. Now that Conan was officially retired, the married couple decided to finally prepare for the trip they had been dreaming of for the last decade.

Conan thought it would take him a few days to find the right destination, but both he and Sonia agreed that there would be no better choice than Hawaii.

"The good thing is, this is my first month of retirement. I am still excited and full of energy. I am not going to be one of those guys who is tired of going on holiday. This is going to be the most amazing holiday ever! No more sleepless nights, no more working myself to the point where I become sick of a boss who underappreciates me! This is going to be the best holiday of our lives!" Conan cried as he embraced his wife Sonia, who was equally excited.

The couple spent the week before the flight getting everything ready for the trip. The five days they were together in the house without having any other commitments was strange.

As excited as they were about the trip, there seemed to be nothing else to talk about, and since they were forced to stay up late to find accommodation, transport, and someone to housesit, they were too exhausted to speak.

When the day finally came for them to depart, Conan and Sonia couldn't be happier.

The flight to Hawaii was long, and unfortunately, due to a crying baby sitting next to them, they were unable to get a wink of sleep the entire time they were on the plane.

Once they were safely at the hotel, Conan and Sonia received a comprehensive itinerary from the concierge with activities for all of the five days they would be staying there.

"That is a lot of activities!" Sonia said, "And all of them so early!"

"Great," Conan cried.

Conan and Sonia ran to their bedrooms to freshen up and get ready to go to the downstairs hotel restaurant for dinner. However, once showering presented itself to be too demanding a task for the weary travelers, Conan and Sonia decided to skip dinner and go to bed early instead.

Unfortunately, the couple's exhaustion did not wear off that night. Conan and Sonia slept the entire next day, and as for the following days, Conan and Sonia attended only one activity each day and slept through the whole thing.

Upon returning home, Conan and Sonia couldn't help but laugh at the fact that they had just paid for two very expensive plane tickets to get the sleep they had been missing for several years in a beautiful and exotic location.

"Well, at least now we're full of energy to talk and get to know each other again in this new phase of our relationship!" Sonia said as she lifted a glass of champagne in her kitchen.

"Here's to retirement and Hawaii, the best sleep destination in the world!" Conan exclaimed as he cheered his wife.

CURLING

Serge was excited about meeting his daughter's new boyfriend, James. The last couple of boyfriends his daughter Florence had brought to the winter chalet to join the family for a week of skiing had been far from what he imagined and hoped for Florence.

However, from what he had heard, Florence was finally bringing home an erudite and professionally successful young man who treated her right and made her happy.

Serge had never found any common ground with the previous contenders, which made for uncomfortable moments whenever he was left alone with them. This time, however, Serge was looking forward to speaking to someone who understood business the way James surely would, given his senior position at a large multinational company. Moreover, being the only man in the family during these yearly reunions could be tiresome at times.

"Apparently, he hasn't skied in a very long time, but he used to be quite good," Miriam, Serge's wife, and Florence's mother, explained as she went around the little chalet cleaning and getting everything ready for the happiness which would be arriving in a few hours.

"Oh well, I'll be glad to teach him how it's done!" Serge boasted as he took a sip of his coffee and read the paper.

"Let's just hope that the bad weather doesn't cause the slopes to close. If they close, we'll need to think of something to do tomorrow," Miriam added.

Serge glanced out the window and shrugged his shoulders assuredly, "The slopes will be fine, don't worry!"

Once Florence and James arrived, Serge immediately approved of his daughter's amiable and presentable boyfriend. It did not take Serge long to urge James to sit down next to him so they could talk business while Miriam and Florence looked on with contended smiles, especially when they noticed Serge perk up with joy when James began asking his father-in-law advice on how to manage difficult managerial situations.

"Well, the important thing is to understand if the situation can be improved or not. If it can be improved, improve it; if not, turn the fault or inconvenience into strength and market it as such to the public," Serge explained as James listened intently.

The conversation was interrupted by Miriam, who announced that dinner was ready and that, unfortunately, the ski slopes would be closed tomorrow due to bad weather.

"So what will we do? Stay in and play cards?" Florence asked.

"No! Surely we can find something fun to do outside," Serge responded, knowing that as charming as the chalet was, it was too small a space to spend the entire day inside.

"Yes, I looked into the activities around town, and I saw that we can go curling!" Miriam announced.

"Curling?" Florence asked, "The sport with the broom on ice?"

Miriam nodded excitedly.

"Sounds fun!" James exclaimed.

Serge had never gone curling and had been looking forward to mentoring James on how to ski, considering Serge had long prided himself on his skiing abilities, so he was trepidatious about trying it out but decided to be optimistic when noticing how excited everyone else was about the idea.

"Sure does!" Serge added.

***

Once everyone had their ice skates on and had listened to the curling instructor's explanation of how to play the game, James went first.

Everyone looked on expectantly to get an idea of what to do or perhaps what not to do if James fumbled.

James executed the game perfectly, which gave way to rapturous applause from Florence and Miriam.

Next up was Florence, who did just as good as James and received loud applause too from everyone, including the instructor, who looked at Serge to indicate that it was his turn.

"What about you, sweetheart?" Serge asked, looking back at his wife, who explained that because of her knee, she would rather not partake but that she would watch enthusiastically.

"Oh, c'mon! There's nothing to it; surely, this won't affect your knee. Watch!" Serge cried as he prepared to have his go at curling.

Serge kneeled on the ice like everyone else and went about executing the exercise as the previous two contestants had but failed terribly by slipping and falling on his butt immediately.

The instructor allowed Serge to try a few times again, but every time Serge went about throwing the curling stone across the ice, he would slip and fall on his behind.

Serge tried to mask his embarrassment but immediately began dreading the moment when it was his turn. After going a second time and continuing to slip, Serge decided to take control of the situation.

"Ok, everyone, watch this!" Serge cried as he kneeled on the ice, propelled himself forward, and then fell onto the ice, only this on purpose and with conviction!

The awkward and comical-looking strategy actually worked to his advantage as the curling stone he launched forward went much farther than the others. Everyone was shocked, and Serge was brandishing a smug smile, even though his behind was wetter than anyone else.

Serge continued using his strategy until the very end and eventually won the entire game.

James walked up to Serge and congratulated him.

"You see, James, it's like I told you, if it can't be improved, then use the problem to your advantage!" Serge announced.

CHAPTER 9

FIVE FUNNY AND UPLIFTING STORIES

PHOTO OPPORTUNITY

Paola was irate. She had traveled all the way to Italy with her friends and had brought her brand new camera to take plenty of pictures to show to her family back home, but had forgotten to charge the battery and therefore hadn't been able to take a single photo during her very long outing with her friends.

The first thing Paola did once she and her friends finally arrived back at the hotel was charge her camera and close her bedroom door so she could sulk uninterruptedly.

During dinner, Paola was not as talkative as she usually was because of how disappointed she was in herself for not having had the camera ready to capture the amazing sights she and her friends had witnessed earlier that day.

"Well, then bring your camera out tonight when we go for drinks by the hotel!" Liliana suggested.

"Oh, why? So I can take pictures of the cocktail menu? It doesn't matter," Paola replied dejectedly.

"C'mon! You don't know what you will see; that's the magic of places like this!" Liliana insisted, to which Paola finally acquiesced and agreed to bring the fully-charged camera.

***

As the excitable group of ladies walked through the lively streets of Rome, Liliana pointed to the large square to their left that was full of street performers, musicians, and pigeons, "Paola, take a picture of the square!"

"Nah, it's ok. We have artists back home, too," Paola replied.

Liliana seized Paola's camera from her and ordered her to go into the square so Liliana could take a picture of her and the lively nightlife.

Overwhelmed by her friend's insistence, Paola ambled over to the square and stood in the middle of the bustling scene.

"What do I do?" Paola cried.

"Just stand there; the backdrop is amazing!" Liliana responded.

Paola wasn't as enthusiastic about the photograph as her amazing friend envisioned but presented a forced smile for the camera.

"Look excited!" Liliana cried.

"How?!" Paola argued.

"Extend your arms!"

Slightly hesitant, Paola extended her arms as if she were about to embrace an elephant. Almost immediately after, a seemingly endless surge of pigeons flew and landed upon Paola's outstretched arms and shoulders.

Despite her desire to shriek, Paola remained quiet so as not to scare the birds away.

"That's perfect!" Liliana insisted as she took several pictures.

Paola remained quiet but was smiling from ear to ear.

Liliana kept taking pictures, and after a minute of doing so, it seemed as though she was never going to stop.

"Enough?" Paola exclaimed; at this point, she looked more like a scarecrow than an actual person.

"Not yet! These are great!"

Finally, Liliana put the camera down. Paola lowered her arms and sprinted towards Liliana.

"These pictures are great!" Liliana said excitedly as she watched Paola approach her but then kept running past her toward the hotel.

"Where are you going?!" Liliana exclaimed.

"To the hotel!" Paola responded without turning around.

"Why?!"

"Because the pigeons pooped all over me!" Paola responded before she disappeared into the crowd.

Liliana shot her eyes at the camera, perused the photographs she had taken, and laughed as she noticed Paola's horrified expression as the pigeons pooped all over her arms.

"Well, these are definitely better than any building or landscape!" Liliana exclaimed as she and the rest of the ladies laughed hysterically.

DRIVING LESSONS

Donnie had been attracted to Camilla for a very long time, which is why he was ecstatic to know that she would be coming to his BBQ in a few days. He was even more excited about the fact that he would be spending some alone time with her since she didn't know how to drive yet, despite being in her early 20s like Donnie. Donnie would have to pick her up from her apartment before anyone else arrived.

It was the day before the BBQ, and Donnie kept fantasizing about the conversations they would have in the car as Donnie picked her up. He imagined her being impressed by his driving skills, which were not necessarily that impressive but would surely seem advanced to someone who had never driven a car before.

Although Camilla did not know how to drive, Donnie was still intimidated by her achievements. Camilla was already working as a senior manager at a prestigious multinational and therefore lived in a very luxurious apartment, one that Donnie would never be able to afford with his current salary.

Furthermore, Donnie also felt intimidated by Camilla's dating record. Her past two boyfriends owned their own businesses and had enough money to take her traveling around the world and accommodate her in the fanciest hotels.

I better do a good job at driving her around, Donnie reasoned.

***

It was an hour before his BBQ was due to start, so Donnie wrote Camilla that he was on his way to pick her up and got into his car.

Donnie had spent an hour cleaning and making sure his car was as impeccable and presentable as he could possibly make it.

Once he arrived at Camilla's' apartment, he felt his heartbeat accelerate considerably. Not long after, Camilla walked outside. She was dressed in a red top and ripped blue jeans. She had just come back from holiday, so her skin was a darker tone than normal, which perfectly complemented her green eyes, freckles, and blonde hair.

Donnie was outside waiting and holding the door open for her, which made him feel a little foolish, but he felt it was better than simply waiting inside the car.

"Thank you so much!" Camilla thanked Donnie, and she slid into the passenger seat.

Donnie sprinted back to the driver's seat and started driving back home.

***

Donnie and Camilla had been on the road for about ten minutes when Camilla informed Donnie that the people coming to the BBQ were delayed by almost an hour because of some problem with the train they were all taking.

"Almost an hour?" Donnie asked.

"That's what they wrote to me!" Camilla confirmed.

Donnie was nervous about spending so much alone time with Camilla but then thought of a great way to use the time.

"I have an idea. Why don't I give you a short driving lesson when we get home?" Donnie asked, without any idea of how Camilla would react to this proposition.

"Oh no!" Camilla cried, "I am terrible. I would kill both of us instantly!"

Somehow, this response made Donnie feel better because it allowed him to assuage Camilla's concerns with his expertise.

"No, you won't kill anyone; I will be right there with you. This is a ghost town. There will be nobody around. We can just go very slow around the block, which is how I learned to drive too, pretty much," Donnie insisted.

Camilla looked very hesitant, but after a little more convincing, she finally accepted Donnie to give her a short elementary driving lesson.

"Perfect!" Donnie rejoiced as he slightly accelerated the car to get home as quickly as possible so he could give Camilla a driving lesson she hopefully would never forget.

***

Once Camilla's things were inside Donnie's apartment and she was back inside the car, ready for her lesson, Donnie ignited the engine and looked at Camilla with a comforting smile.

"You're going to be ok, trust me. First, you'll just watch me drive a circle around the block, and then you'll do the same with me right next to you," Donnie explained.

Camilla presented a sheepish smile, which Donnie immediately recognized as trepidation.

"If you really don't want to do it, then we don't have to!" Donnie added.

"Maybe we shouldn't. This is a nice car, and I wouldn't want to start the BBQ by destroying it…" Camilla responded.

Donnie realized how much he wanted to conduct this lesson and how dejected he would feel if he didn't get to go through with it.

"Are you sure?" Donnie asked, hoping she would reconsider and go through with the driving lesson.

Camilla remained silent for almost a minute as she considered her options and finally agreed to let Donnie teach her.

"Awesome!" Donnie rejoiced.

***

Donnie drove around the block a couple of times and did it slow enough for him to explain what he was doing as he was doing it so Camilla could have a vivid picture of how to go about replicating his maneuvers.

Once Donnie parked the car a few blocks away from his apartment, he told Camilla it was finally her turn to drive around.

"I don't know; I feel nervous. These kinds of things make me anxious," Camilla explained as she stared at her lap.

Suddenly, Donnie felt guilty for what he was doing and decided he had already spent enough quality time with Camilla and that there was no point making her uncomfortable by doing something she did not feel prepared to do.

"That is absolutely fine; let's go home, yeah?" Donnie asked, to which Camilla replied with a sullen and silent nod.

As Donnie drove back to his apartment, he knew he needed to do something to cheer Camilla up, so he put on loud pop music, which seemed to lift her spirit slightly.

"I'm sorry, I'm so scared. I just need to be braver, I guess..." Camilla said.

"Don't be silly; you just need to stop thinking about it and have some fun!" Donnie retorted as he spun the wheel from side to side in a forceful manner which made Camilla laugh.

"My dad used to do the same when the road was empty just to make my sister, and I laugh!" Camilla explained, which prompted Donnie to do the same thing again, only that this time he almost hit an oncoming car that was turning from the right.

Donnie swerved to the right and stopped the car on top of the pavement, where there were luckily no pedestrians, and the car he almost hit stopped too.

Oh no, Donnie thought.

Donnie saw a terrifyingly tall man leap out of his car and begin walking toward Donnie.

"Stay in the car!" Donnie told Camilla as he immediately got out of the car himself and walked toward the oncoming heavily tattooed man.

"What do you think you're doing? Are you drunk, stupid, or both?!" the man demanded furiously.

"I'm so sorry; I am driving my sister home because she is feeling really sick!" Donnie explained, "She suffers from a medical condition, and we left the medicine at home. I just wanted to make sure you are OK! Are you OK, sir?" Donnie asked.

The man towering over Donnie looked bewildered. He looked at Donnie's car and noticed Camilla looking severely terrified.

"Oh, I see her. She doesn't look well at all. I'm sorry, please go! Go!" the man responded.

Donnie thanked the stranger and raced back to his car. Donnie ignited the engine, drove past the other parked car, and finally made it home.

I am such an idiot, Donnie thought as he parked the car in front of his apartment; *Camilla must be terrified now.*

"That was SO brave!" Camilla exclaimed.

"Really?" Donnie asked.

"Yes!" Camilla replied with gleaming eyes, "I would *never* have been able to confront someone that way. I am *really* impressed!"

Donnie's spirits lifted. The two laughed about the incident before Donnie suggested that he should carry her into the apartment just in case the man was watching from somewhere.

"You know what? I think that's a great idea!" Camilla responded.

Donnie got out of the car and carried Camilla into the apartment in his arms.

"If I would've known this was part of the driving lesson experience, I wouldn't have been so reluctant!" Camilla said as she looked at Donnie inches away from his face and her arms wrapped around him.

"If I would've known, I would have offered much sooner," Donnie responded with a satisfied smile.

COOL AUNT

Martina thoroughly enjoyed and was proud to know that she was considered the cool aunt by her nephew Jared, her sister's eight-year-old boy.

Martina, her sister Carmen, Carmen's husband Oscar, and Jared were taking a short day trip together to a neighboring town to have ice cream together at a new place that everyone was raving about as having the best ice cream.

The three family members got into Carmen's car, with Jared carrying his favorite pillow with him.

"Why are you bringing your Disney pillow with you, J?" Martina asked as she scootched more to the right to make room for Jared and his pillow in the backseat.

"It helps me sleep," Jared responded as she showed his aunt the pillow and explained how he got it at Disneyland and that nobody in his school had one like it.

"He didn't sleep well last night. He was very excited about the ice cream," Carmen explained.

"And not to mention to see his favorite aunt!" Oscar added.

Martina listened intently to her nephew talk about the pillow until he fell asleep with his head resting on it against the window.

The drive to the nearby town took about an hour and a half; Jared was asleep for the entire trip until he heard the much-desired sound of the car engine switching off.

"Are we there, Auntie?!" Jared asked enthusiastically.

"Yes, we are!" Martina responded.

The entire family got out of the car and made their way to the ice cream shop.

The town was filled with families. By looking at the way Jared was holding Martina's hand the entire time, one would have surmised that Jared was Martina's son as opposed to his nephew.

Once they arrived at the ice cream shop, Martina and Jared went up first.

"What would you like, J?" Martina asked her nephew, who was gleaming at all the different available flavors in dazed euphoria.

As Jared failed to answer due to his state of shock, Martina began to tell the vendor what flavor she wanted.

"No, wait! I was supposed to go first!" Jared protested as he pulled on his aunt's brand-new summer dress.

"Ok, ok. I just wanted to give you some time to decide. What do you want?" Martina inquired yet again. Still, there was no reply.

"J, what do you want?" Martina repeated.

"I don't know!" Jared responded frustratedly.

"Ok. Well, in that case, please get me two scoops of—" Martina began before she felt a small yet insistent hand pull on her new dress even more forcibly than last time.

"Auntie, I haven't ordered yet!" Jared declared as if some great injustice was trying to befall him.

"I've asked you three times now, J. What kind of ice cream do you want?"

Jared finally looked ready to answer as he brandished a satisfied smile.

"All of them!"

Martina looked bemused.

"You can't have all of them, J. You have to pick a maximum of three," Martina explained, getting slightly impatient.

"Why can't I have all of them?" Jared asked.

"Because you won't be able to eat them all, and they won't serve it."

Jared looked at the vendor in desperation.

"Could I have all the flavors?" Jared asked the vendor.

"Technically… yes," the vendor replied, finding Jared amusing.

"Jared. I told you no, now pick up to three flavors," Martina ordered.

"I want ALL of them!" Jared protested as he pulled on his aunt's dress so strongly that she feared the people around her would soon be able to see more of her than she intended.

"I said NO, and if you don't like it, then you don't get ANY ice cream!" Martina cried frustratedly.

Everyone, including Martina herself, looked shocked at this outburst. Without saying a word or making a sound, Jared sprinted away from his aunt and from the ice cream shop as if frightened by the apparition of a ghost.

***

The walk back to the car after an excruciatingly awkward afternoon felt endless.

"Don't worry, Martina. You are still his favorite aunt—favorite family member in general, and that includes immediate family too, I think," Carlos said as he walked back to the car with Martina as Jared walked ahead holding hands with his mother.

"I just feel awful. I've never spoken like that to any child, and I can't believe it happened to him. I think I've ruined my chances of him ever looking at me the same way again," Martina lamented.

Carlos scoffed, "Before you know it, he will have forgotten about the whole thing, as will you. Don't force it, just be there for him when he needs a shoulder to lean on, and it will be like nothing ever happened."

As much as Martina wanted to believe her brother-in-law's words, she was inundated with guilt. Martina wanted children of her own, and she had always viewed her relationship with Jared as a sign that she was ready to be a mother—and a great one at that, which meant that she was now starting to doubt her own motherly abilities.

Even Martina knew that she was letting her mind play tricks on her and make a bad situation seem worse than it really was. Still, she couldn't help but wonder if perhaps she had severed one of the relationships she valued most in her life as she saw Jared walking ahead of her instead of happily by her side like most times.

***

Martina sat in the backseat of the car next to Jared as she had on the way to the ice cream shop. Jared looked at Martina apprehensively, but Martina stopped herself from apologizing because she had already done so too many times.

Jared's eyes eventually closed, and his head began swaying side to side.

Martina furtively reached over past Jared and made sure his favorite pillow was at the right angle for him to rest his head on it and fall asleep as they reached home. However, instead of falling asleep on the pillow, Jared turned his head the other way and fell asleep on Martina's shoulder.

Although this was potentially an involuntary move—or perhaps, not—Martina felt rejuvenated as a smile bloomed on her face.

After a few minutes, Carmen turned around from the passenger seat and looked contently at her sister.

"Are you crying?" Carmen asked incredulously.

Martina nodded, although her face was red and her eyes were scrunched together.

"It looks like you are," Carmen insisted.

"I'm laughing," Martina whispered, trying not to wake up Jared.

"Why?" Carmen asked.

"Because he is drooling all over my shoulder!" Martina responded as she failed to stifle a chuckle that luckily didn't wake up Jared, "And I don't mind at all. I'm just glad I'm a better alternative than his favorite pillow."

MANGO SLICES

Jimmy felt overwhelmed at the prospect of being alone in a car with his uncle Leo and cousin Enrique. These two men were potentially the biggest pranksters and loudmouths of the entire family, and whenever they were together, there was no saying what kind of chaos would ensue.

Since Jimmy lived abroad with his parents and rarely visited Colombia, the country he was born in, except for Christmas and summer holidays when there was no school, Jimmy had very little exposure to his extended family.

However, this particular Christmas, the entire family had gathered in a summer villa to celebrate the holidays together, including Jimmy and his parents, who flew from Europe to participate in the festivities.

Jimmy found it hard to keep up with the conversations since his Spanish was not as good as everyone else's, and he was accustomed to a more tranquil environment, which greatly contrasted the faced pace and sometimes chaotic ambiance that was so integral to any family reunion in Colombia.

However, on this particular occasion, Jimmy was in a van with his uncle Leo and older cousin Enrique since both these men were tasked with bringing home some more beer, and out of the blue, Leo had insisted that Jimmy join them so that Jimmy could break out of his shell and learn to speak Spanish with the locals.

The entire car ride to the supermarket, Leo and Enrique asked Jimmy questions about Europe in Spanish, and Jimmy struggled to provide sensical answers. Although the supermarket was only a few blocks away from the summer house where everyone was staying, the few minutes that Jared spent in the van with his two cousins felt endless.

Leo and Enrique continued being boisterous and jovial as they purchased copious amounts of beer, none of which Jimmy would be able to have due to him being underage.

Once all three family members and all three six-packs of beer were safely loaded into the car, Leo caught something out of the corner of his eye that filled him with excitement. Leo pointed to the street and brought Enrique and Jimmy's attention to a fruit vendor on the street who was selling mango slices in a plastic cup.

Jimmy asked what was so special about those mango slices, and Leo explained that they were unlike anything else Jimmy had ever tasted when it came to fruit. Leo went on to elucidate Jimmy on the gastronomic wonder that was ripe mango slices covered in salt, pepper, and spicy sauce.

Enrique laughed as he noticed Jimmy cringe at the idea of fruit being anything other than sweet.

After further elaboration on the matter, Leo told Jimmy that he had to try it or at least buy two cups for Leo and Enrique.

Wanting to show his uncle and cousin that he was capable of handling a simple street transaction, such as the purchase of exotic fruit, Jimmy accepted. After being handed the money, Jimmy lept out of the van and sprinted to the street vendor.

At first, Jimmy struggled more than he imagined he would, but to his surprise and great elation, he found out that the street vendor spoke almost perfect English.

"How many mango slices would you like?" the street vendor, who identified himself as Hector, asked Jimmy.

"Just two, please," Jimmy responded, excited at the prospect of his uncle and cousin seeing him complete the transaction so quickly and with so much ease without knowing that he was communicating in English the entire time.

"Perfect!" Hector replied as he filled up two plastic cups with mango slices. Jimmy extended his hands to receive his order but wasn't handed the cups just yet.

"I'm sorry, I forgot to ask. Did you want small, medium, or large?" Hector asked.

Not knowing the answer, since the snack was not for him, Jimmy asked Hector to wait as he returned to the van to ask Leo and Enrique what size cup they wanted.

Once he had the answer he needed, Jimmy walked back to Hector and asked for two large cups of mango slices.

"Perfect!" Hector replied but still refrained from handing Jimmy the cups he was already holding in his hands.

"Did they want the mango slices with salt and pepper and spicy sauce?" Hector asked.

Jimmy knew Leo had explained the treats as slices of mango covered in spices, but he was unsure if he specifically wanted his order to be prepared as such. It would be hard to remove salt, pepper, and spicy sauce if either Leo or Enrique wanted the slices without any seasoning.

Jimmy once again sprinted to the van and asked before returning to Hector and telling him that both cups should have salt and pepper but very little spicy sauce.

Hector smiled and proceeded to complete the order.

"Do they want a fork and knife or not?" Hector asked.

Jimmy sighed. He had no idea.

After yet another quick run to the van, Jimmy returned and confirmed that he did indeed need two sets of cutleries.

Finally, Jimmy handed Hector the money his uncle Leo had given him for the order and relished at the prospect of no longer having to be the intermediary between Hector and his uncle and cousin.

"Oh, sorry. Do you have smaller bills?" Hector asked Jimmy.

Jimmy had no bills. The money he had was from his uncle Leo.

Jimmy didn't even excuse himself this time.

A dejected and tired Jimmy walked over to the van and asked his smiling family members if they had smaller bills.

"How small does he want?" Enrique asked with a red face and gleaming eyes.

Jimmy had enough. "Give me all the small bills you have!" Jimmy cried.

Upon hearing this outburst, Leo and Enrique could no longer contain their laughter and ended up almost crying from their gasps of hilarity.

**

The entire ride home, Jimmy listened to his uncle and cousin talk about how they had planned the whole thing with Hector, which meant that they knew that Hector would have had endless questions for Jimmy and that this would have frustrated Jimmy.

Once the van arrived at the summer house, Jimmy walked out feeling sheepish and went straight to the bedroom. A few moments later, his mother, Marie, stepped inside.

"What's wrong, sweetheart?" Marie asked as she stroked her son's head, who was resting on the bed staring at the white ceiling.

"They played a prank on me. They wanted Hector to ask me a million questions and drive me crazy."

Marie looked befuddled.

"That's not true. They just came in and explained the whole thing. Leo and Enrique are friends with Hector, and they know that his English is perfect, which is why they asked you to get some mango slices so that you would be able to speak English with Hector and feel more confident. They were trying to make you feel good.

As Jimmy recalled the conversation he overheard from the backseat of the car after the mango incident, he realized that he had misheard and that what his mother was saying was true.

"Oh, I misunderstood. They really did that just to make me feel good?" Jimmy asked.

Marie nodded.

Jimmy felt a lot better.

"But why were they laughing so much, then?" Jimmy demanded.

"Because they forgot how ineffective Hector is when trying to sell mango slices and that he asks every question individually as opposed to just once. They laughed because they have been in your situation too!" Marie explained.

"Oh, I see," Jimmy replied as he, too, began laughing as he comprehended the reality of the situation.

CARNIVAL

Kyle had just moved to Germany to live with his girlfriend, Emilia. Kyle had never lived in Germany and therefore spoke no Germany or knew nothing of the family customs or traditions, which was why he was so nervous about attending what Emilia described to him as the yearly carnival celebration, an event dedicated to bidding winter farewell and usher forward spring.

"In reality, it's just an excuse to drink a lot of beer and dance!" Emilia explained as she attempted to assuage Kyles's concerns that the family would find him boring since he would be unable to communicate or understand the stand-up comedy event that would be taking place at the carnival.

"I know. I just want to make a good impression, and I fear that when they see me just sitting there not talking to anyone, they're going to think I'm anti-social!" Kyle explained as he got ready for the evening.

"Everyone knows that you don't speak German, and just because my family is a little crazy and likes to party, it doesn't mean that they won't respect what you are going through with the move to come live with me," Emilia insisted. Kyle was still trepidatious.

"I just wish I could meet them in different circumstances," Kyle added.

"Do you want me to hold your hand and take you there?" Emilia asked mockingly.

***

As predicted, Kyle felt very self-conscious about the fact that he couldn't speak to anyone. During the stand-up comedy routine, he smiled and pretended to know what was going on, which was the strategy he implemented whenever people got on stage and talked endlessly in German about things that clearly excited everyone in the prodigious dining hall.

As the night progressed, Kyle drank a lot to loosen up. He mostly accepted drinks from some of Emilia's family members and friends of the family, and, at one point in the night, just strangers, it seemed.

It did not take long for Kyle to feel unable to walk, which unfortunately did not stop him from continuing to consume copious amounts of alcohol.

After taking one last shot of Jägermeister with a group of very large German men, Kyle began jumping around the dining hall and screaming nonsensical German words, much to Emilia's horror.

***

The next morning, Kyle woke up with what felt like a life-threatening headache and stomach ache. After paying the necessary visits to the bathroom, Kyle collapsed on the living room sofa where Emilia was waiting for him with a judgmental face.

"I know, I know. I made a fool of myself in front of your family. I ruined my chances of anyone liking me. I'll just move back home. It's fine," Kyle said as he massaged his throbbing forehead.

"Unbelievable," Emilia protested, clearly dissatisfied.

"Look, I'm sorry ok?" Kyle insisted, his eyes firmly shut and his mind thinking of only water and coffee but feeling too weak to go get either, "I will personally apologize to everyone who was there."

"That's not the problem!" Emilia cried.

"What is it then?" Kyle inquired.

"They LOVED you. They say you are just as crazy as them, and they can't wait to invite you to their private little after-carnival party in their beer garden!"

Kyle smiled, "Really?"

"Yes, really!" Emilia responded.

Kyle shot his arms up joyfully, "That makes me happy!"

Emilia was tapping her foot furiously, "They never invited me to their after-carnival party!"

Kyle smiled, "Do you want me to take your hand and walk you there?"

Emilia couldn't help but giggle.

Chapter 10

Five Stories About the Simple Things in Life

Time (A Joe and Robin Story)

Joe was frustrated over being unable to assuage the concerns that both he and his girlfriend, Robin, had been having lately. Between the rising tensions growing between them concerning the way Robin was spending a lot of time with her ex-boyfriend ever since she joined a yoga class that he instructed, and Robin's issue with the way Joe wasn't devoting enough time to her due to his overwhelming workload, the relationship was under a lot of strain.

The issue that always made it difficult for Robin and Joe to understand each other whenever an argument arose was that Joe was used to continually striving to find a way to resolve the issue, even if it meant going through sleepless nights and talking endlessly to find a solution, which was the way he was brought up and also reflected the way he managed his professional responsibilities at work.

On the other hand, Robin embodied a completely different approach to conflict resolution. Robin felt overwhelmed at times when Joe would attempt to force a resolution, which made her apprehensive and somewhat defensive.

It seemed that the more Joe tried to push forward a solution to their relationship woes, the further the couple got to understand each other.

In this particular instance, it was Joe who had started the argument that led the couple to completely skip the movie night they had planned after work and instead go into yet another heated discussion.

Joe had been cognizant of his girlfriend's desire for him to spend less time at work and to devote more of his time to her, so instead of working late as he usually did on Friday evenings, Joe decided to leave all the work he had to next week and leave at a normal time to surprise Robin.

On the way to the small one-bedroom apartment they shared, Joe gleefully imagined how happy he would make Robin once she noticed he was home early, meaning that perhaps they could even go to dinner together or something before the movie night.

However, once Joe arrived home, ready to surprise Robin, he found a completely empty apartment, except for their dog Buckley.

"Where is momma, Buck? Do you know where she went?" Joe asked the chocolate labrador retriever, who, by the sheer amount of energy he was displaying as he sprinted across the living room when questioned about his mother's whereabouts, was clear that he hadn't been walked in a while.

Joe considered calling Robin to ask her where she was but then rejected the notion of doing so because he did not want to spoil the surprise.

"I will walk you in a bit, Buckley. I want to surprise Momma when she comes home! Can you help me do that?" Joe asked.

Buckley barked excitedly, which made Joe worry that the surprise might be ruined if Robin was to approach the apartment in the next minute since Buckley never barked when left alone.

Joe proceeded to open a bottle of red wine and serve a glass for himself and Robin. He also considered sprinting downstairs to the flower shop by the apartment to get her flowers but was worried that Robin would arrive before he was back.

"Do you think I have enough time, Buck?" Joe asked his restless dog.

Joe decided that it was worth a try, so he raced out of the apartment, struggling to keep Buckley from following him, and leaped down the three flights of stairs to avoid having to wait for the elevator that always took longer to arrive than it would to simply use the staircase.

Joe purchased the first flowers he could find, worried that Robin would cross the street and catch him in the act, and ran back upstairs.

Breathing heavily and slightly sweaty, Joe carefully placed the flowers in a plastic shaker cup because the only vase they had in the apartment had shattered a few weeks ago when Buckley accidentally slammed against the kitchen table and caused it to fall, and put the cup and the flowers within it next to the glass of wine he had previously served.

Not knowing what else to do, Joe collapsed on the sofa and braced for impact as Buckley leaped on top of him and waited for Robin to arrive finally.

***

It had been an hour. Robin was still not home.

Joe had been fiddling with his phone the entire time, entertaining the idea of calling Robin and asking her where she was.

The more time passed, the more Joe wanted to call her, but at the same time, the more groundwork he would be destroying by letting her know he had come home early.

"Oh, this is ridiculous!" Joe exclaimed to himself.

Joe decided to call Robin. Joe didn't want to come off as aggressive, even though he was slightly frustrated over the situation, so he took a couple of deep breaths before he called.

No answer.

Joe called again.

No answer.

***

Joe was beginning to fall asleep on the couch, which he would have done a long time ago if it wasn't for Buckley's heavy snoring, when the door finally opened. It was Robin in yoga clothes.

Robin looked genuinely surprised.

"You're home!" Robin cried elatedly.

"Where have you been?" Joe demanded, in an almost involuntarily aggressive tone, as if he had emptied all of his patience in the past two hours.

"Yoga," Robin replied apprehensively as she opened her arms to receive a very excitable and loud Buckley, who was giving Robin the reception Joe had been meaning to give her before he was made to wait endlessly.

"Yoga finished two hours ago," Joe replied.

"I stayed and had a coffee with the class," Robin explained.

Joe felt his blood boil. If there was any chance of the situation not escalating and getting out of hand, it hung entirely on how he managed the next couple of seconds.

"In the studio?" Joe inquired.

"No, at the café by the studio."

"With the instructor?"

Robin looked at Joe disappointedly.

"Yes, Jared was there, too. Are we going to argue about this again?" Robin asked frustratedly as she went about putting her things away with a much more subdued attitude than the one she had walked in with.

"No, this isn't about you stretching and gyrating in front of your ex-boyfriend every day. This is about you constantly being on my case about not being available for you because I focus too much on work!" Joe cried, "You, of all people, know how much stress I am under and how important the next couple of weeks is for me, my job, and consequently us. Still, I listen to your words, and I decide to abandon my work and leave early to surprise you, only to find that YOU are the one who is unavailable for me, and why? Because you are too busy putting your phone on silent so you can give all your undivided attention to your ex-boyfriend, who has all the time in the world for you because he is a yoga teacher who works three days a week which I guess is exactly what you're looking for, isn't it?! Maybe I should just quit my job so you can be happy!"

"How was I supposed to know you were coming home early? Normally at this time, you would still be in the office for another two hours!" Robin retorted, "You should have told me."

"How am I supposed to surprise you if I tell you when I'm planning to surprise you!"

The couple continued to argue up to the point where Buckley's willing participation in the elevated voices proved to be too much for both Joe and Robin.

"You know what? I'm going to go walk the dog since he clearly was also ignored today so that you could spend more quality weekend time with your ex-boyfriend," Joe sneered as he got Buckley ready for a walk.

Robin looked on in with a woeful countenance.

Joe was unsure if he heard her apologize before he made his passionate exit but did not go back to check.

***

During the evening walk, Joe knew he had to come up with a solution to the predicament he and Robin were in. Things could not continue the way they were, or the relationship would eventually fall apart.

"Buck, we're going to have a short walk tonight, and you're going to have to behave because I need to concentrate so I can come up with a solution on how to fix the relationship. So let's be calm—" Joe was interrupted by Buckley seeing a bird bounce past him, who he immediately tried to chase.

Joe had been switching hands to grab Buckley's leash when it was suddenly pulled out of his grip, allowing Buckley to run free through the dimly lit streets of the neighborhood.

"BUCKLEY!" Joe cried to no avail.

Buckley ran toward the bird as it flew away, dodging night-time pedestrians and joggers.

Joe raced toward his dog, but when Buckley turned a corner, Joe lost sight of him and couldn't see him anywhere.

***

Joe had walked around the block for over half an hour and still couldn't find his dog, no matter how loudly he called for him.

Joe asked local street vendors if they had seen him, but no one had.

I can't believe this, Joe thought.

Joe had long believed that when one thing goes wrong, everything else follows suit, and this seemed like a shining example of that logic.

There were so many birds flying and hopping around the neighborhood that Buckley could literally have followed his prey all the way to a different town.

Normally, by this time, Joe would have already come up with a solution on how to resolve things with Robin, but this time, he hadn't had time to think about anything else other than finding Buckley, which frustrated him greatly.

Joe pulled out his phone and contemplated asking Robin to come outside and help him search for Buckley when suddenly he felt an impressive force slam against his back. Joe turned around and saw Buckley.

"Buckley!" Joe cried when he saw his dog. Rather than getting mad, Joe felt a surge of relief and happiness.

Joe kneeled on the pavement and embraced his dog, which was significantly calmer now that he had potentially run close to a marathon through the town.

"You can't do that to me!" Joe said as he pulled his dog in for a tighter hug, getting his neck and ear wet with drool that leaked from the exhausted dog's open and heavy breathing mouth, which luckily was not transporting any dead bird.

***

Joe entered the apartment feeling defeated. He had no idea how to manage the situation with him and Robin. After having searched for Buckley all around the neighborhood, his mental stamina was depleted, and he had no energy to try and conceive a solution.

As he shut the door behind him, he noticed Robin sitting by the living room table, slowly drinking the wine that Joe had served her hours ago. Joe imagined Robin was going to ask what had taken him so long to come home.

Instead, there was silence from both.

Buckley collapsed on the carpet, and Joe did the same on the sofa as he took a deep breath and fought the fatigue he was feeling at that moment.

"I see what you just did," Robin said sheepishly.

"Excuse me?" Joe asked, hoping that Robin was not about to start arguing again.

"You said I didn't notice you wanting to surprise me and that I am blind to the things you do, but I am seeing them now," Robin explained.

Joe looked at Robin, befuddled.

"You know that I do not like it when you come in here and try to control the situation with your solutions, so you stayed out longer and gave me the time I have always told you I need in these moments, and I know how you don't like to go on long walks with Buckley at night. I deeply appreciate you giving me time to process things, and I appreciate you recognizing that that is important to me," Robin said as she approached Joe and sat by him on the sofa.

Joe had not expected this, but it was true that he hadn't come in with any solutions or any intentions of continuing to converse about their issues as he normally did, mainly because he barely had the energy to get himself a glass of water to quench the thirst, he had built up with the unintentional exercise Buckley had just put him through.

"Thank you for the surprise and the time you gave me this evening. I appreciate it a lot. I used that time to think about what you said, which is why I always ask you to give me some space whenever we argue, so I can consider your feelings as opposed to just experiencing my own."

Not only did Joe not have the energy to refute her surmising of the reason why Joe had taken so long during his walk with Buckley, but he was also interested in continuing to hear the positive effects of having done so.

"I understand why you are frustrated and seeing as you have been meeting me halfway, I will meet you halfway, too. If you want, I can change yoga classes and find one where Jared isn't the instructor. I'd be willing to do that for you."

Joe felt taken aback by Robin's words. He was unsure whether he should divulge the truth or pretend that his extended absence was not intentional.

"You don't need to do that. I trust you completely," Joe replied almost involuntarily, as if his subconscious were speaking for him, "now that I think about it, it has nothing to do with that. I suppose I've just been frustrated at myself for not knowing how to handle the relationship, and how to make communication work to our advantage. I suppose, tonight is the only time I've learned to handle things the right way. I'm sorry, I haven't given you the space you need at times. From now on, I will learn to do so."

"But you already have! And I appreciate it so much. I know it couldn't have been easy for you to suppress your inherent desire to fix things. It is your job and what you get paid to do after all and I am starting to understand that."

Joe shuffled in his place.

"Well, the truth is—" Joe began.

Once Joe explained that the cause for his tardiness was due to Buckley's antics, Robin couldn't help but laugh and nod approvingly.

"That makes complete sense. Buckley is a very wise teacher, you were right to seek his counsel," Robin quipped.

"Funny, how a dog can know that something as simple as time, is enough to mend the rifts of a troubled relationship at times. He truly is remarkable," Joe contemplated as he stroked Buckley's brown fur, who was recuperating from his frantic sprint on the sofa by Joe.

"Oh, that's not even what I meant," Robin added.

"What did you mean, then?" Joe asked.

"Well, you know. There are a lot of robins in the city, it is quite a common bird in this town. Now I don't know what a robin looks like so even if you showed me the subject of Buckley's fascination from earlier, I would not be able to confirm whether it was or wasn't, but I think Buckley was sending you a very clear message," Robin suggested.

"Go to Robin," Joe said.

"Yes!" Robin.

"But!" Joe clarified, "Not immediately, just after some time!"

Robin nodded in agreement as she looked at Buckley lovingly.

"You're such a wise boy, Buckley!" Robin cried, which prompted Buckley to leap out of the sofa and do a big stretch on the carpet in front of the couple.

"What message is he sending me here, Robin?" Joe asked.

"I think that downward dog position he is showing you right now is his way of saying that you should join me at yoga!" Robin replied.

Although Robin was clearly joking, Joe nodded in agreement.

By that time next week, Joe was enrolled in Robin's yoga class, which forced him to leave work earlier and to realize that there was nothing to worry about when it came to Jared being Robin's yoga teacher because the relationship had had trust all along, it was just being obscured all along.

However, when Robin and Jared brought Buckley to the yoga studio one day before class, Joe had to smile when Buckley leaped on Jared and caused him to fall flat on the floor.

"He *is* a very wise boy, indeed," Joe whispered to Robin a couple of minutes after it happened, to which Robin responded by vaguely stifling a laugh.

Airport Pickup

Jonah was struggling to believe that his marriage was over. He had devoted so much of his life to making his relationship work for it to end so suddenly and inexplicably.

Although the marriage had been facing challenges for a couple of years before the divorce, Jonah had always maintained hope that he would find a way to fix things. However, he did not expect things to end that fateful night when Jonah came home to find that his dog Mickey, a two-year-old beagle, had destroyed his wife's favorite necklace.

Although it had been Mickey who destroyed the pearls, Jonah knew that it had been partially his fault that it happened because he had been lazy that week when it came to exercising Mickey, which prompted Mickey to wreak havoc as a means to blow off steam as dogs do.

However, Jonah's wife had come home from a very tiring work day, and seeing her necklace destroyed was the last straw. Naturally, the passionate argument that ensued stopped being about the necklace and became about the overriding issues that were crippling the foundation of Jonah and his wife's relationship.

Even though the marriage was over, and Jonah had now moved in back with his mother, who had lived alone ever since her husband, Jonah's father Carl, had died a decade ago from a liver disease caused by excessive drinking, Jonah never harbored any resentment toward his dog which he loved dearly.

It's not your fault; you are a very special dog, and what happened was my fault for not exercising you, Joe would continuously remind Mickey, worried that Mickey would be feeling guilty over the situation as people who form a close bond with their dogs do without contemplating the notion that dogs have no idea what is going on for the most part.

Unfortunately, Jonah's mother, Eve, was not fond of the dog. She would constantly retreat whenever she saw him and had forbidden Jonah from allowing him to be anywhere other than the living room and Jonah's bedroom.

Jonah had finally found a place for him to stay. He searched for a permanent residence and would be moving out of his mother's place in a couple of weeks, since his mother would be gone for the next three days visiting a friend for her birthday, Jonah decided to break the rules and let Mickey roam free through the house. Still, he made sure to give him plenty of exercises beforehand to ensure no more unfortunate accidents.

***

It was the day when Jonah was due to pick up his mother from the airport and drive her back home. It was also the day that Jonah was supposed to go over to his new apartment and sign the final papers to move in the following week.

Unfortunately, the realtor had made Jonah wait an hour due to traffic, which gave Jonah no time to exercise Mickey before leaving for the airport.

Once Jonah was back home, he considered leaving Mickey in the house and locking all the doors to ensure Mickey didn't wander into anyone and destroy any personal belongings. Still, he decided he did not want to run that chance, primarily since he had heard his mother say that she was feeling a bit upset and was not in the best spirits.

"OK, Mickey. You are coming to the airport with me, which is not ideal since we know that your grandmother is not a fan of you just yet. So please, I implore you to behave and not take her reaction too personally if she does not become overwhelmed with joy when she sees you, OK?" Jonah reasoned with his very confused-looking beagle.

***

As Jonah arrived at the airport, he immediately noticed how busy it was. Several people were walking past Jonah, who made adoring noises at Mickey and tried to pet him as they walked past.

"Remember these moments when people fall in love with you in case grandma is not the most affectionate person in the world right now, Mickey!" Jonah reminded his dog.

The last message Jonah received from his mother detailed how tired she felt and how all she wanted to do was arrive home and go to sleep, even though it was still the afternoon.

Jonah was not the tallest of people, so he struggled to see the passengers exiting through the sliding doors and would definitely struggle to find his mother, considering she was even shorter than he was!

Eve finally walked out of baggage claim and gave Jonah a lackluster wave hello.

Jonah moved past the people to approach his mother, who stopped in her tracks when she saw Mickey.

Oh no, Jonah thought, immediately becoming infuriated with the realtor who made him wait.

However, Eve shot her hands up to her cheeks and held up an elated smile at the sight of Mickey.

Mickey started barking excitedly, and Eve asked Jonah to let the dog run to her. Jonah let go of the leash, which prompted Mickey to race toward Eve, who scooped him up and began kissing his excitable cheeks as if they had been best friends all along.

Jonah witnessed the surprising scene and failed to understand what was happening, yet he dared not interfere.

Eve spoke lovingly to Mickey, who proceeded to lick her face, which seemed to supply Eve with a fresh batch of energy and endorphins.

Finally, Jonah approached his mother, who seemed not even to notice his presence over the elation she felt at being around Mickey.

"I see you're in better spirits!" Jonah observed.

"Oh, I am now. Thank you for picking me up, and thank you for bringing Mickey; it was a lovely surprise!" Eve replied.

"No worries," Jonah said, not explaining that he had originally meant to leave Mickey at home.

As Eve lowered Mickey back to the ground and the three of them began heading to the car, Jonah couldn't contain his curiosity any longer and asked his mother what had prompted the sudden change of heart.

"It literally happened the second I saw his little face waiting for me. I didn't expect it at all," Eve explained.

"To see him or to be happy to see him?"

"Both!" Eve replied.

Mickey was pulling hard on Jonah's leash, but Jonah was intent on listening to his mother's explanation.

"I didn't have the best time over there, and I suppose I just felt a bit sorry for myself on the way here. As I walked out of the plane, I remembered how your dad would surprise me at the airport whenever I arrived back from anywhere. He would always say that he couldn't make it, and yet he would always be there. It was funny how he believed I would fall for his lies; I knew he would always be there waiting for me regardless of how hard he would try to convince me that he genuinely would not be able to make it," Eve said. "And for some reason, when I saw little Mickey's face waiting for me, I was reminded of that feeling. I was reminded of the first couple of times your father would surprise me at the airport and how happy it made me. I can't explain it; I guess today was a day I needed to be surprised at the airport by a loving soul."

Jonah had never heard his mother tell that story, so it touched him very much, especially considering that he was happy to see his mother finally forge a bond with Mickey, something he had been trying to do for a very long time, especially after his divorce and the two were constantly around each other.

"He really is such a great boy!" Eve exclaimed as she looked down at Mickey, who suddenly sprinted toward a cement column to his right and started peeing all over it, to the horror of many people watching.

Jonah scolded his dog and pulled him back, which made Eve laugh.

"I don't suppose this kind of behavior reminds you of Dad, too, huh?" Jonah quipped as he picked up the pace to escape the embarrassment he was feeling.

"Oh honey, your father was a heavy drinker. Now that I'm around public urination, I really feel reminded of your father!" Eve exclaimed as she proceeded to laugh even louder before she looked down at Mickey and assured him that he was still a very good boy.

THE FIRST DATE

David was very nervous about going on a date with Lauren. David was one of the most—if not the most—unpopular people in his entire school. In fact, Lauren was significantly more popular in David's school, and she didn't even go to the same school!

Lauren went to the British School of Budapest, Hungary, while David went to the American, yet David knew of Lauren because she had more friends in his school than he did.

However, during the summer, David decided he no longer wanted to be the shy boy in class who never spoke and spent all his free time reading books by himself, so he started playing sports and taking care of his physical appearance for the first time in his life.

One day, David was buying books in the bookstore by his school when he received a text from his brother Paul saying that if David wanted, he could give him a ride home. David accepted and headed to the bar where his brother was hanging out with some friends.

As David entered the underground bar, he noticed that all the popular people from his school and the other schools from the local area were there drinking. Among those people was Lauren, who looked stunningly beautiful as she always did.

David felt overwhelmed when he saw her notice him. David quickly looked away and went over to his brother, who asked David to wait outside for him as he finished his drink.

Slightly frustrated, David exited the bar fast enough to avoid anyone from his school recognizing him.

David had been outside the bar for a couple of minutes when Lauren suddenly arrived and walked up to him.

"You dropped this!" Lauren said as she handed David one of the books he had purchased from the bookstore.

"Oh, thanks!" David said, feeling more nervous than he had in a very long time.

Lauren had long blonde hair and brown eyes that matched the freckles on her cheeks.

"Are you Paul's brother?" Lauren asked.

"Yes," David responded.

"I have an older sister too. Do you get along with your brother?" Lauren asked.

The two continued talking for a while, and eventually, David mustered up the courage to ask Lauren on a date. Fully expecting her to say no,

David asked Lauren if she would like to go for dinner next week and was elated when Lauren said she would love to.

However, now that the day of the date was finally happening, David was more nervous than he had planned. David had been on a few dates before, but this was the first time he was going on a date with someone he found truly beautiful and who he considered way out of his league.

David asked his brother Paul for advice, but all he got in return was a comprehensive list of bars that Paul frequented, and thought would make a good setting for David's first date.

David knew that he had to pull out all the stops when it came to his dinner with Lauren. David surmised that Lauren had probably been on several dates with guys much more popular and interesting than David, so there was no room to make mistakes.

In fact, David was aware that Lauren had been the girlfriend of one of the coolest and most good-looking guys in David's school, someone who had never said a single word to David since they were in entirely different social circles. However, what frustrated David the most was that if David were to approach this more popular schoolmate of his and try to converse with him, he would most likely oblige since he also appeared to be one of the nicest people David had ever encountered.

Feeling like the odds were firmly against him, David sat in his room and counted his savings to see how much he could spend on this date. Typically, David was quite good at sticking to his weekly budget to ensure he didn't unnecessarily run out of funds. Still, he was also fully aware that this circumstance merited straying from his responsible money-saving tactics.

Knowing that he would not be able to buy any snacks in school or go out with his friends after this weekend, David decided to use all his money to ensure he could provide Lauren with the date he felt she was probably used to and deserved.

David had only driven his parent's car a few times since he had only gotten his license very recently, but he assured his parents that he would take good care of it and that nothing would happen.

Once David's parents saw how important the date was to him and how the car would be in safe hands, considering David's absolute reluctance to have an accident with Lauren on board, they allowed him this one time to use the car in the evening.

***

It was the day of the date. David had gone to get a haircut the day before that his brother had suggested but was struggling to style his hair the way he liked since the hairdresser had decided to ignore David's instruction and go rogue with creativity.

"It's fine; just go, or you'll be late!" Paul cried from his bedroom.

David sprinted out of the bathroom and into the car to pick up Lauren, ignoring his parent's well wishes and assurances that everything would go well.

As David drove to pick up Lauren at her parent's house, he obsessively repeated in his head that everything was going to go well and that there was no need to feel this nervous.

David had reserved a table at an amazing Italian restaurant that he frequented with his parents, which would surely impress Lauren, and just outside the restaurant, there was a long boardwalk filled with music and little shops that David planned on walking with Lauren once they were finished with dinner.

Luckily, the drive to Lauren's place was quite short, and he managed to get there early.

Oh wow, David thought as he looked at the time. He was 20 minutes early.

Realizing that it was too early to knock on the front door, David started detesting his brother, who frightened him by advising him to leave immediately and stop fiddling with his hair in front of the mirror.

I could have been on time and done a better job at fixing this horrendous haircut, David thought.

David decided to drive around the block a few times to not come off as overzealous in front of Lauren and her parents, but his attempt to drive away was stifled when the front door opened and Lauren's mother, Claire, walked outside with a jubilant and expectant smile.

Oh no.

"David?" Claire beckoned from the open front door.

David waved sheepishly and knew there was no other course of action to take at that time other than to switch off the engine and enter the house he was not supposed to be at for another 20 minutes.

***

David was already apprehensive about his early arrival. Still, he tried his best to present a confident front as he drove Lauren, who was smiling in the passenger seat next to him, to the Italian restaurant.

"I love that place!" Lauren exclaimed as David told her where they were going for dinner, "I go there with my parents all the time! It's strange that I've never seen you!"

David smiled. In fact, he had seen Lauren there once with her parents, but his natural instinct at that moment had been to be as inconspicuous as possible when being around very beautiful women.

"Yeah, strange!" David replied.

David had practiced the drive to the restaurant several times before going on the date just to make sure that he knew where to go and wouldn't arrive late to his reservation.

However, as David approached the left turn that he was supposed to take, he noticed—to his great dismay—that the road was closed.

"Oh wow, that road is never closed!" Lauren observed.

But of course, it closes the one time it is me driving, David lamented.

To make matters worse, the next left turn was closed too, which forced David to keep driving and completely lose his sense of where he was and where he needed to go—something he was working very hard at concealing from Lauren.

"I wish I could help you, but I have never driven through here. I just sit in the back and let my parents drive me," Lauren said as she looked around, trying to help David find his way back to where they needed to be.

"Oh, it's fine. I'm pretty sure I can take this turn," David replied as he took a gamble on the next right, which unfortunately did not pay off and made him get even more lost than he already was.

This is just great, David thought, *only I would arrive extremely early to pick up my date, to arrive too late to get the table at the restaurant.*

***

Luckily, David was able to arrive on time so as not to lose his table.

Despite the setbacks, Lauren seemed elated to be on the date with David and utterly impervious to his frustrations, which were getting increasingly harder to conceal.

Lauren spoke passionately about her dance classes and her many international travels with her friends. Her energy was intoxicating, and David wanted to match it, but his intrusive thoughts regarding what he considered to be a lackluster performance as a date were weighing him down significantly.

Finally, Lauren and David breached the topic about the reason why they were on a date in the first place.

"How come you never talked to me before?" Lauren asked.

David paused. He could not find a good way to say that he hadn't because she was clearly out of his league, and she was probably making an error in judgment even being on a date with him.

To avoid simply ignoring Lauren's question, David acquiesced to his inability to think of a less embarrassing reason and confessed that it was because he was too shy.

Lauren's charming smile beamed and doubled in size, but David knew that she was probably just feeling pity for him.

The rest of the dinner went well except for when it came time to pay. David knew he was not supposed to let Lauren pay, so he immediately reached for his wallet when the bill came, only to realize that he had left it in the car, which was parked a good 600 meters from the restaurant.

David excused himself and sprinted as fast as he could to the car, hoping Lauren wouldn't get bored and pay for the entire meal herself. Luckily, Lauren was still waiting with the bill unpaid and with her usual disarming smile, which made David feel all the more guilty and foolish.

***

David was once again parked in front of Lauren's house. Lauren was sitting next to him, looking slightly trepid, as if she had finally had enough of David's mistakes and underwhelming performance as a date.

David walked Lauren to her front door but didn't have the heart to look her in the eye; instead, he kept his eyes glued to the floor as if he were terrified of slipping on the dry concrete.

"Thank you so much; I had an amazing time!" Lauren declared as she waited for her parents to open the door.

"Me too. Have a goodnight!" David replied as he almost immediately turned around and walked back to the car, which drove him to feel defeated.

As David walked through the front door, he was inundated with questions from his parents, but he quickly informed them that he was not in the mood to reply or recount anything about the date and that he simply wanted to go to bed, which he did.

Why can't I ever just be smooth and have things go my way? David pondered as he lay awake for hours on his bed, staring at the white ceiling, hoping to either receive an answer or have his concerns magically dissipate and let him rest, none of which happened.

***

It had been a week since David's date with Lauren, and he hadn't spoken to or written to her in any way.

David was in his room after school working on some homework when there was a knock on the door.

"Come in," David cried. It was Paul.

"What are you doing, man?" Paul demanded.

"What do you mean?"

"I just hung out with some people after school, and Lauren was there," Paul explained. David turned around on his chair so fast that he almost continued spinning.

"And?" David inquired.

"And?! She said you totally blew her off! Are you crazy?! Even I can't get a girl like that!"

"Blew her off? That's not true!" David cried.

"She said she had an amazing time and that you didn't even wait to speak to her parents, and that you haven't called her or written to her once. That is totally blowing someone off. If you didn't like her, that's fine, but you shouldn't ignore her," Paul exclaimed.

David explained what had happened and how he felt that he hadn't been as charming or as impressive as he had intended, which made him feel that there was no point in attempting to pursue things further with Lauren.

"Well, I don't know what date you went on, but Lauren told me an entirely different story," Paul explained.

"What did she say?" David asked.

"Go ask her yourself. She's still at the bar. If you run, you can probably catch her," Paul replied.

David looked at his brother, befuddled. Unsure of what to do.

"If you're thinking of checking your hair first, don't. Run!" Paul cried.

David got up and did as he was told.

***

As David walked into the bar, he immediately made eye contact with Lauren. Who waved at him unenthusiastically. David walked up to her and asked her if they could talk.

"Sure," Lauren said as she got up and walked outside the bar with David.

David explained what had happened and how he had felt so insecure the entire time because of how so many things had gone wrong on the date and how attracted he was to Lauren.

"But then, why didn't you tell me all that stuff?" Lauren demanded.

"I was too shy, and I didn't want you to see it. I thought you wanted me to be confident and sure of myself. I thought that I had made too many mistakes on the date to confess how I felt because I thought it would make things even worse."

"So you thought I didn't like you? I thought it was obvious that I did," Lauren added.

"I just thought you were being nice. I guess I was too much in my own head to notice what was really going on," David confessed.

"I think that's true," Lauren confirmed.

"But, you liked me? All my mistakes didn't put you off?"

"Well, I noticed every time you became flustered and nervous about things not going right," Lauren confessed.

"You did?" David asked, feeling his heart sink in shame.

"But that is exactly why I enjoyed the date so much and started to like you. Most guys don't really care, and they just treat me like any other girl. I could see how focused and self-conscious you were every minute. I wanted you to feel better, so I tried to show you that it wasn't bothering me, just the opposite; it was making me feel a lot of things toward you. The truth is I think the date wouldn't have been as good if you wouldn't have made all those mistakes," Lauren explained.

David was at a loss for words. He could see everyone in the bar looking at him and Lauren through the window.

"So, I didn't ruin my chances of going on a second date with you?" David asked timidly.

"Well, you almost did when you ignored me completely while you walked me to my door. But now that you've been honest about why you did it, I think you're OK."

"Would you like to go out again tomorrow night?" David asked.

Lauren squinted playfully at David.

"On one condition," Lauren replied.

"Yes?"

"That you fix that awful haircut of yours," Lauren replied.

David almost fainted.

"I'm kidding. Your brother told me about how long you spent obsessing over your new haircut!" Lauren explained as she laughed and gave David a peck on the cheek, which prompted everyone in the bar to start banging their hands excitedly at the glass.

David walked back inside the bar with Lauren and sat with her and her friends, knowing that it was OK to feel shy or nervous at times but that the important thing was not to let that keep him from showing his true self to the people he knew would appreciate it.

The Plastic Vase (A Joe and Robin Story)

Joe had never been apart from Robin, his girlfriend of several years, for longer than a week since they met that fateful day in the local bar.

Not only had they now been apart for almost a month, but Joe was on a different continent altogether for work. A couple of months ago, Joe had been offered to manage a very high-profile project which was attractive to him because of how well it paid and because the added responsibility that it awarded him would surely make him a top contender for the open senior executive position he had been working to obtain for a long time.

However, the job required Joe to travel to Europe and be away from his girlfriend for a long time. Originally, it was supposed to be a couple of weeks, but at the last minute, Joe heard from his boss that it would likely take two months.

At first, Joe considered stepping back from the opportunity and saying that he had changed his mind and could no longer spearhead the project. Still, Robin had made him realize that if they were talking about starting a family soon, which they were, then maybe this was a small sacrifice they would have to endure to secure a profitable future temporarily.

Joe was unsure and remained unsure until he finally agreed to lead the team and travel to Europe for what potentially could become a very long time.

The first week was alright because there was a lot of work to do, and there were many moving parts that Joe had to address to keep the project moving forward productively. However, once he began to approach the one-month mark, he felt something he had not felt for a very long time—not since he had enthusiastically gone camping with his elementary school friends and some teachers during the summer holiday and later realized the dire implications of his actions—Joe was homesick.

The longing to be home with Robin and Buckley intensified with each passing day, and it seemed with every passing second.

Joe wanted to call Robin every hour, but because of the time difference, it was very difficult to stay in touch.

Joe would wander aimlessly around his small rented studio apartment and dislike everything about it, even though it was a pristine and impeccably clean place that was just as impressive in real life as it had been in pictures when he was searching with Robin for a place to stay during his absence.

The thing that frustrated Joe the most was that before leaving, he and Robin were thriving in their relationship. No longer were Joe and Robin quarreling every other week over banal and insignificant things, but they were very supportive and loving with each other. Much of the improvement that occurred in the relationship had to do with Joe's realization that he had to stop trying to micromanage the relationship and allow things to resolve themselves naturally since love would always find a way to bring Joe and Robin back together.

"I know that I learned the importance of giving you space and time, but even this seems excessive to me!" Joe quipped as he spoke to a very tired Robin on the phone.

"I know, this is not ideal. I wish you were here," Robin replied, stifling a yawn.

"I just feel like this place is getting smaller. Maybe not smaller, but more foreign. The longer I have to wait to find out when I will be coming home, the colder this place becomes, and the more I want to run as far away from it as possible," Joe explained.

"Are you referring to the apartment, the project, or the country?" Robin asked.

"All three. Nothing about my life feels right here. I don't know how productive I can be while feeling like this, and if I can't be productive at my work, then what is the point of going through all of this?!" Joe exclaimed frustratedly.

Robin didn't reply, but Joe could hear her concern in the silence she was providing—he knew her that well.

"I wish I knew what to do. I wish I could fly over there with Buckley and make you feel at home," Robin said.

Joe looked at his watch and realized that it was very late back home and that he should let Robin get some sleep.

"Ok, I love you. Soon you will be home," Robin said before hanging up the phone.

Joe looked around and detested the silence that now seemed to be engulfing every corner of the cold studio apartment.

For the following week, Joe found it hard to focus on the task at hand, and found himself overthinking every aspect of his life and what he was doing, to the point where he thought the only solution to his woes would be to fly back home and be back with Robin and Buckley, even if it meant no longer having a job—which was the most likely scenario if he went ahead with that desire.

The issue was aggravated by the fact that Robin was clearly very busy at work since it became virtually impossible to get a hold of her. Every time Joe tried to reach her, she would reply that she was busy.

Joe was no longer a jealous person, but he felt uncomfortable not knowing what Robin was doing so late in the evening on the last couple of nights he had tried to reach her.

Maybe she is just enjoying her space, as she normally does, and is tired of me constantly complaining and bringing the mood down, Joe considered, which prompted him to stop constantly trying to get in touch with her and Buckley.

One day, after a long shift at work that had left Joe exhausted and slightly demoralized, not to mention that at some point during the day, Joe's boss had submitted the notion that Joe might need to stay yet another month supervising the project to ensure that everything went well, Joe arrived to his apartment and without even removing his smart business shoes, collapsed on the sofa and fell asleep immediately, with the TV's remote control stabbing him in the stomach but not creating enough discomfort to prompt Joe to find it necessary to move a single muscle.

The only thing that made Joe move was that the telephone kept ringing.

"Go away!" Joe shouted at the telephone, which blatantly ignored him as it continued to ring.

Reluctantly, Joe dragged himself out of the sofa and picked up the phone. It was reception. There was a package marked urgent for him.

Great, more work stuff, Joe reasoned.

Luckily, the receptionist offered to bring it up to him, much to Joe's elation.

Staying upright as he waited for the package to be delivered proved to be quite a demanding task, which he managed to do only because he knew he would throw himself back on the sofa and fall back asleep the second he received the package that he had no intention of opening that night.

The door opened, and Joe received the package.

Joe walked over to the kitchen table, dropped the small cardboard box on the table, and was about to walk past it when he saw something in the corner of his eye that caught his attention.

Joe returned to the box and saw a letter attached to it with Robin's unmistakable cursive handwriting.

Joe grabbed the letter, opened it, and read it:

Hi Joe, I know things have been difficult for both of us and that it has been hard to accept that things are different than they used to be. I know you miss home, and I miss you having you here, but what bothers me most is knowing that you are sad. Therefore, I got to thinking about the time that you surprised me with flowers but remembered that you didn't have a vase in the apartment because Buckley had broken it a while ago. Yet, that didn't stop you from working with what you had to present me with flowers. I didn't need a glass vase; I just needed you to do whatever you could to make me smile, even if the situation wasn't ideal. For that reason, I am sending you something to remind you that you can always work with what you have to be happy, regardless of not being surrounded by the thing you wish you had. I love you. Let your creativity make you feel at home.

Joe read the letter a second time before opening the small box the letter had been attached to.

Just as he predicted, a couple of seconds before finally seeing the contents of the box, he noticed that the plastic shaker cup was inside.

Joe pulled it out and admired it as if it were a prestigious trophy. Holding the cup in his hand was the closest he had felt to being back home in a long time, especially considering what Robin had just written in the letter.

Joe put the cup down because he knew he would never be able to take himself seriously again if he began crying over a piece of plastic that had carried his water and protein powder for several years. He looked at his watch and realized that it was probably too late for him to call Robin, so instead, he went into the kitchen to make himself a drink.

A few minutes later, as Joe was sitting on the sofa watching TV, he got a call from Robin.

"Honey? You're awake?" Joe asked.

"I am now! I got a notification that the package was delivered and signed by you!" Robin replied.

Joe explained how emotional he had gotten over the cup and how it had done precisely what Robin intended, and that he felt a lot more at peace and calm now that he had it.

"You are right, as always. It's the simple things that make a big difference. You have no idea how much your letter meant to me. I will find ways to make something great out of this unfortunate situation," Joe asserted.

"Have you put anything in the cup already?" Robin asked.

Joe smiled, "Of course, I did immediately once I got it and understood its purpose."

"What's inside it?" Robin asked excitedly.

"A generous serving of Irish Scotch Whisky!" Joe replied.

"Joe!" Robin exclaimed.

"Well, I don't have any flowers here, and it is definitely a simple solution to make me feel right at home!" Joe explained, which made both him and Robin laugh together for a full two minutes.

THE ART SHOW

Martin had been dating Carole for almost four years when he was accepted to do a full-time MBA at a very prestigious university, something he never envisioned for himself back when he was a slacking teenager who nobody believed in and who many people thought would not amount to anything in the future.

However, Martin was now attending business classes every day at a postgraduate level, something even his father—a very successful executive—had never done but wanted to do his whole life.

Martin had met Carole back when he was still drinking every day and hanging out with his high-school friends who, like Martin, seemed to be perpetually stuck in the same carefree mindset of not worrying about the future or taking their studies seriously.

It had been on one of Martin's regular nights out with his friends when he met Carole by chance at one of Martin's local bars that he frequented most weekends.

Martin hadn't planned on meeting someone he would eventually end up dating for so many years; in fact, he was convinced he would remain single for a very long time because most girls got tired of his attitude and his lack of ambition.

However, Carole immediately saw something inside Martin that even he could not see in himself, which prompted Martin to immediately change his immature ways and seek to improve his life, which he felt he was achieving now that he was enrolled in the full-time MBA.

When Martin got accepted, he ran to Carole and told her the good news.

"Can you believe it? You can finally be proud of me!" Martin cried, to which Carole replied that she had always been proud of him, and that this MBA did not prove anything to her that she didn't know.

"I'm going to let all of my high-school friends who said I was making a mistake by dating you and no longer hanging out with them know so they can see how wrong they were!" Martin announced excitedly.

Once again, Carole corrected Martin in his thinking and let him know that he shouldn't do anything to prove his worth to anyone other than himself.

"I think there is more worth in you deciding to distance yourself from them by your own accord than getting accepted to do an MBA," Carole explained.

"No way! I think the distancing happened naturally. Their party lifestyle simply didn't fit into the life I was creating with you. I had to work really hard to get accepted to do this course!" Martin exclaimed.

"I know you did, but sometimes it's the little things that mean the most and carry the most weight. If you wouldn't have decided to improve your life, which I think was symbolized by the space you created between you and your old friends, I don't think you would have ever even contemplated doing an MBA. You always spoke about it as something your father wanted to do but something you would never consider. Do not underestimate the power of the little things," Carole declared.

Martin knew she was right—as usual—but it was hard for him not to feel the incessant urge to gloat or prove the people he considered his doubters wrong.

Now, Martin was in his second term at the MBA and had managed to make a new group of friends from his business classes who were the exact opposite of his old friends from high school. His new group of friends loved to talk about art, business, and politics, and they already had high-profile jobs and continuously boasted about all the charities they continuously supported through the years.

Martin had invited Carole to meet them several times since none of them lived relatively close to Martin, so it was always Martin who had to travel to them. Although Carole was perfectly pleasant to everyone, as she always was, it was evident that there was a slight disconnect between her and the people from the MBA.

Martin knew that Carole came from very humble beginnings, so he knew it would be strange for her to be surrounded by people who came from such tremendous wealth. Martin, too, would sometimes feel overwhelmed when he heard his friends talk about all the places, they would visit during holidays to luxuriate and spend copious amounts of money on frivolities.

"They are lovely people!" Carole would always respond when questioned by Martin on what she thought about his new friends.

"Really? But you seem slightly uncomfortable around them at times," Martin retorted.

"Well, I don't really have anything in common with them, but that's not their fault. I'm just happy to see you excited and positive about your future!" Carole replied.

As much as Martin loved hearing this type of answer from Carole, he couldn't help but be worried about the fact that whenever he asked his friends about Carole, no one had anything that lasted more than a single adjective to say.

**

Martin and Carole were hanging out together at a shopping center near where they lived because it was Carole's mother's birthday next week, and they were shopping for a present to surprise her with now that prices were discounted, and it was more affordable for them both.

Later that evening, there was an art show that Martin's friends from the MBA were going to and that Martin was invited to join. Martin had asked if

Carole could go, even though art was not really her thing, but she had expressed an interest in joining but had received a unanimous response from his friends that it was only for people from the university.

"That's ok," Carole said when Martin said that he would have to go alone, "can you at least walk me home from the train station before you go?"

"Of course!" Martin had responded.

Once both Martin and Carole had each purchased a birthday present for Carole's mother and were ready to head home, they noticed that the public transport they needed to take to get home was temporarily shut.

"Oh no," Carole lamented, "we're going to have to walk home."

Martin quickly did the math in his head and realized that if he walked Carole home, he would not have enough time to meet his friends for dinner before going to the art show right next to the restaurant.

"Why don't you just walk with me to the other train station I will take to get to the art show?" Martin asked Carole.

"Because that one doesn't stop by the house, you know that. The fastest way is to walk; every other station is farther from the house than where we are now."

Carole was right. Martin would need to walk Carole all the way home and then walk back past the shopping center they were at present and then walk another 20 minutes to the other station that could take him to where he was due to meet his friends.

"Can you please walk me home? You know how I get about these things," Carole pleaded.

Martin despised the unfairness of the situation; either way, no matter what decision he made, he disappointed someone.

"I just don't get why you feel so worried about walking home just because something happened to your mother twenty years ago in a completely different town that is nowhere near as safe as this one. I have spent years trying to tell you that it's fine, and even though we have never had an incident, you still are as scared as you have always been. If I walk you, I will arrive late to the dinner, and you know that I hate being late to things," Martin protested.

"Can't you just ask them if they can wait for you like for thirty minutes?" Carole asked.

"I did. They just wrote me that they'd rather not because they don't want the restaurant to get too busy so that they can eat and pay quickly and then head straight to the art show," Martin explained.

Carole looked askance at Martin as if he had answered a question she hadn't even asked.

"That doesn't seem like much of an excuse, does it?" Carole asked.

Martin felt himself getting frustrated.

"Fine, I'll walk you home and be super late. Let's go," David said with an irate tone, which Carole immediately clocked and realized was not going to lead to anything productive if she stayed in close proximity to it.

"No, I'm sorry. You're right; this is important to you, so you should go. I'll be fine. As you said, we've always been fine. Just go and have fun," Carole said.

Luckily, Martin knew that Carole was not the type to hold a grudge or to pretend that things were fine just to build ammunition for a later argument. If she said things were fine, she was willing to follow through with that assertion.

"Are you sure?" Martin asked.

Carole nodded with a smile.

***

Martin sat on the train, glad that he would not be late for dinner with his friends but also feeling slightly guilty over the whole situation.

Martin felt his phone buzz in his back pocket, so he removed it and glanced at the screen. He had two text messages, one from his friends, who he was on his way to meet, and the other from Carole.

The one from the group chat with his friends read:

Harold: Hey, man. Everyone got here early, so we were already eating dinner. We were going to have some drinks at a friend's pub before heading to the art show. Let us know when you plan on getting here to see if you catch us in time before having to go in.

Martin winced as he read the text. This was not what he was expecting from a group of people he was starting to regard as his close friends, considering the way he had practically abandoned Carole in the shopping center to be with them.

Under that text message was a previous one from Carole:

Carole: Hi sweetheart. I am sorry if I came off as unsupportive. You are amazing, and I fully support the path you are taking in your life. Have fun, and I hope you meet a lot of amazing people and see very interesting art. I love you.

Martin put his phone down and glanced at an ad plastered on the train wall above his eye line. The ad was for some online marketplace that delivered products to people's doors at affordable prices. Martin read the tagline:

Comparing the right value has never been simpler!

As Martin pondered the meaning of the tagline, he looked down and compared the intrinsic value of the two text messages that were now side by side on his telephone screen.

Quite simple indeed, Martin reasoned.

Martin got up and got off at the next stop, which luckily was only two stops away from the shopping center he had just exited, but many stops away from where he was due to meet his friends but no longer would.

As Martin walked home, he smiled at the serenity he was feeling over having made such a small but clearly poignant and significant decision. He also realized that his new friends were simply the other side of the same coin and that it was high time for him to stop spending time with people who did not value him the same way Carole did.

The most profitable decision he had made in his life had not been to pursue an MBA but to be with Carole, which is something he was not going to invest all his time and effort into, starting at that moment.

Martin picked up the pace and could not wait to be back home.

Once he arrived at the apartment he shared with Carole, he explained everything he had realized on the train and how he had been wrong to behave the way he did.

"I now realize how right you are and how I need to stop doubting everything you say. I am now fully invested in you in every way!" Martin declared amorously.

Carole smiled as her eyes got teary, and she hugged her boyfriend as tightly as she could.

"Does this mean you are going to stop doubting me?" Carole asked.

"Of course!" Martin assured her.

"Good, then I want you to know I still firmly believe we should invest in turning the guest room into the yoga studio I've always wanted!" Carole declared with a jocular smile.

"This might be one of those times when you are wrong!" Martin quipped as Carole once again fell into his arms and locked in a passionate embrace.

"You could even use that online marketplace you saw advertised on the train to get all the equipment here. You don't want to ignore both me and the mystical train sign, do you?" Carole quipped.

Martin smiled.

Bonus

Family (A Story About Cherishing What You Have)

Anna had a natural proclivity for arriving later than she was supposed to during weekends when her father, Joe, was home and announced that he would be cooking for the family.

Joe had recently been promoted to CFO of the company he had worked at since before Anna was born. However, before taking on the job, Joe had sat down with his wife, Robin, and his daughter Anna to assure them that even though things were undoubtedly about to change, he would never allow his work to interfere with his time at home.

"Many years ago, I learned the importance of being together with the people who support you," Joe explained to his daughter Anna, who had finally come down to have dinner with her family after various attempts from both Joe and Robin to make her come down to the table while the food was still warm.

"I had to spend a lot of time away from your mother once, and if it hadn't been for her amazing support, I don't know if I would have been able to handle it. Luckily, your mother was very supportive of me, and I managed to get through that challenge. Still, I learned the importance of surrounding yourself with the things you truly cherish, which for me is family, so you two," Joe explained over the dinner table.

Anna smiled accordingly but just thought that her father was once again being over-philosophical as he always was.

"You don't have to worry about me. I know your new role will take up a lot of your time. You can focus on that!" Anna retorted, fully expecting to see her father less and less as the weeks went on.

However, to her surprise, Joe kept his word and never arrived home after seven, which was the specified time for the family to have dinner as a unit.

In the past, Anna had been very good at going down to have dinner on time, but as she grew and began going through the typical changes that most high students do, her desire to sit with her parents every night to discuss current events and interesting anecdotes began to wane considerably, which was noticed by Joe and Robin.

"Have you told your father about the boy you like?" Robin asked at the dinner table one night, trying to find a way to engage Anna's interest so that she would stop looking at her phone the entire time and converse with her parents instead of ignoring them throughout the entire meal.

"Mom!" Anna cried.

"Well, it's not like he's your boyfriend. Why don't you ask your dad for advice on how to approach him?" Robin suggested.

"I told you it was a secret!" Anna protested.

"I know, but I thought you meant in school, not at home," Robin replied.

"Who is the boy?" Joe asked.

Anna sighed and continued looking at her phone and distancing herself from the conversation she refused to be a part of.

"Kenny is actually quite a nice boy, from what Anna tells me; he is the student representative of the entire class, isn't he?" Robin inquired.

Once again, Anna shot a disapproving look at her mother, only even more infuriated this time.

"What's wrong? If you don't want me to tell it, then you tell it. We just want you to talk to us…" Robin declared.

"May I be excused?" Anna demanded, looking at her father.

"But you barely touched your food," Joe responded.

"I lost my appetite. Please?" Anna continued.

"You know relationships are a two-way street, Annie. We listen to you when you say you don't want anyone to bother you when you are in your room because we know it is important to you, but you also have to respect our desire for you to be an active participant in this family. You can't just have things your way all the time," Joe explained.

"I just need my space, please?" Anna pleaded.

Before Joe could finish nodding, Anna was already up from her table and running up the stairs to her room.

Anna closed the door and jumped on top of her bed as she tried to calm herself. Anna detested the way whenever she told her mother anything, she would immediately tell Joe. Anna recognized that she perhaps could have been a little more specific when it came to explaining to her mother that she wanted it to be a secret in the household, too, and not just at school.

***

The school was finally over, and Anna was waiting outside the front door with her friend Anthony. Anthony had been Anna's friend since middle school and had been inseparable ever since that time.

Anthony did not have many friends, nor did Anna, so they relied a lot on each other, and since they lived so close to each other, they would often spend most weekends together getting ice cream in the town and listening to each other vent their frustrations, which in Anna's case was mostly regarding her parents.

When Anna's mother—who cherished the friendship between Anna and Anthony—arrived, she informed Anthony that his mother was being held up at the dentist and, therefore, that she would be bringing Anthony home.

"It will give you two more time together!" Robin exclaimed as she opened the door for her daughter and Anthony.

During the drive home, Anthony and Anna started talking about Kenny, the boy Anna liked.

"Oh, so you get so mad at me for talking about it with you, but it's not a secret with Anthony?!" Robin quipped as she drove Anthony home first.

"Oh, Anna tells me everything, Mrs. Barish," Anthony asserted.

"I can see that," Robin replied.

"And she wouldn't be capable of concealing a crush from me for longer than two seconds!" Anthony added.

Anna looked thoroughly uncomfortable and refused to say a word.

"Has she told you the name of the boy?" Robin asked, trying not to overstep her bounds again.

"Yes, of course, Kenny, but I only know him by name; I haven't had the pleasure yet," Anthony explained.

Robin looked confused, "Really? That's strange. Do you not know everyone in your class?"

Now Anthony looked confused, "Our class?"

"Yes, Anna says he is the student representative of your class. Isn't he the boy who put the dead frog in the teacher's back pocket during science class? Do you not know him?" Robin asked.

There was a prolonged silence in the car that was only broken by an irritated scoff by Anna, who had turned a bright shade of red and was looking out the window as if a life-threatening toxin had just been released into the car.

"*I* am class representative, and *I* put the dead frog in Ms. Carter's back pocket during science class…" Anthony declared.

There was another long silence.

"Oh," Robin responded, knowing she had just severely put her foot in her mouth and that she would be hearing all about it the moment she got home.

***

Once Anna finally came down to dinner, even later than usual, she walked down with a sense of purpose.

"If you're coming down to berate me again, please don't. How was I supposed to know you were lying to both me and your friend about the fact that you like him!" Robin cried, to which Joe responded by taking her hand and giving her a comforting smile.

Anna brandished a stoic countenance as she refused to sit down at the table but merely stood by it, holding some documents in her hand.

"No, don't worry; this is not about how you once again ruined things for me and now alienated me from my friend, who now knows that I have had a secret crush on him for a very long time; this is about the future," Anna explained, trying very hard to exude no emotion whatsoever even though she was inundated with anger and several other confusing and muddled emotions.

"The future?" Joe asked as he put his knife and fork down.

"Yes. My school offers a student exchange program, and there are places available for students wanting to spend six to seven weeks abroad. I have signed up to go to England for that program which means that you will have to house a British student who would come here. Would that be OK with the both of you?" Anna asked with the tranquility of someone asking whether it would be OK to play an instrument quietly in their room late at night.

Joe and Robin bombarded Anna with questions about the program, but it was clear that there was no deviating Anna from her resolve to go abroad for a while.

"Anna, if you are doing this to punish us—" Joe began.

"—No, it is not that. I just need some space. I think that I am not getting the privacy I need and deserve, and perhaps there being distance between us can help me get what I am not getting here and help you two appreciate how important space is for me when I am still living here," Anna explained.

"Anna, no one knows more than me how important space is for a person; if I didn't know it, then I wouldn't have been able to make my relationship with your mother work, but I think what you are doing is the opposite of looking to improve things but to damage things. But, if you are really set on doing this, then there is nothing we can do; maybe it will end up being a good experience," Joe stated.

Anna had not expected her father to be so understanding, which made her slightly trepidatious about what she was proposing.

This is his plan, to simply say yes so I get cold feet, Anna reasoned with herself.

"Fine, I will finish the paperwork upstairs and bring it down when it is ready," Anna asserted.

"What about dinner?" Joe demanded.

"I'm bringing up some ice cream to my room!" Anna responded.

"You can't just have ice cream for dinner, Anna!" Joe exclaimed but was completely ignored by his determined and defiant daughter.

***

It was finally time. Anna was standing at the airport with her two suitcases on her left and her school backpack hanging off her back.

Joe and Robin were standing before Anna as they prepared to say their final goodbyes before Anna had to go through the security check and finally depart to England.

"Be safe. We love you, and we will be waiting for you here in case you want to come home early. Whatever you need, just call us," Joe said as he kissed his daughter on the forehead and stepped back so Robin could say goodbye to her.

Robin was unable to say anything as she broke down in tears and simply kissed her daughter on the cheek and begged her to be safe.

"It's OK, Mother, it's England. Jack the Ripper doesn't exist anymore; I'll be fine," Anna reassured her inconsolable mother.

Anna felt her stomach twist into a knot as she began rolling her suitcases along with her and gave her parents one final wave.

Once I get there, everything will be fine, Anna reassured herself. However, the farther away she walked from her parents, the more challenging each step became. Anna had never been apart for so long and so far away from her family, and as much as she tried to withhold it from her parents, she had been feeling overwhelmed for the past week.

As Anna got her things from the security check and proceeded to leave the place where she could still catch a faraway glimpse of her parents, she lifted her hand to give her parents one final wave, to which they responded immediately and enthusiastically.

Anna felt reluctant. She did not want to leave, but she knew she had to.

Anna lowered her hand and disappeared amongst the frenzied airport crowd as she fumbled her way toward the gate.

***

As Anna struggled to carry all her bags through the airport, she went over the instructions she had received from her host mom about where they would find each other.

Anna hadn't slept much at the airport, and it turned out that the sandwich she had packed for the flight wasn't going to be enough to satiate her for the long flight.

Anna tried to focus on going where she needed to, but she struggled not to admire all the different things about this airport and become excited about the foreign accent that she was unaccustomed to.

Finally, she met with her host mother, Erica, who had a husband and a young daughter who would be staying with Anna's family back home.

Anna approached Erica enthusiastically, even though she hadn't slept on the plane as a way to get off on the right foot, considering they would be living together for the next five weeks. However, Erica appeared to be rushing to be elsewhere other than the airport, as her greeting was not as amiable or lively as Anna had hoped.

"How was the flight?" Erica asked as she sprinted toward the car park, forcing Anna to do the same as she struggled to keep up with the luggage slowing her down.

"It was alright, but I was seated next to someone who snored the entire way, so that made it impossible for me to fall asleep!" Anna explained in between, trying to catch her breath as she pulled her bags with all her might.

"That's nice!" Erica responded.

Even though Erica was a couple of feet away from Anna, Anna still did not have any clearer image of what she looked like other than what she had seen in photos since Erica was wearing huge round sunglasses that almost covered her entire face and had her back to Anna for most of their time together at the airport.

Once they were in the car, Erica proceeded to ask Anna a litany of questions regarding the student exchange as if she had only found out about it that very morning.

"So how long is it, again?" Erica asked.

"Seven weeks in total!" Anna replied, wondering how Erica hadn't been interested in finding out previously how long her daughter would be out of the country.

"And do you come with your own money, or do we have to provide for you too?" Erica asked nonchalantly.

Anna remained silent for a couple of beats as she was unsure if the question was genuine until Erica turned around to look at Anna for the first time since they encountered each other at the airport to demonstrate that she was waiting for an answer.

"I have a little pocket money with me," Anna replied, unsure of how to let Erica know that the host family was supposed to provide for her during her stay.

"OK, that's good," Erica replied.

***

It was late, and Anna was still in her bedroom waiting to know when dinner would be served. Generally, at this time, Anna would already have cleaned up the dirty dishes alongside her mother and been sneaking into the freezer for some ice cream. However, not only had no one come up to speak to Anna for the entire evening, but Erica had made it clear that no sugar was allowed in the house and that if any sweets or unhealthy snacks were found in the house, they would be immediately thrown away.

Finally, as Anna was starting to get sleepy, there was a knock on the door.

"Come in!" Anna responded.

"Are you not going to eat?" Erica's husband, Corbin, replied.

Anna was befuddled.

"Is dinner ready?" Anna asked as she looked down at her watch—it was almost ten in the evening.

"Well, everyone has eaten. Please don't have dinner later than ten because the noise from cleaning the kitchen keeps us up," Corbin explained.

"Oh, OK," Anna replied as she got up from her bed and walked outside the bedroom. Corbin was already gone.

Anna walked down the stairs, trying to remember where everything was in the house she had received a haphazard and rushed tour of from Erica, and rejoiced when she found the kitchen.

There were several stacked Tupperware inside the fridge, all with sticky notes attached that specified who the Tupperware belonged to, which Anna took to mean that they were not for her to eat or even touch.

There were very few things not contained in the Tupperware, so Anna made herself a turkey sandwich and took it to the large dinner table with a glass of water to eat by herself.

The dinner table at this house was significantly larger than the one back home. It was also pristine in its cleanliness as if nobody had ever used it before.

As Anna sat down to eat, the already prodigious table seemed to double in size due to the silence and emptiness around it.

Well, at least you can have your privacy here, Anna reasoned.

Anna's phone buzzed. Anna took out her phone and saw that she had a message from Anthony:

Anthony: Hey, how's it going with the host family?

Anna stared at the message as if it was in a foreign language for a long time before refusing to reply and putting it back in her phone. Anna was unsure if her reluctance to answer was due to her inability to accept that the experience was proving to be significantly less enjoyable than she had expected or if she was still in the throes of shame after the incident in the car with her mother. It was probably a mixture of both reasons.

***

Anna found herself thoroughly enjoying her time at school and taking part in the activities and excursions organized for her by the school.

Anna had befriended a girl named Grace, who was fascinated with Anna being an exchange student from abroad.

Anna and Grace became fast friends and were inseparable while they were together.

During a day trip to a nearby museum, Grace seemed more interested in finding out what would compel Anna to leave her family for so long.

"I just felt like I didn't have my space. Whenever I shared anything with my mother, she would immediately ask a million follow-up questions and then continue to talk about it until it was no longer a secret and everyone knew about it!" Anna explained.

Grace looked at Anna in a contemplative way, as if she had to struggle to imagine a scenario like the one Anna had just depicted.

"So, you want your mother to talk to you less?" Grace asked.

"Maybe a little. Or at least know when the right time is to talk to me and when is the right time to give me some space," Anna responded.

"And when is the right time, and when is the wrong time?"

Anna opened her mouth to respond but quickly realized she did not have an answer ready. She felt inclined to say that a bad time to speak to her was right after school when she was exhausted. All she wanted to do was sleep on her bed and not have to engage with anyone or any activity for a while. Still, given the underwhelming experience she was having at Erica and Corbin's home, where she felt like a ghost that no one could see, Anna reconsidered her initial theory.

"To be honest, I'm not sure," Anna finally replied.

"My parents work all the time," Grace began, "they both have full-time jobs that they started when I got accepted into this school, which is not cheap. I don't really get to see them that much, but I can't imagine ever being away from them for so long. I know it would be harder on them than it would be for me, and that's saying something."

Anna contemplated Grace's response.

"But what about your personal space? Do you ever feel like it is not respected at home?" Anna asked.

"I suppose that I consider my time away from them my personal space. When I go to school, I feel I've had a break from seeing everyone from my class, and when I arrive home, I feel the same way about my parents. I am lucky enough to go to school, but I know that some of my friends are not, and they have to be with their parents constantly, which I can imagine can get quite tiresome," Grace explained.

Anna thought about Grace's response and imagined how her family would feel if she adopted Grace's ideology and arrived home excited to be around her parents and spend time with them. Anna had to admit that considering how she was feeling presently, the idea of coming home to her parents seemed more attractive a proposition than ever before.

Anna had rarely spoken to her parents ever since she left, which she knew was mostly because she had asked her parents to use their time without her to let her have her space and have the break from the family life she so desperately was seeking. However, Anna caught herself regularly checking her phone to see if her mother or father had written to her, only to see that Anthony was the one who kept writing to her even though Anna refused to respond to his messages.

"How come you don't respond to your friend?" Grace asked as both she and Anna followed the class through yet another corridor of the prodigious museum.

Anna recounted the incident in the car with her mother and Anthony to Grace, which prompted Grace to laugh so loud that the teacher turned around and gave Grace a disapproving glare.

"Well, it sounds to me like your mother helped you out there," Grace suggested.

"How so?" Anna inquired.

"Well, if you've liked this boy for so long but have been too afraid to do anything about it out of fear that he would not reciprocate your feelings, only to have your mother spill the beans and make you discover that this boy has not attempted to flee from your presence or ignore you, then it seems that you can finally be open and honest about your feelings towards Anthony."

The teacher turned around again and instructed the girls to talk more quietly and to pay attention to the tour, which they did.

However, the entire time Anna followed the class through the various rooms of the museum, she could not help but think about how Grace was reframing everything in her mind. Perhaps Anna was seeing things differently because of how vulnerable she felt over the sadness she felt whenever she arrived home at Erica and Corbin's house, or maybe this experience was quickly becoming a teaching moment that allowed her to see the mistakes of her past.

***

Anna arrived home late that night after hanging out with Grace and some other classmates from her school. Since Anna despised scrounging through the marked Tupperware in the fridge to find her daily options in terms of food, she had come home with some takeaway that she had picked up with Grace on the way.

Anna sat down by the dinner table by herself as she did every night and started eating. Almost immediately after, Corbin emerged from the kitchen with a plate of hot leftovers from the day before, which he had microwaved and was carrying over to the dinner table.

Although Anna did not think much of her host parents, she was happy to have some company for once.

"Oh, I'm sorry. I'll be in the kitchen," Corbin said as he noticed Anna eating at the table before turning around and heading back to eat by himself in the kitchen.

"I don't mind," Anna responded as she stopped unwrapping her takeaway food.

"No, it's fine!" Corbin replied without any attempt to veil his frustration at being unable to eat at the occupied dinner table.

Anna sighed quietly and proceeded to once again eat by herself. A few minutes later, Erica came downstairs. Anna almost didn't recognize her without her giant sunglasses, which she sometimes even wore in the evening.

"Where's Corbin?" Erica asked, confused.

Anna placed her hand over her mouth, which had just taken a generous bite out of her sandwich, and attempted to chew quicker to provide Erica with an answer.

Erica glared at Anna as if expecting her to simply spit the food out and respond immediately.

"He is in the kitchen," Anna informed Erica, who did not seem surprised but definitely unimpressed.

Anna felt compelled to stand up and take her plate upstairs to her room as if she had committed some sort of felony by opting to eat at the dinner table.

Following that incident, even though it did not involve much of an actual interaction, Anna decided to eat her food by herself in her room. She would constantly bump into Erica and Corbin in the kitchen but never with both at the same time since no one ate together at their house.

As the days passed, Anna began to become frustrated that her parents were not getting in touch with her as much as she wanted them to, even though she knew it was because of her specifically asking them not to, which frustrated her all the more.

One night, when Anna still had a couple of weeks left abroad, she received a call from her mother.

"Hi, Anna," Robin said, "I know you said you didn't want us to get in touch so much, but I just missed you and wanted to know how you were doing."

Anna had barely said two words before finally breaking down in tears and spilling the beans about what an awful time she was having.

Robin immediately offered to buy her daughter a plane ticket that evening to get Anna back home.

"No!" Anna cried, "It's OK, I want to finish it. Hearing your voice helps a lot. Can we keep talking these last two weeks so it's not so hard for me?"

Now it was Robin who was sobbing.

***

It was Anna's last day. As excited as she was about leaving the house she was living in and being reunited with her parents, she was sad about having to say bye to Grace.

"Just remember what I told you!" Grace said as she wiped away the tears from her cheeks, "If Anthony is writing you, it's because he likes you too. Don't be scared to see him."

Anna nodded in agreement before the two friends embraced each other and promised to visit whenever they could.

Erica's car horn made both Anna and Grace jump in terror as it did most people standing outside the school.

Anna waved at Erica to signal that she would be right there.

"Is it OK if I stay with you next time I visit?" Anna asked in a quieter tone.

"Oh man, I was looking forward to sitting alone in your old bedroom while you, Erica, and Corbin took turns eating without each other. I still can't believe that's real," Grace quipped as she shot a disapproving glare at Erica, who was sitting behind the wheel of the car with her unnecessarily large glasses on.

"You're just going to have to take my word for it because there is no way I am going back there!" Anna responded as she gave her friend one final hug before saying goodbye and ambled into Erica's car.

***

The drive to the airport was completely silent, much to Anna's delight, as she had no intention of trying to conjure up a conversation with Erica at this point.

Once Erica dropped Anna off at the airport and continued driving as if she had just dropped off some dirty laundry, Anna felt a reinvigorating sense of relief and freedom that she had not felt for a very long time.

Anna checked her phone to see that it was blowing up with messages from her mom asking her if she was OK and reminding Anna that if Erica did anything disrespectful, she was willing to find a British hitman to take care of her.

Anna laughed and called her mother to let her know that she had arrived at the airport on time and would be making her way to the gate in about an hour since Erica had dropped her off excessively early.

Anna walked around the airport looking for something to eat while still talking to her mother until she received a text message from Anthony.

Anthony: Hi, I heard your flight is today. I hope you arrive home safe and that you no longer have to deal with that horrible woman who shows the glory that is ice cream.

"Mom?" Anna asked over the phone, "Did you tell Anthony about Erica?"

Robin sounded flustered.

"He came by the house one day to ask if you were OK because, apparently, you hadn't responded to his messages. I'm sorry; I hope I didn't do something wrong again!" Robin replied.

Anna chuckled, "It's fine. It is my own fault for not responding to him."

"What are you going to write him?" Robin asked.

Anna thought of what the right response would be but ultimately decided that the best thing to do would be to speak to him in person.

Once it was time to board the plane, Anna told her mother she had to hang up and then had to continue reminding her every five minutes when Robin refused to let her go.

"OK, fine. I'm only hanging up because if you miss your flight, I will cry every day until you're here! Be safe, and I love you. Write to me the second you land, please!" Robin implored.

Anna once again agreed to do what her mother requested and hung up the phone before getting in line to board the plane.

***

Anna was sitting in her room and was taking a break from unpacking to speak to Grace on the phone.

"So, what are you going to do?" Grace asked Anna.

"I am going to let him know how I feel and see if he wants to be more than friends," Anna explained, which made Grace shriek with excitement.

The two girls laughed and conversed about possible scenarios to the point where Grace demanded that she be the maid of honor for Anna and Anthony's wedding.

"When are you two going to talk?" Grace asked.

"I told him I was home, and he said he would come when he was finished helping his dad with something, so any minute, I guess," Anna explained.

Robin knocked on the door.

"Come in!" Anna cried.

"Dinner is served," Robin said.

"OK, perfect. Grace, can I call you later?" Anna asked.

"Is that Grace? Hi Grace!" Robin exclaimed as she sprinted closer to Anna's telephone.

Anna handed her mother her phone and walked over to her open bedroom door to wait for her mother to be done talking to her friend.

"Mom?" Anna asked after about a minute.

"Yes, sweetie?" Robin asked.

"Dinner?"

"Oh, yes, sorry! Grace, it has been a pleasure, and you are welcome here anytime!" Robin said as she said her final goodbyes to Grace and walked down with Anna to the dinner table.

During dinner, Joe and Robin were in disbelief over how cold and distant Erica and her husband had been the entire time.

"We should say something to the school!" Joe said frustratedly.

At that moment, the doorbell rang.

Anna stood up and opened the door for Anthony, who was standing outside with a nervous smile.

"You're back!" Anthony exclaimed awkwardly.

"Yeah!" Anna replied.

The two stood idly before each other, unsure of what to say.

"I was wondering if maybe you wanted to go for a walk and talk?" Anthony suggested.

"I would love to! But I am having dinner with my parents right now. Can we do it after?" Anna responded.

"Of course!" Anthony replied.

"OK, I'll call you!" Anna said as she waved goodbye to Anthony and shut the door.

Joe and Robin both grinned at Anna as she sat back down.

"So, back to what we were talking about; even though the exchange experience was not pleasant, do you think you learned anything from it or took with you a positive lesson that you can carry with you moving forward?" Joe asked as he put his knife and fork down on his empty plate.

Anna nodded with a timid smile.

"I learned that I need to be more appreciative of what I have and that—as you said—I need to surround myself with the things I truly cherish, which is my family," Anna responded.

Robins's lip quivered as she practiced restraint and attempted not to cry. Joe smiled and extended his hand to Anna, who grabbed it along with Robin's.

"We're glad you're back home," Joe said as the family let go of each other's hands.

"I am definitely glad to be home. I'm sorry for the way I was behaving; I know it wasn't right," Anna admitted.

"It's OK. It's like your mother and our old dog Buckley taught me many years ago; sometimes, people just need to have a little space from each other to see things clearly. Just remember that this is always your house," Joe reminded his daughter, who was smiling so hard her cheeks were beginning to hurt.

"So, what are you going to do with Anthony?!" Robin inquired.

"Well, once I am done with dinner, I will go over to his place, and maybe we can go for a walk and talk about how we feel and stuff," Anna responded.

"But we're all finished with dinner already, sweetheart. If you want, you can go now, and we can clear up!" Robin offered.

"No, I'm not quite ready yet," Anna responded, "there is still something that I cherish deeply that I haven't been surrounded by yet since I got home, and I think I shouldn't wait any longer."

"What is it, sweetheart?" Joe asked.

"There is a lot that I want and need to say to Anthony, but I also know that moving forward, I need to prioritize the things that matter in my life, and like I said—that is you two. However, there is something else that now holds a special place in my heart and that I cannot ignore for much longer," Anna explained.

Joe and Robin looked at Anna, waiting for an explanation as to what she was referring to.

Noticing her parents' confusion, Anna lifted her index finger with a playful smile to suggest that she would be right back before getting up without saying a word and disappearing from the table.

Joe and Robin looked at each other befuddled.

Suddenly, both Joe and Robin erupted into rapturous laughter when they noticed their daughter strut back into the dining room carrying two enormous pints of ice cream with a sense of elation that made it seem as if she had just walked in with two Olympic trophies.

Anna slammed the ice cream on the table and looked at it delightfully.

"Boy is it good to be back home," Anna exclaimed, which made her parents laugh even harder.